MW00438705

THE KUMULIPO

A Hawaiian Creation Chant

Translated and Edited with Commentary by

MARTHA WARREN BECKWITH

THE UNIVERSITY OF CHICAGO PRESS

THE UNIVERSITY OF CHICAGO PRESS, CHICAGO 37
CAMBRIDGE UNIVERSITY PRESS, London, N.W. 1, England
W. J. GAGE & Co , LIMITED, Toronto, 2B, Canada

Copyright 1951 by The University of Chicago
All rights reserved. Published 1951
Composed and printed by THE UNIVERSITY OF CHICAGO PRESS
Chicago, Illinois, U.S.A.

To the memory of

ANNIE M. ALEXANDER

*Lifelong Friend and Comrade from
early days in Hawaii*

*Whose generous sponsorship has made
the author's research possible*

247128

Contents

PART III. THE POLYNESIAN CHANT
OF CREATION

APPENDIXES

CHANTS

Introduction

THE Kalakaua text of the Hawaiian genealogical prayer chant called the "Kumulipo" covers sixty-six pages of a small pamphlet printed in Honolulu in 1889 after a manuscript copy at that time in the possession of the ruling King Kalakaua but now the property of the Bishop Museum in Honolulu, to which it passed in 1922 from the estate of Prince Kalanianaole, nephew of the former rulers. A prose note of two pages attached to the text tells the circumstances under which the chant was allegedly composed and recited in old days. Except for the third paragraph relating the connection of the chant to the line of ruling chiefs from whom the Hawaiian monarchy of that period claimed descent, the prose note derives from the manuscript source.

A European scholar, the eminent German anthropologist Adolf Bastian, first called attention to the manuscript of the Kumulipo. During a month's stay in Honolulu in the course of a tour of the Far East, he learned of the existence of a Hawaiian cosmogonic chant, borrowed the king's copy, and was able to translate passages from the first eleven sections and to obtain some light on their meaning. This text and translation, together with comparison with other cosmogonies from Polynesia and from ancient Asiatic as well as European civilizations, Bastian incorporated into a volume called *Die heilige Sage der Polynesier*, published in 1881 in Leipzig.

The interest shown in the chant by this European scholar probably influenced the king to have the text printed. He saw also a chance to strengthen his own hereditary claim to the throne among subjects who regarded genealogical descent as the ultimate test of rank. Six years later his sister and successor, the deposed Queen Lili'uokalani, while under de-

tention at Washington Place in Honolulu after the attempted
revolt of 1894–95, began a line-by-line translation of the
Kalakaua text. This translation was later completed and published in Boston in 1897.

In 1902 a native scholar of Kona district on the island of
Hawaii, named Joseph Kukahi, printed in Hawaiian, together with other traditional lore, a text with commentary
of the Kumulipo through the eighth section. Except for considerable abridgment, the edition differs but little from the
Kalakaua text. Kukahi is said to have held a post at the palace
as a member of Kalakaua's household. His version must have
come from a common source with the manuscript copy, if it
is not a direct variant from it. In 1928 Kukahi's first seven
sections, in still further abridged form and with an attempted
English translation, were reprinted in consecutive numbers
of a short-lived bilingual journal called *Aloha*. Unfortunately this praiseworthy effort to revive interest among Hawaiians in their literary heritage is without importance for this
study.

As a printed text the Kumulipo chant is thus buried in obscure libraries out of reach of scholars today and unknown
even to the few Hawaiians left who read their own language
and might be able to interpret its meaning. Of manuscript
texts, the most important after that reproduced by Kalakaua
in his printed edition is an unsigned book of genealogies attributed to "Kamokuiki." The late J. M. Poepoe called this
Kamokuiki "one of those who were instructed with David
Malo under Auwae, the great genealogist of Kamehameha's
last days," who "filled in the genealogy left incomplete by
Malo . . . from Puanue back to Kumulipo and forward to
Wakea." Of the two thousand one hundred and two lines of
the Kumulipo chant as it appears in the Kalakaua text, over
one-half are straight listings of names of man and wife, *kane*
and *wahine*. The Kamokuiki book gives all these genealogies,

each under its own heading and with variations unimportant in themselves, but proving an independent transcription.

Poepoe, who was Rivers' Hawaiian informant for his volumes on Melanesian society, himself left an unfinished text and commentary on what he calls "Kamokuiki's Genealogy of Kumulipo." Another manuscript by an unknown hand gives a genealogy of La'ila'i from the "creation" to Kalakaua. Still another consists in a translation into English of Bastian's German rendering of the Kumulipo manuscript text, made at the request of Dr. Handy by the Austrian philologist Dr. Joseph Rock. Finally, a fifth manuscript called "Helps in Studying the Kumulipo" contains classified name lists chiefly of plants and animals. These, though important in themselves, have no direct bearing upon the interpretation of the Kumulipo chant.

Besides these written sources I have gone over the text with living Hawaiians familiar with native chant style. In two cases these informants were introduced to me by Theodore Kelsey of the Hawaiian Village, to whom I am indebted for paving the way to the establishment of friendly relations. David Malo Kupihea is from a Molokai priestly family who held an inherited post under the late monarchy as keeper of the royal fishponds below Palama. The late Daniel Ho'olapa belonged to an old Kona family on the island of Hawaii, and his wife was also of chief blood. A third helper was the late Mrs. Pokini Robinson, an old family friend of exceptional qualities of mind belonging to an important chief family of the island of Maui and, although given an English education in a mission household, preserving a constant connection with Hawaiian life and tradition as she knew it in old days under the best native environment and as she followed it through the Hawaiian press. She read the Kumulipo for the first time from the copy I lent her and exclaimed with enthusiasm, "How I should like to hear this chanted!" Finally I am especially indebted to Mrs. Mary Kawena Pukui, of the

Bishop Museum, for her unfailing helpfulness as interpreter and for her sound advice on questions of detail. Hers has been the final authority in correction of both text and translation. Both have in almost every case been based upon manuscript readings or have been suggested or approved by these Hawaiian interpreters.

Acknowledgment should also be made to the editor of the *Journal of American Folklore* for permission to use the article on ceremonial birth chants in Polynesia which appeared in the oceanic number of that periodical. I wish also to thank the trustees and director of the Bishop Museum for their courtesy in permitting access to manuscript material needed for this study and in furnishing every facility for work during various visits to Honolulu, and the librarian and staff for helpful co-operation. Discussion of textual and social problems with Sir Peter Buck, Dr. Kenneth Emory, Dr. Samuel H. Elbert, and other members of the staff has been a constant source of stimulus. Although for the final form of the work I must hold myself alone responsible, my appreciation of their aid is here gratefully acknowledged. Finally, I owe a debt of gratitude to Professor Robert Redfield for his exceedingly helpful interest in arranging for the publication of the manuscript, and to the officers of the Press for their cordial co-operation.

PART I

Social and Historical Background

CHAPTER ONE

The Prose Note

THE Hawaiian Kumulipo is a genealogical prayer chant linking the royal family to which it belonged not only to primary gods belonging to the whole people and worshiped in common with allied Polynesian groups, not only to deified chiefs born into the living world, the Ao, within the family line, but to the stars in the heavens and the plants and animals useful to life on earth, who must also be named within the chain of birth and their representatives in the spirit world thus be brought into the service of their children who live to carry on the line in the world of mankind. To understand such a family chant, it is necessary to know what we can of its social and political background, how it came to be composed, the part it played in the ceremonial life of a chief's household, its importance as a perquisite of rank.

Some of these questions are answered on the title-pages of the published text and the queen's translation, others in the prose note affixed to the Kalakaua text, amplified from the original Hawaiian manuscript by the insertion of a paragraph, the third, explaining more fully the family connection of the child to whom the chant is said to have been dedicated. "A prayer of dedication of a chief, A *Kumulipo* for Ka-'I-amamao and (passed on by him) to Alapa'i-wahine (woman)," reads the title-page of the Kalakaua text. Queen Liliuokalani is more specific. "An ancient prayer for the dedication of the high chief Lono-i-ka-makahiki to the gods soon after his birth," she writes, a discrepancy in name explained in the note itself, and she adds the date 1700 for the time of its compo-

7

sition and the name of Keaulumoku as its composer. The
prose note as translated under the direction of Mrs. Mary
Pukui and checked with the queen's rendering of certain
passages reads as follows:

Hewahewa and Ahukai were the persons who recited this chant
to Alapaʻi-wahine at Koko on Oahu. Keʻeaumoku was lying on his
deathbed. The Lono-i-ka-makahiki mentioned in the chant was
Ka-ʻI-ʻi-mamao. Lono-i-ka-makahiki was the name given to him by
his mother at his birth. She was Lono-ma-ʻI-kanaka. It was Keakea-
laniwahine [his paternal grandmother] who gave him his new name
at the time when he was consecrated and given the Taboo, the Burning, the Fearful, the Prostrating Taboo, at the time when his naval
cord was cut at the heiau of Kueku at Kahaluʻu in Kona, Hawaii.
Ka-ʻI-ʻi-mamao was the correct name. That was the true name
Keakea gave the child, but the composers of the chant "Kekoaulikoʻ-
okea ka Lani" called him by the name of Ka-lani-nui-ʻI-ʻi-mamao.
The "Lani-nui" was just inserted by the composers; Ka-ʻI-ʻi-mamao
was the correct form. The meaning of the word [*mamao*] is this.
When Keawe lived with Lono-ma-ʻI-kanaka, a new strain was introduced into the family of ʻI the father of Ahu and grandfather of
Lono-ma-ʻI-kanaka; as if to say that this ʻI was greater than all the
other ʻI's. This was the meaning of the word "mamao" ["far off,"
hence "removed," that is, high in rank] added to the first half of
the name.

Before his banishment by the commoners of Ka-u for his evil
deeds, [because of] his sleeping with his own daughter, with Kao-
lanialiʻi, he was called by the name of "Wakea." It was under this
name that he went with his kahu, Kapaʻihi-a-Hilina, to Kauai, to
Kalihi-by-the-sea and Kalihi-by-the-streams, and to Hanalei, and he
went to the bush country of Kahihikolo and became demented and
wandered about in the uplands.

This was not the Lono-i-ka-makahiki who riddled with Kaku-
hihewa. A number of different chiefs were called Lono-i-ka-makahiki
and they lived at different times. There were three Lono-i-ka-makahiki's. The first Lono-i-ka-makahiki was the son of Keawe-nui-a-
ʻUmi; another was Lono-i-ka-makahiki the humpbacked. His time
came later. He was the son of Kapulehuwaihele by Makakaualiʻi.
The Lono-i-ka-makahiki whose prayer this was, that Lono-i-ka-
makahiki was the son of Keawe-i-kekahi-aliʻi-o-ka-moku by
Lono-ma-ʻI-kanaka. That was the Ka-ʻI-ʻi-mamao here mentioned,

the father of Ka-lai-opu'u and the grandparent fifth removed of the King Kalakaua now on the throne and grandparent fifth and fourth removed of Ka-pi'o-lani the present Queen Consort.

This chant of Kumulipo is the chant recited by Pu'ou to Lono (Captain Cook) as he stood while a sacrifice of pork was offered to him at the heiau of Hikiau at Kealakekua.

The priest had said at the time of Ka-'I-'i-mamao's death that Lono would come again, that is, Ka-'I-'i-mamao, and would return by sea on the canoes 'Auwa'alalua.

That was why Captain Cook was called Lono.

Besides explaining the dedication of the chant under two different names, the prose note seems to connect it with the consecration of Keawe's son in the temple at the time of his birth, as well as with two other occasions at which its recitation is definitely stated. The first of these recitations was at the ceremony in the temple for Captain Cook when he was received as the god Lono; the second was at the time of Ke'eaumoku's death. The sacred character of the chant is thus clearly established. In two instances it was apparently connected with a religious ceremony within a heiau. In the two instances in which the reciters are named they are priests and two in number, since a chant of such importance could not be intrusted to the memory of a single individual and the technical effort involved must have been of an exacting nature. The reciters seem also to have been priests of rank. Of Hewahewa who chanted as Ke'eaumoku lay dying, we are told that he claimed lineal descent from the priest Paao whom tradition claimed to have migrated to Hawaii before intercourse with southern groups had ceased and to have introduced reforms on that island at a time of decay of the chiefship. After the death of Kamehameha, who had striven to retain ancient religious practices, and the acceptance by the chiefs of Christianity, Hewahewa himself is said to have been active in demolishing the images that embellished the old temple structures.

The death of Ke'eaumoku, dated 1804 by Hawaiian chronology, like that of Captain Cook's landing on Hawaii in

1779, falls well within known history. Ke'eaumoku was uncle and supporter of Kamehameha and father of his favorite wife. The lady Alapa'i the queen identifies with the child of Ka-'I-'i-mamao by his own daughter, "a woman chief of the highest rank then at Koko, Oahu." The alliance had earned for the chief the joking sobriquet of "Wakea" in allusion to the myth that the original ancestor of the race was child of the Sky-god Wakea by the daughter born to him by the Earth-mother Papa, but this does not appear to have been one of the "evil deeds" for which the chief was banished, such unions seeming to have been accepted among persons of rank. A younger woman of the same name, granddaughter by his daughter Kauwa'a of that Alapa'i who was at one time ruling chief of the island of Hawaii, married John Young the younger, later premier under Kamahameha III. It may have been a last honor paid to her dying relative by the chiefess to whom it already belonged, or the younger Alapa'i-wahine may have been the final inheritor, to whom the family chant was at this time dedicated, or "named," as the Hawaiians say. To understand what such a chant contributed to the prestige of a family of rank, it will be necessary to know something of the terms upon which a ruling chief held his title to control over land rights and ultimately over the lives and activities of his followers.

CHAPTER TWO

Rank in Hawaii

POSITION in old Hawaii, both social and political, depended in the first instance upon rank, and rank upon blood descent—hence the importance of genealogy as proof of high ancestry. Grades of rank were distinguished and divine honors paid to those chiefs alone who could show such an accumulation of inherited sacredness as to class with the gods among men. Since a child inherited from both parents, he might claim higher rank than either one. The stories of usurping chiefs show how a successful inferior might seek intermarriage with a chiefess of rank in order that his heir might be in a better position to succeed his parent as ruling chief. In any case, a virgin wife must be taken in order to be sure of her child's paternity, hence the careful guarding of a highborn girl's virginity until her first child was born. Laxness in enforcing taboo rights lowered rank. Political power also had its bearing upon rank, perhaps because a ruling chief was in a position to enforce the taboos. Nevertheless, a chief might be himself dispossessed of lands and followers and forced to live like a commoner and yet claim the right of rank for his posterity.[1]

The system by which closeness of blood relationship between parents of high birth was reckoned in determining the rank inherited by their offspring is described in four published sources.[2] David Malo's account must date before 1853. Judge Fornander died in 1887, and his notes on the subject

1. Fornander, *Polynesian Race*, I, 113–14, II, 28–30, Kepelino, pp. 130–42, 143.
2. Malo, pp. 80–84, Kepelino, Appendix, pp. 195–98; Fornander, *Collection* ("Memoirs," No. 6), pp. 307–11; Rivers, I, 380–82.

may belong to Kalakaua's time. The Hon. E. K. Lilikalani
was court genealogist during the last period of the monarchy,
and his manuscript, prepared "for the information of Liliuokalani" and published in 1932 by the Bishop Museum as an
Appendix to Kepelino, must fall within the queen's reign.
He dictated its contents to me in substantially the same form
in 1914. Rivers must have obtained his similar information
from Poepoe at about the same time.

David Malo is our earliest and probably best authority of
the four on the system of reckoning rank in Hawaii before
the intrusion of Western culture, since he lived at a time
when the taboos were still in practice. Malo came from
Keauhou, North Kona, on the island of Hawaii, where he
was associated with the high chief Kuakini, acquired Hawaiian learning under Auwae, the favorite genealogist of
Kamehameha, and took an active part as master of ceremonies at court entertainments. About 1820 he came to Lahaina on the island of Maui. There he became the friend of
the Rev. William Richards of the American mission. Aban-
doning the old faith, he studied for the ministry in the Lahainaluna mission school and occupied a parish on West Maui
until his death in 1853.[3]

As Malo is our most reliable native source for ancient practice, so Fornander is the leading foreign authority. Son of a
distinguished Swedish clergyman and himself a man of education, he was a resident of the Hawaiian Islands from 1842
until his death in 1887. Much of the time he was engaged in
government service. He was married to a Hawaiian chiefess,
spoke the language fluently, and was able to claim personal
acquaintance with all classes "from the King to the poorest
fisherman of the remotest hamlet." He thus won the respect
and confidence of native and foreigner alike.[4]

3. N. B. Emerson, "Biographical Sketch," in Malo, pp. 5–14.
4. W. D. Alexander, "A Brief Memoir of Abraham Fornander," in
Stokes, *Index to "The Polynesian Race,"* pp. v–vi.

Malo, Lilikalani, and Poepoe do not differ essentially in their grading of the ranking system. All would give highest rank to the child of own brother and sister, the grades descending according to distance in kinship blood between the two parents, provided these are themselves of high chief, that is, of *niaupi'o* rank. The union of brother and sister, says Malo, is a *pi'o* ("arching") union symbolized by the figure of a bow. That between children of younger or elder brothers and sisters (first cousins) is a *ho'i* ("return") union. Less desirable is the union between half-brother and sister, called a *naha*, probably correctly a *nahá* ("broken") union. The child in all three cases would be of the *niaupi'o* class but entitled to different degrees of veneration in the form of taboos. The child of a *pi'o* union was an *akua*, a god. So sacred is the child of such a union that he is spoken of as "a fire, a blaze, a raging heat, only at night is it possible for such children to speak with men," this lest the shadow of the god falling upon a house render it sacred, hence uninhabitable. A person even accidentally profaning thus the sacred taboo chief was in danger of death. A chief of divine rank therefore went abroad at night, and the most sacred chiefs were always carried about in a litter (*manele*) lest their very footsteps make the ground forbidden. Offspring of both *pi'o* and *ho'i* unions were entitled to the prostrating taboo, *tapu-moe*, but the child of a *naha* union had only the crouching taboo, *tapu-a-noho*.

Judge Fornander understands the system slightly differently. He would give the *tapu-moe* to all three of these unions. Under the highest or *pi'o* grade he would include children of a half- as well as own brother and sister. By a *naha* union he understands the child of parents of the same family but of different generations and instances the union of father and daughter or of a girl with her mother's brother. As example of the *pi'o* rank he cites the child of Keawe by his half-sister Kaulele. Ka-'I-'i-mamao, child of Keawe by a *niaupi'o* chiefess of different parents, has only the *niaupi'o* rank. A girl born to Keawe by his own daughter was reckoned of *naha* rank.

Judge Fornander does not mention marriages between first cousins; Malo makes no reference to marriages in different generations. Since the whole ranking system seems to consist in an effort to distinguish the prerogatives of chiefs from those of commoners, it would not be surprising if unions considered favorable among chiefs were exactly those not practiced or even held to be incestuous among commoners. Rivers was told that marriages between first cousins were not permitted by Hawaiians and that their tolerance by the mission at first stood in the way of Hawaiian acceptance of the new teaching.[5]

From these informants we gain only a partial view of family relationships and attitudes as they affected rank among chiefs in ancient days, only such as were preserved up to the time of the last days of the monarchy. Certain it is that there existed a developed system of rank based primarily upon blood descent but also dependent to some extent upon political power and marked by a severe etiquette designed to mark off the chief class from that of commoners through the claim of direct descent from ancestral gods. Hence the preservation of such a genealogical chant of beginnings as the Kumulipo was of the highest importance in establishing the rank of a ruling family.

5. Rivers, I, 382, Cf. Firth, *We the Tikopia*, pp. 330-33.

CHAPTER THREE

The First-born Son and the Taboo

O F THE ceremonies attending the birth of a chief's son who is the first-born of his mother, two accounts are available, one an unsigned text with translation by John Wise included in the Fornander *Collection*, the other a translation by Dr. Emerson from Malo's *Hawaiian Antiquities*.[1] The Fornander paper stresses the precautions taken to keep the highborn couple apart and virgin until the time for their first mating. This takes place in a kind of tent under guard, and thereafter the girl is closely watched in order to make sure of the parentage of her expected offspring. At the first sign of pregnancy she is placed under taboo lest evil befall the child through sorcery or inadvertently through offended deities. The people are meanwhile urged to "dance in honor of my child, all ye men, all ye chiefs." Name songs (*na inoa*) are composed and sung about the countryside. At the time of birth a priest is summoned, sacrifices are offered, "drums are beaten and prayers at intervals are offered from a separate place, in honor of the child." If a son is born, he is "taken before the deity in the presence of the priests," that is, to the heiau, or temple. There the priest ties the umbilical cord and cuts it with a bamboo knife.

David Malo's in some respects more specific account does not differ essentially from that given in the Fornander paper. The composition and chanting of songs before the birth of the young taboo chief is similarly described. Malo writes:

If after this [the formal mating] it is found that the princess is with child there is great rejoicing among all the people that a chief

1. Fornander, *Collection* ("Memoirs," No. 6), pp. 2-7, Malo, pp. 179-84.

15

of rank has been begotten. If the two parents are of the same family, the offspring will be of the highest possible rank.

Then those who composed the meles (*haku mele*) were sent for to compose a *mele inoa* that should eulogize and blazon the ancestry of the new chief-to-be, in order to add distinction to him when he should be born.

And when the bards had composed their meles satisfactorily (*a holo na mele*), they were imparted to the hula dancers to be committed to memory. It was also their business to decide upon the attitudes and gestures, and to teach the *inoa* to the men and women of the hula [i.e., the chorus].

After that the men and women of the hula company danced and recited the *mele inoa* of the unborn chief with great rejoicing, keeping it up until such time as the prince was born; then the hula ceased. . . .

. . . and when the child was born . . . if a boy, it was carried to the heiau, there to have the navel string cut in a ceremonious fashion.

When the cord had first been tied with *olona* [fiber], the kahuna, having taken the bamboo [knife], offered prayer, supplicating the gods of heaven and earth and the king's *kaai* gods [bones of ancestors preserved in woven baskets] whose images were standing there. . . .

The child Ka-'I-'i-mamao to whom the Kumulipo chant is said to have been "named," was undoubtedly born to the purple, as we say. The family name 'I means "supreme" and the epithet *mamao* expressed the further "remoteness" to which his rank entitled him as first-born of a daughter of the ruling 'I family of Hilo district to that Keawe who was called "foremost chief of the island," Keawe-i-kekahi-ali'i-o-ka-moku. The two families were closely related by blood; the child was the first-born of his mother, hence he was held to be a god among men, with from infancy the rank of a *niaupi'o* chief entitled to the strictest of taboo rights, the *kapu moe* or prostrating taboo, the *kapu wela* or burning taboo. Commoners must fall on their faces before him, chiefs of low rank must crouch in approaching him. If he went abroad by day he was preceded by the cry *Tapu! moe!* If an object connected with his person such as clothing or bath water was being carried by, the officer who bore it, a close relative with the title of *wohi*, warned with the cry *Tapu! a noho!* and all must drop to a squatting posture. To remain standing in either case was punishable by death. Even chiefs, if of lower rank, must uncover the upper part of the body in coming into his presence, as a token of reverence.

The length to which taboo was carried in Hawaii must have developed locally under the stress of competition among ruling houses. It was also a means of power to the priesthood. The prostration taboo with the penalty for its infraction of death by burning, the terrible *Kapu wela o na li'i,* tradition says was brought from the island of Kauai to Oahu whence it was introduced into Maui at the time of the ruling chief Kekaulike, who must have been a near contemporary of Ka-'I-'i-mamao, since his daughter Kalola became wife to that chief's son; Malo indeed calls its introduction "modern."[2] Only the uncovering of the upper part of the body in coming into the presence of a high chief is noticed by Ellis in Tahiti.[3] Firth speaks of the crouching position taken in Tikopia by one who brings a gift to appease a chief whose anger he has incurred, and Alexander reports from the Marshall Islands in the early seventies: "The people of . . . Kusaie and Ponape are all serfs. The chiefs own all the land and when a common native approaches the chief, he comes crouching."[4] Certainly the idea of the divinity of ruling chiefs and the consequent sacredness attaching to their persons and effects is not unique in the Polynesian area. A position of humility as an acknowledgment of rank was, as we know, widespread throughout Asiatic courts. The custom served to increase among the commoners fear and awe for their rulers as representatives of the gods on earth, as well as to preserve, by means of a severe etiquette, respect for blood descent among the chief class itself.

2. Fornander, *Polynesian Race,* II, 277; Malo, p. 83.
3. Ellis, *Polynesian Researches,* III, 105.
4. Alexander, p. 493.

CHAPTER FOUR

Lono of the Makahiki

THE prose note explains the name Lono-i-ka-makahiki with which the final genealogy of the chant concludes—"To Ahu, to Ahu-a-'I, to Lono-i-ka-makahiki"—as the name given to the infant by his mother at his birth, to be replaced after his consecration in the temple by the name by which he is known in history. The word *maka*, "eye," refers to the constellation of the Pleiades, *hiki* is a sign of movement; the word translated liberally hence refers to the rising of the Pleiades in the heavens corresponding with the time of the sun's turn northward, bringing warmth again to earth, the growth of plants, and the spawning of fish. At this time a festival was celebrated in honor of the fertility god Lono, god of cultivated food plants not alone in Hawaii but throughout marginal Polynesian islands, and prayed to in Hawaiian households to send rain and sunshine upon the growing crops, spawn to fill the fishing stations, offspring to mankind. His signs were observed in the clouds. Heiau were built to Lono not in time of war but under stress of famine or scarcity. His worship was mild, without human sacrifice such as belonged to the severer worship of the war god Ku. Any man might set up a temple to Lono, a ruling chief alone to the god Ku as a prayer for success in war, for life in case of illness, or upon the birth of a first-born son.

During the Makahiki period athletic sports were celebrated, said to have been inaugurated by the god Lono in person. "Father Lono," symbolized by a long pole with a strip of tapa and other embellishments attached, was carried about from district to district to collect taxes (*'auhau*) in the shape of products given in return for the use of the land distributed by each overlord among his family group. There was also a ceremony in which "a structure of basket-work, called the *wa'a-'auhau,*" literally "tribute-canoe," was sent adrift "to represent the canoe in which Lono returned to Tahiti," or more probably the tribute paid to the absent god from the food supply of the past year, earnest of similar gifts in the year to follow.[1]

Symbolic forms of this sort look as if Lono of the Makahiki had once appeared in the person of some voyager who brought culture gifts, introduced athletic sports, perhaps also the Polynesian custom of the *ho'okupu* or tributary offering, a word meaning literally "to cause to grow, as a vegetable; to spring up, as a seed." The offering sent to sea to feed the god was hence to come back to the people in abundant crops for the coming season. The basket of food was to provide for the god's "return" in symbol in the year to follow.

There was indeed a tradition that such a human manifestation of the god had actually appeared, established games and perhaps the annual taxing, and then departed to "Kahiki," promising to return "by sea on the canoes 'Auwa'a-lalua" according to the prose note. "A Spanish man of war" translates the queen, remembering a tradition of arrival of a Spanish galleon beaten out of its course in the early days of exploration of the Pacific; "a very large double canoe" is Mrs. Pukui's more literal rendering, from 'Au[hau]-wa'a-l[o]a-lua. The blue-sailed jellyfish we call "Portuguese man-of-war" Hawaiians speak of, perhaps half in derision, as 'Auwa'alalua. The mother honored Keawe's son, perhaps born propitiously during the period of the Makahiki, by giving him the name of Lono-i-ka-Makahiki, seeing perhaps in the child a symbol of the god's promised return.

1. Malo, pp. 186–210; Makemson, pp. 82–84, Beckwith, *Hawaiian Mythology*, chap. iii.

Another and earlier Lono-i-ka-makahiki on the 'Umi line of ruling chiefs of Hawaii is better known to Hawaiian legendary history. This Lono was born and brought up not far from the place where were laid away the bones of Keawe and his descendants, woven into basket-work like those of his ancestors from the time of Liloa, near the place where Captain Cook's grave stands, a monument to a brave but in the end too highhanded a visitor among an aristocratic race such as the Polynesian. This Lono cultivated the arts of war and of word-play and was famous as a dodger of spears and expert riddler. He too may have contributed to the tests of skill observed during the ceremony of the Makahiki.[2]

It is not, however, likely that either of these comparatively late ruling chiefs on the 'Umi line was the Lono whose departure was dramatized in the Makahiki festival and whose "return" the priests of the Lono cult on Hawaii anticipated so eagerly. Both were born in Hawaii, and no legend tells of either of them sailing away with a promise to return. A more plausible candidate for the divine impersonation is the legendary La'a-mai-Kahiki, "Sacred-one-from-Tahiti," who belongs to a period several hundred years earlier, before intercourse had been broken off with southern groups. La'a came as a younger member of the Moikeha family of North Tahiti, older members of whom had settled earlier in the Hawaiian group. He brought with him the small hand drum and flute of the hula dance. As his canoe passed along the coast and the people heard the sound of the flute and the rhythm of the new drum-beat, they said, "It is the god Kupulupulu!" and brought offerings. Kupulupulu is Laka, worshiped as god of the hula in the form of the flowering *lehua* tree and welcomed also as god of wild plant growth upon which the earliest settlers had subsisted and still continued to subsist to some extent during the cold winter months before staple crops were ready to gather. This La'a-mai-kahiki took wives

2. Beckwith, *Hawaiian Mythology*, pp. 392–94.

in various districts, especially on Oahu, stronghold of Lono worship, from whom families now living claim descent. He seems to have sailed back to Tahiti at least once before his final departure.[3] In this sojourner belonging to a great family from the south, who came like a god, enriched the festival of the New Year with games and drama, possibly organized the collection of tribute on a southern pattern, and departed leaving behind him a legend of divine embodiment, one is tempted to recognize a far earlier appearance of that Lono of the Makahiki in whose name the Kumulipo chant was dedicated to Keawe's infant son and heir.

Not that it is necessary to attach the symbol of divine incarnation to any actual historical event. Arrival and departure by canoe would be the normal way to dramatize the advent of a god. Just as Vedic hymns visualize the arrival of invited gods to the sacrifice in chariots drawn by steeds each of a distinctive color because thus they were accustomed to see their own superiors approach, so Lono would come to island dwellers in a double canoe of divine proportions such as their own chiefs employed. Not this chief or that was the unique god of the Makahiki. In each human birth of a *niaupi'o* child there lived anew a Lono to preserve and carry forward the sacred stock. Each year when the sun turned its course northward and warmth and quiet weather prevailed, there returned to his worshipers this procreative force, the beneficent god of the Makahiki.

3. Fornander, *Collection* ("Memoirs," No. 4), pp. 152–55.

CHAPTER FIVE

Captain Cook as Lono

WE KNOW that once, indeed, in historic times, the god Lono's looked-for return seemed to have become a reality. The British officer Captain James Cook, sailing north under orders to explore the Pacific Coast of North America for a northwest passage to the Atlantic, touched upon a hitherto uncharted island, northernmost of the Hawaiian group, and on his return, on January 17, 1779, anchored off Kealakekua, "Pathway-of-the-gods," on the larger island of Hawaii. The wondering multitude crowding the shore to witness this marvel were easily persuaded by their priests of the Lono cult that the prophesied day was at hand.

The story is told circumstantially by Cook's underofficer, Captain James King, who often accompanied Cook on his visits to shore and was taken by the natives for his son.[1] Upon first landing, King writes that they "were received by four men, who carried wands tipped with dog's hair, and marched before us, pronouncing with a loud voice a short sentence, in which we could only distinguish the word Orono. . . . The crowd, which had been collected on the shore, retired at our approach; and not a person was to be seen, except a few lying prostrate on the ground, near the huts of the adjoining village."[2] The account tallies well with what we know of the prostrating taboo in the presence of deity and of the identification of the visitor with the god of the Makahiki, about the time of which festival Cook's arrival

1. King, III, 4 ff., Fornander, *Polynesian Race*, II, 157–65, 167–79.
2. King, III, 5–6.

took place. Hence the invocation to "O Rono" (Lono), as a note adds: "Captain Cook generally went by this name among the natives of Owhyee [Hawaii]; but we could never learn its direct meaning. Sometimes they applied it to an invisible being, who, they said, lived in the heavens. We also found that it was a title belonging to a person of great rank and power in the island, who resembles pretty much the Delai Lama of the Tartars, and the celestial emperor of Japan."

The stone platform is still standing that marks the site of the heiau to which the priests of Lono conducted Cook and his companion for the ceremony of chanting and offerings appropriate to the welcome of a god. The prose note asserts that at this time the Kumulipo prayer chant was recited, with "Puou" as the officiating priest. Unfortunately King's full description of the occasion neither confirms nor disproves the tradition. Puou is easily to be identified with the old chief called "Koah" in King's account, who seems to have taken the lead throughout in the reception of the visitors. He had been a great warrior but at this time is described as "a little old man, of an emaciated figure; his eyes exceedingly sore and red, and his body covered with a white leprous scurf." Another priest, described by King as "a tall young man with a long beard," also took part in the chanting. King writes the name as "Kairekeekeea," possibly to be identified with Pailili or Pailiki, who, according to Fornander, substituted at this time for his absent father.[3]

This younger priest chanted "a kind of hymn . . . in which he was joined by Koah." Of their manner of chanting King writes: "Their speeches, or prayers, were delivered . . . with a readiness and volubility that indicated them to be according to some formulary." At the presentation of a dressed hog to the captain, Koah "addressed him in a long speech, pronounced with much vehemence and rapidity." With Cook

3. Fornander, *Polynesian Race*, II, 173 n.

perched on a kind of scaffolding, the two priests further delivered a chant "sometimes in concert, and sometimes alter-
nately" and lasting "a considerable time." Finally, before the
guests were fed, the younger priest "began the same kind of
chant as before, his companion making regular responses."
These diminished to a single "Orono," an invocation plainly
addressed to the god Lono, believed to be there present in
the person of the distinguished stranger.

It is not surprising that during the days that followed the
successful attack against a god who had proved fallible to
weapons, the old warrior advised putting to rout the whole
expedition, while the young chief, who had acted as political
head during the absence of his superior, remained friendly.
The matter-of-fact way in which the multitude regarded
the death of a god has curious confirmation in King's statement that after Cook's death the people inquired anxiously
of King when "the Orono" would come again.[4]

4. King, p. 69.

CHAPTER SIX

Two Dynasties

THE year 1700 for the date of composition of the Kumulipo chant and the name of Keaulumoku for its composer appear on the title-page of the queen's translation. Both statements are highly conjectural. To a song-maker called "Keaulumoku" is ascribed the famous prophetic vision still extant, describing the conquest of Hawaii by Kamehameha and dated 1782 by Hawaiian chronologists. This was only a few years after Cook's visit. The poet's dates are given from 1716 to 1784. However inexact, they certainly preclude the possibility that the same man composed a birth chant for Keawe's son and heir and a threnody for the defeat of the young heir who inherited the overlordship after the long rule ended of Keawe's grandson born to the same parent for whom the Kumulipo prayer chant is claimed. Possibly the name was titular and passed from one court poet to another. Possibly to the renowned poet of Kamehameha's time was intrusted the task of weaving together family genealogies and eulogistic songs into an integrated whole such as we have in the Kumulipo chant as it exists today. Such was undoubtedly the custom within a great house risen to power.

For the date, if the chant was actually originally recited to celebrate the birth of Keawe's son, the year 1700 may not be inexact. Ka-'I-'i-mamao had no long rule after Keawe's death, and his son Kalani-opu'u was certainly ruling chief at the time of Cook's arrival in 1779. Chronology gives 1752 as the date of his succession. Keawe's period must date back to the early eighteenth century. Eulogistic chants call him "Lord [Haku] of Hawaii," the term Mo'i, "Supreme," not having been used, says Stokes, before the time of Kamehameha III. In chant he is named

> Kane the Earth-shaker,
> The chief Keawe from the thunder-cloud,
> The Heavenly-one who joined together the island.

The boast of divine origin put forth in the chant of his rival Kuali'i of Oahu is said to be an attempt to offset the prestige derived by Keawe from the long lineage claimed for his family stock in the Kumulipo. "Are you two equal?" asks the poet, and he answers:

> He [Keawe] is not equal to Ku [Kuali'i],
> Not equal to the Heavenly-one,
> No comparison is here,
> A man is he,
> A god is Ku,
> A messenger is Ku from the heavens,
> A stranger is Ku from Kahiki.

With such boasts the Oahu peerage sought to discredit the claims of its powerful rival on the island of Hawaii.[1]

The system of inheritance according to rank has always proved itself one well calculated to stir up discord between rival aspirants. Hawaii was no exception to this rule. Kamehameha's conquest, which finally brought the whole group under the one ruling family, began with a struggle for land of a disinherited faction after the death of Kalani-opu'u, grandson of Keawe. It was indeed from two sons of Keawe by different mothers, not without later intertwinings of family relationship, that were descended the two lines who ruled over the united kingdom throughout the period of the monarchy from the opening of the nineteenth century to its last decade; on the one side the ruling house of the Kameha-

---

1. Fornander, *Collection* ("Memoirs," No. 4), pp. 394-95.

meha kings, on the other that of Kalakaua and his sister successor.

A brief sketch of the history of these family relations during the eighteenth century leading up to the monarchy of the nineteenth will make this clear. Keawe's title of "foremost chief over the island" had been fairly nominal. The powerful 'I family descended on the Maui line from 'Umi dominated Hilo district, the Mahi family ruled Kohala and probably Hamakua. It was the districts of Ka-u and Kona that Keawe's sons actually inherited. To the first-born son to his chiefess of the 'I family went the lands of Ka-u district, to another son born to Keawe by his half-sister Kaulele fell the coveted lands of Kona. From this son the Kamehameha dynasty was descended; from Ka-'I-'i-mamao the King Kalakaua and his sister Lili'uokalani claimed descent.

To Kaulele tradition gives a rank above that of her half-brother and a corresponding place as co-ruler with him. "Excessive" the word means, perhaps referring to her size of frame. Certainly "excessive" she was in her favors according to the custom of chiefs in high-ranking circles, so that the story of struggle and turmoil throughout the turbulent eighteenth century on the island, marked toward its close by the intrusion of foreigners and culminating in the conquest of the group under Kamehameha I, is bound up in great part with the activities of the rival offspring of this restless and accommodating chiefess. To a chief of the Mahi family she bore that Alapa'i who rose in rebellion against the sons of Keawe and ruled wisely over their lands during the nonage of their sons. By a visiting high chief from the island of Kauai she became grandparent of that Ke'eaumoku who listened on his deathbed to the chant of the Kumulipo at the turn of the century, the man who had been most active in inciting Kamehameha to rebellion, father also of that remarkable woman called "Cape-of-bird-feathers," Ka'ahumanu, who became the favorite wife of the conqueror. For

Kamehameha himself genealogists claim direct descent in the
fourth generation from the union of Kaulele with her half-
brother Keawe.

It was, however, through the 'I family union that the
ruling power returned to Keawe's line. After Alapa'i's death
his weak son was overpowered and slain, and the son of
Ka-'I-'i-mamao became ruling chief over Hawaii. This was
that Kalani-opu'u who appears as "Tereeboo" in King's
account of the events surrounding the death of Captain
Cook. His life was one of constant strife, first against Alapa'i's son, then in continual sorties against the island of Maui,
where he seems to have claimed lands not only in his own
right through direct descent from the great Pi'ilani family of
East Maui but also through marriage with Kalola, own sister
of the ruling chief of that island and a lady of very high taboo
rank. Her son Kiwala'o succeeded his father, and it was the
divison of lands by this new overlord after Kalani-opu'u's
death that precipitated the revolt of the Kamehameha faction. Kiwala'o fell in battle. His half-brother Keoua by
another mother of inferior rank, the Kane-kapolei who appears as the chief's consort in King's account under the name
of "Kanee-Kabareea," yielded to treachery.

Conquest over the one island was quickly followed by that
over the whole group, aided by superior weapons purchased
or seized from the foreigners. In order firmly to establish his
position, the conqueror sought marriage alliances with the
blue-blooded families of Maui as well as with those of his
own island, who looked upon him as a usurper against the
legitimate line of out-ranking chiefs from Keawe. The
Maui chiefess Kalola was, after the affable custom of chief
wives, both mother of Kiwala'o as consort of Kalani-opu'u
and, by this husband's half-brother of Kona—the same who
became father of Kamehameha—she was mother also of Kiwala'o's chief wife. She bore to him a daughter, and this girl
Kamehameha took as his own chief wife and parent of the

succeeding line of Kamehameha kings who ruled after the death of their great ancestor. On her father's side she belonged to the legitimate Ka-u branch, on her mother's to the Kona, and on both sides she could claim connection with the purest blood of Maui, besides the culminating sacredness imposed by the close mingling of half-brother and sister blood. Of so lofty a rank indeed was this chiefess that Kamehameha himself must uncover the upper part of his body on coming into her presence.

By 1874 the line of the Kamehameha family was extinct. Prince David Kalakaua became king by a stormy election and ruled until his death in 1891. He was succeeded by his sister Lydia, the Queen Lili'uokalani, who was the last representative of the Hawaiian monarchy before its overthrow and the setting-up of a provisional government in 1893, followed in 1898 by annexation of the islands to the United States as the Territory of Hawaii. The election of Kalakaua had not been without bitter opposition. It was to his interest and later to that of his sister as queen to uphold in every way the family claim to blood descent from the fountain source of Keawe's line. With the freeing of the slave class, the abolition of the taboos, the development of a constitutional form of government participated in by foreigners to whom the native rules of rank were alien, and the opening-up of lands to individual ownership, the outward marks distinguishing the chief class had disappeared. Only the name chants and genealogies remained to preserve a family's claim to noble ancestry.[2] The king sought to revive interest in old tradition. A society was formed, and proof of such ancestry was demanded for membership. The printing of the Kumulipo seems to have come as one result of this movement back to old court practices and the ancient clash of rank between the sons of Keawe.

It must be parenthetically observed that, in summarizing

2. Fornander, Collection ("Memoirs," No. 6), pp. 310–11.

the path of events leading up to the publication of the Kumulipo, I have followed Fornander without calling in question
the factual accuracy of genealogies handed down from
Keawe. Actual blood relationship must always be a debatable
point under the social etiquette then prevailing in court
circles. It is their conventional acceptance that gives them
social and political importance for the historian. Sexual
freedom for a chiefess after the birth of her first child was
accepted or even encouraged by court custom. The father
of Kalani-opu'u is said to have been, not Ka-'I-'i-mamao, but
Peleioholani, son of Kuali'i and ruling chief of Oahu. The
ruling chief Kahekili of Maui was almost certainly the father
of Kamehameha. Keawe himself has the name of having
mingled his strain with that of every family in the realm,
chief or commoner. But for genealogical purposes a wife's
children were generally accepted as his own by the nominal
husband unless the actual parent was in a position of advan-
tage in rank and power which made him worth cultivating
by an ambitious offspring. The journey of a first-born child
of his mother to seek recognition of a highborn father in a
distant land is hence a favorite theme of Hawaiian saga
and romance.

The effect of such loose matrimonial relations in a land
where inherited blood counted above all things in establishing the perquisites of rank is to be seen in the dual pattern of
court genealogies, where an unbroken line of descent often
depends upon the female when a male parent fails. The
Keawe line from 'Umi is twice so preserved on the 'Ulu
genealogy. Both genealogies for the Kalakaua family derive
finally through the mother.

1. △ ——— = ○ Keakealani = △ ———

2. ○ Lono-ma-'I-kanaka = △ Keawe-i-kekahi-ali'i-o-ka-moku = ○ Kaulele

3. △ Ka-'I-'i-mamao = ○ Kamaka'imoku

4. ○ Kanekapolei = △ Kalani-opu'u = ○ Kalola

5. △ Keoua Kuahu'ula(Kau) △ Kiwala'o(Kona) = ○ Keku'iapoiwa Liliha

6. ○ Keopuolani = △ Kamehameha

2. ○ Kaulele = △ Keawe-i-kekahi-ali'i-o-ka-moku

3. △ Kalanike'eaumoku = ○ Kamaka'imoku

4. △ Keoua = ○ Keku'iapoiwa II = ○ Kalola

5. △ Kamehameha   ○ Keku'iapoiwa Liliha

2. ○ Kaulele = △ Kauaua-a-Mahi(Kohala) = △ Lono-i-ka-ho'upu(Kauai) = ○ ———

3. △ Alapa'i-nui = ○ Keaka = ○ Keawepoepoe = ○ Kuma'iku = ○ Kanoena

4. △ Keawe'opala   ○ Namahana(Maui) = △ Ke'eaumoku   △ Kamanawa
                                                         △ Kame'eamoku

5. △ Kamehameha = ○ Ka'ahumanu

Kaumuali'i(Kauai)

Symbols △, male, ○, female, =, parents, |, child

PART II

The Chant

CHAPTER SEVEN

The Master of Song

WHETHER Kamehameha's favorite genealogist or an earlier poet is responsible for the composition of the Kumulipo as we have it today, the chant represents a master-work in the aristocratic art of song employed throughout eastern Polynesia in the families of chiefs to extol their family nobility.[1] This particular class of genealogical prayer chant is known in Hawaii as a *Ku'auhau*, a word referred by Parker to *Ku(amo'o)* meaning a "pathway" and *'auhau*, "lineage," the analogy belonging rather to the meanderings of a roadway trodden out by human feet than to the more familiar symbol of a tree and its branches.

The work of weaving genealogies into a hymnlike chant commemorating the family antecedents was the work of a *Haku-mele* or "Master-of-song," attached to the court of a chief, one who occupied also the special post of a Ku'auhau or genealogist. He held an honored place in the household. It was his duty to compose name chants glorifying the family exploits and to preserve those handed down by tradition, but especially to memorize the genealogical line through all its branches. Since writing was unknown in Polynesia before contact with foreign culture, a master of song usually gathered together two or more of his fellows to edit and memorize the lines or themselves to contribute passages. Especially must genealogies be memorized by more than one reciter. The oral recitation of a completed chant of eulogy required a special technique in handling the voice. Its utterance was

1. Luomala, "Polynesian Mythology, Introduction," *Encyclopedia of Literature*, Vol. II (1946).

in the nature of a charm. Evenness of voice was obligatory. A breath taken before the close of a phrase, a mistake, or even hesitation in pronouncing a word was a sign of ill-luck to the person or family thus honored. Kamakau writes: "The voice took a tone almost on one note and each word was enunciated distinctly. There was a vibration [*kuolo*] in the chanting together with a gutteral sound [*kaohi*] in the throat and a gurgling [*alala*] in the voice box. The voice was to be brought out with strength [*ha'ano'u*] and so held in control [*kohi*] that every word would be clear." Such a feat of memory as must have been involved in the composition and recitation of a sacred chant like the Kumulipo was hence common to the gifted expert in Polynesia.

The importance of such name chants in establishing a chief's claim of birth is illustrated in a legend of a certain exiled chief from the island of Hawaii who claimed asylum with a powerful chief of Oahu, unattended by any of his followers. Upon his name chant being demanded as proof of his title to rank, he is said to have escaped disgrace by gaining the favor of a visiting chiefess just come from Kauai and reciting as his own a new chant taught him by the complacent visitor. A similar story tells of a surfing competition where jealous rivals concealed from the winner the ruling that a surfing chant proving his rank must be recited before a contestant would be permitted to beach his board after the race, and how he was saved from drowning only by the impromptu composition of an old retainer, the famous "Surfing Song of Naihe" still chanted to extol the waves of Kona that comb the surfing beaches of the young chief's home.[2] In both cases it is clear that the chief himself would have been helpless to recall his family chant or to improvise one for himself that would have met the severe standard of expert court composition.

The Kumulipo as we have it today is popularly known as

2. Pukui, *Journal of American Folklore*, LXII, 255–56.

the Hawaiian "Song of Creation," from its name Kumu-
(u)li-po, "Beginning-(in)-deep-darkness." It consists in
sixteen sections called *wa*, a word used for an interval in time
or space. The first seven sections fall within a period called
the *Po*, the next nine belong to the *Ao*, words generally explained as referring to the world of "Night" before the advent of "Day"; to "Darkness" before "Light"; or, as some
say, to the "Spirit world" in contrast to the "World of living
men," with whom the "World of reason" began. In the first
division are "born" (*hanau*) or "come forth" (*puka*) species
belonging to the plant and animal world, in the second appear gods and men. Of the over two thousand lines that
make up the whole chant, more than a thousand are straight
genealogies listing by pairs, male and female, the various
branches (*lala*) making up the family lines of descent. Thus,
although the whole is strung together within a unified
framework, it may in fact consist of a collection of independent family genealogies pieced together with name songs
and hymns memorializing the gods venerated by different
branches of the ancestral stock.

The highly conventionalized form employed in poetic
composition by court poets throughout marginal Polynesian groups has thus far discouraged an intensive study of so
important a contribution to the oral literature of this isolated
people. Each year the difficulty of editing and translating
becomes greater. The Kalakaua text itself contains misprints,
besides puzzling elisions in the manuscript due to oral memo-
rizing. Since the chant has already died on the lips of a
reciter, the absence of any sign for the unvocalized glottal
catch makes it necessary to distinguish, by the probable
meaning alone, words from quite different roots that are
spelled alike in the text. The language is often archaic, con-
taining many words completely unknown to modern Hawaiians. Little is known with any assurance of the court use

of words once common to chiefs within their own inner circle.

Under the tension of court etiquette, moreover, poetic phrasing was purposely allusive, with elision and the play of fairly complex symbol obscuring the surface meaning and rendering doubly ambiguous the hidden and inner intention which was the real subject of the passage. It heaped up mythical or legendary allusions with which the modern reader can hardly be familiar. It used poetical devices of sound, such as repetition, assonance, and linked lines, often as a mnemonic device but also with a deeper implication, since an accumulation of words of like sound had power in determining the fates of men. Endless listing, arranged seemingly for sound even in genealogies, employed a constant parallelism, a balance in pairs, often of opposites such as male and female, above and below, plant and animal, sometimes perhaps with inclusive intent in order to take in the whole range between, lest the grudge of offended deities bring ill-luck to the family eulogized, but I think primarily for the rhythmic balance so noticeable in the formation of a line and especially of a pair of lines, although I have not myself detected any use of this parallelism in the management of the voice in recitation.

Most puzzling to the uninitiated today is the passion for puns together with a double court usage of words destined to land the translator in unexpected pitfalls as he ventures along unfamiliar ways obscured by so rich a verbiage of language. The use of a double meaning in a word extends to whole passages. A vivid description of natural scenes or activities, some mood of nature or inthrust of myth, may conceal an allusion recognized by the native listener but wholly misinterpreted by us of another culture who attempt translation. To the initiated such a passage attains value, sometimes even intelligibility as part of the context, only through such symbolic meaning. This is the "theme" or

kaona called the dominant characteristic of native art—the
more deftly hidden, the more delightful to those who catch
the application.[3] The meaning of a separate passage must
hence be referred for its interpretation to this double significance, often to the meaning of the chant as a whole, and this,
as we shall presently see, is a subject for argument in the case
of the Kumulipo even among Hawaiians themselves who are
familiar to some extent with the requirements of old poetic
style.

Nor is this trick of allusion confined to court poetry. It
exists today among the most simple with a taste for the turning of verses. A mele given me by a countryman of the island
of Maui recites the various scandals within his own family in
similar cryptic terms but drawn from a completely banal
sphere of allusion. A schoolteacher at Kailua, where we
went ashore while our boat was taking on freight, enter-
tained us with some verses he had just composed and was
careful to point out the symbol contained within the charming natural scene which the words were ostensibly meant to
portray.

One has but to study the rich and picturesque vocabulary
of the Hawaiian proverbial saying to become aware of the
fondness for indirect speech in the everyday language of the
people. The feeling for analogy governs their wit, their gift
of naming, their swift use of a concrete example rather than
abstract definition. As instance, a Hawaiian in a remote sea-
side village, wishing to describe to me the character for nig-
gardliness earned by the inhabitants of a neighboring village,
picked up a bit of close-grained stone to illustrate his thesis.

Especially are sex and the natural bodily functions subject
to conventionalized word-play. Whole passages lost in the
literal reading are to be understood only through such application. This obscurity of language is why the Hawaiian
taunts the foreigner who tries to interpret his lore. "Always

3. *Ibid.*, p. 247.

keep something back" is the thought in the mind of every native informant, however helpful he may seem and really wishes to be in his relation with the foreign inquirer.

There is, moreover, a hesitation inherent in the character of the content in the case of a sacred chant like the Kumulipo that hinders frank explanation even when the meaning is clear to the one questioned. This is not necessarily because he knows that allusions which are to him the natural subjects of jest and story may be considered indelicate by a foreigner. It is also because of the sacred nature of such a revelation and the fact that knowledge has been intrusted to him as a kind of charm to be guarded for his own prestige in commanding the favor of the gods. So Bastian reports the bitter reply of the old man whom he was prodding with questions about the meaning of certain allusions in the chant, "Wollt ihr mir meinen einzigen Schatz rauben?" ("Would you rob me of my only treasure?")

Because of this dominant part played by symbolism in Hawaiian poetic style, it is important to know the theme or *kaona* of the whole composition in order to catch the drift of each part. In the case of the Kumulipo a number of such underlying meanings have been proposed, each sufficiently plausible in itself, but difficult of application in relation to the text as a whole.

The general and orthodox view has been to look upon the chant as an actual history of life on earth from its beginning (*kumu*) progressively up to the coming of man, and thence through the family succession in unbroken line to the birth of the child to whom it was dedicated. As a poetic composition it is thus to be compared with the Greek *Theogony* and the Hebrew Genesis.

Kupihea, however, thinks that the chant should be read for its immediate political implications. He thinks that King Kalakaua has changed and adapted the original source material in order to jeer at rival factions among the chiefs of his day and laud his own family rank.

Pokini Robinson was sure, for her part, that the first seven sections composing the period of the Po symbolize stages in the development of the divine taboo chief from infancy to adolescence, when there begins in the second division the symbolic rehearsal of his taking a wife, house building, and the rearing of a family.

Still another idea, put forward, I think, by Dr. Handy, is that the first division depicts, not stages in the growth of the child after birth, but those passed through while still dwelling in the spirit world as an embryo within the womb of his mother.

How decide among these diverse opinions? An informed young modern to whom I put the question replied, "Probably all are right"; and it is on this advice that I have acted, not holding rigidly to a single concept but allowing, as I think is justified by the obviously composite nature of the whole composition, a wider range of analogy. Passages still doubtful to myself and my Hawaiian helpers I follow with parenthetical question marks. These lines as well as others unquestioned specifically may be differently understood when new light is thrown on the matter. I believe, however, that the reading selected is at least true to Hawaiian poetic art and to the intention as I see it of the passage as a whole.

CHAPTER EIGHT

Prologue to the Night World

TO ILLUSTRATE how the slant upon the meaning of
a text may affect translation of a passage, here is the
Prologue to the chant of the first section, to be followed by
the various renderings already published or suggested by my
interpreters. The lines read:

> O ke au i kahuli wela ka honua
> O ke au i kahuli lole ka lani
> O ke au i kuka'iaka ka la
> E ho'omalamalama i ka malama
> O ke au i Makali'i ka po
> O ka Walewale ho'okumu honua ia
> O ke kumu o ka lipo
> O ke kumu o ka Po i po ai
> O ka Lipolipo, o ka lipolipo
> O ka lipo o ka La, o ka lipo o ka Po
> Po wale ho-i

Bastian, who knew the text from the manuscript alone,
was the first to attempt its analysis. His translation into German gives a poetic turn to the thought. The first six lines
give him the picture of a burnt-out world just taking shape
again out of the mists of night under the first faint light of
the moon. The next four stress the idea of remoteness, at the
very roots where darkness begins, far from the sun, far from
the "night." Bastian is thinking in terms of a European concept, that of a world conflagration out of which a new world
rises. He gets his start from the word *wela*, meaning "hot,
fiery." It is, however, doubtful whether this Old World con-

cept had any place in Polynesian cosmic philosophy. Bastian writes:

> Hin dreht der Zeitumschwung zum Ausgebrannten der Welt,
> Zuruck der Zeitumschwung nach aufwarts wieder,
> Noch sonnenlos die Zeit verhullten Lichtes,
> Und schwankend nur im matten Mondgeschimmer
> Aus Makalii's nacht'gem Wolkenschleier
> Durchzittert schaftenhaft das Grundbild kunft'ger Welt.
> Des Dunkels Beginn aus den Tiefen (Wurzeln) des Abgrunds,
> Der Uranfang von Nacht in Nacht,
> Von weitesten Fernen her, von weitesten Fernen,
> Weit aus den Fernen der Sonne, weit aus den Fernen der Nacht,
>   Noch Nacht ringsumher.[1]

Rock translates:

The wheel of time turns to the burnt-out remains of the world,
Back again, then upwards,
Time is as yet sunless with a dull light,
And only floating in the dim moonlight
From Makalii's awful veil of cloud
Tremble through in shadowy fashion the outlines of the future world,
The beginning of darkness from the depths (roots) of the abyss,
The primordial beginning of night in night
From far away, far, far away,
Far from the remoteness of the sun, far from the remoteness of the night,
    Still night all around.

Here again the thought is European. The wheel was unknown in Polynesia; still less could the idea of time as a revolving wheel be a genuine native concept. Nor did the Polynesian poet stand off and view his world in Miltonic form as trembling "in shadowy fashion" through "an awful veil of cloud." He thought of it, if at all, as a land mass upheaved from primeval waters out of a kind of pit leading to underworlds whence life sprang and to which it might return; arched above also by an equivalent number of sky

1. Bastian, p. 70.

worlds inhabited by ancestral gods. In short, neither Bastian nor his translator has contributed to our understanding of the possible meaning of the lines with which the Kumulipo chant opens.

With Queen Liliuokalani the case is different. Her literal rendering keeps fairly within native thought. As an educated Hawaiian of chief stock, she had ample opportunity to consult those still living who knew something of the old chant. She was also herself a composer of charming songs turned in the symbolic style familiar to Hawaiian mele. Her translation pictures the rise of earth out of slime at the time when the first light begins to dawn out of darkness before the sun was. She retains the stylistic features of the original—formal repetition as a mnemonic device and a play of opposites, in this case the idea of earth (*honua*) as opposed to heaven (*lani*); of darkness (*po*) used here with the contrasting word *la*, meaning the light of day or "sun"; of illumination, *ho'omalamalama*, used in contrast to "deep darkness" or "depth of darkness," *lipo, lipolipo*. Emphasis upon the dawn of light bringing heat to earth is conveyed by the word *wela*, meaning "hot" or "fiery," upon the light itself by such specific words as "sun" (*la*), "moon" (*malama*), and in the word *aka* signifying "the first faint light of the rising moon." These words the queen generally renders by some more neutral phrase. The native idea of the word *lipo* is of "dark from the depth of a cavern, or from the depth of the sea." It implies a space concept and at the same time one of degree of shade as applied, for example, to the change in color of the ocean as one gets away from shore into deep water. As a cosmographic term it describes the ocean bottom where lies the slime (*walewale*) out of which life emerges. Its makeup from the words (*u*)*li po*, "darkness of (the) depth," has already been suggested. The queen writes:

> At the time that turned the heat of the earth
> At the time when the heavens turned and changed

At the time when the light of the sun was subdued
To cause light to break forth
At the time of the night of Makalii [winter]
Then began the slime which established the earth,
The source of deepest darkness,
Of the depth of darkness, of the depth of darkness,
Of the darkness of the sun, in the depth of night,
　　It is night,
　　So was night born.

By smoothing out some rough phrasing and allowing for the running of the seventh and eighth lines into one line, we get a quite reasonable version from the cosmic point of view, a character implied also in the reiteration of the word *kumu*, read as "source," and *ho'okumu*, read as "established." The relation of "night" to the establishment of earth is not, however, made clear.

The *Aloha* translation from Kukahi's text follows the same train of thought. The first lines—

The time when the earth was hotly changed
The time when the heavens separately changed—

suggest the Polynesian myth of the forcible separation of Earth and Sky to admit the light of day, but I do not know by what authority the idea is read into the word *lole*, which means "to turn inside out" and is the basis for the cataclysm of world forces read into the text by some commentators, as well as for the idea of the seasonal return of the sun northward at the opening of the new year, as in the queen's rendering. The next lines read:

The time when the sun was rising
To give light to the moon,

but it is doubtful whether Hawaiians knew that the light of the moon came from the sun, and if they did so believe, they were too good observers to represent the sun as "rising" to give such light. In the sixth line *walewale* is changed to *welawela*, meaning "intense heat" or "strong emotion" and

good from the point of view of the link with *wela* of the first
line but ignored in translation, where the line reads:

> Then was the creating of the earth.

In lines seven and eight the word *kumu* is translated by
"reason" in place of the usual "source" or "beginning," and
the lines are written with inverted commas as if quoting a
popular saying,

> 'The reason for the deep, to get depth,
> The reason for night, to get darkness.'

Poepoe's explanatory notes attached to his roughly pen-
ciled text give an even more explicit cosmic meaning to the
lines. The first two he thinks tell of "the coming of fire from
the inside of the earth and leaving in confusion (inside out)
the heavens and the earth." The word *Kuka'iaka* is "the
moon," called "the sun that lighted the period called po."
Makali'i is "the first month of the year," and he adds, "at this
time these materials were made." The phrase *wale ho'okumu
honua* he refers to "the beginning of the earth because of the
melting together of the earthy material and water. They
were mixed this way and that, became melted, and are called
the Kumulipo, the slimey beginning of the earth." Poepoe
is here bringing to bear upon the text the scientific knowledge acquired through foreign culture. He reads into the
lines the formation of earth as a factual process without
recognizing such spiritual forces as become explicit in Tahitian chants and could hardly have been absent from the
thought of ancient Hawaii.

Thus far the cosmic interpretation alone has been illustrated. In the *Honolulu Advertiser* for November 12, 1936,
Theodore Kelsey, born in Hawaii and familiar with the language, although not himself of Hawaiian parentage, printed
a "combined literal and symbolic interpretation." Without
quoting his whole paraphrase, I wish to point out some ideas
it contains that may throw light upon the underlying mean-

ing. He distinguishes the literal interpretation—that of the creation of light and life on earth—from the symbolic, to be found also in the story of the first man Kumu-honua ("Source-of-earth") and the first woman, Lalo-honua ("Earth-beneath-the-surface"), the two called in this chant Kumu-lipo ("Source-of-profundity") and Po'ele ("Darkness"). What is here symbolically pictured as the "earth" (*honua*) is to be interpreted as "Hawaii's original royal line, hot with fiercest tabu—*kapu wela.*" Makali'i is the season when seeds sprout, fish spawn, and the Pleiades (the Makali'i) appear with other stars high in the heavens. At this time the sun was "like a vital fluid of generation that produced life." As the line of Wakea's descendants increased in number, its beginnings stretched far back into the past and this past grew more and more dim in memory. The poet therefore proceeds to explore back into the profound depth of the past for the beginning of the royal ancestral line. Kelsey has here a definite conception of the symbolism under the literal wording of the lines. Life on earth is engendered by the heat of the sun. As the sun symbolizes the procreative power whence life proceeds, whose source is the god of generation in the spirit world, so a chief descended from the god and "hot with fiercest taboo" carries on through procreation the continuity of the family line. "Darkness" Kelsey applies to distance in time rather than in space. The pit idea is absent and attention fixed upon a genealogical beginning of the chief stock in a time so remote as to be lost to memory.

Kupihea, keeper of the king's fishponds, rejects the Prologue altogether. He thinks Kalakaua himself exchanged it for the original two lines with which the chant opened—

> Hanau ka po i ka po, po no,
> Hanau mai a puka i ke ao, malamalama—

to be translated,

> Things born in the night are of the dark,
> Things born from and sprung up in the day are of the light.

Dark and light, *po* and *ao*, he would refer to the intellectual
faculties in man as opposed to plants and animals. The first
seven sections of the chant represent the generation of the
gods in the bodies of beings without the light of reason.
With the eighth section man emerges, and the period of the
Ao has to do with the children of men, who multiply on the
earth from the first birth of the god of procreation in the
body of man. With man dawned the rational powers. The
Ao is peopled by creatures endowed with power to develop
arts and crafts, all cultural activities; the Po, by creatures
"controlled" by gods alone, that is, born not through mankind but through the gods. The Po is a spirit world, the Ao
a world of living men.

Still more specific is Pokini Robinson's interpretation of
the Prologue. Her fresh approach, uninstructed save by long
familiarity with chant practice in chief circles, gives her
opinion special interest. She believes, like Kelsey, that the
lines herald the birth of the divine child whose stages of
development are followed in the succeeding sections of the
chant. He is called a "fire" (*wela*) because of his taboo rank,
"heavenly one" (*lani*) as a customary mark of honor. The
word *walewale* names the seven-day purification period for
the mother after childbirth as well as the "slime" whence
the divine seed sprouted. The shining of the "sun" (*la*) she
refers to the dim opening of the child's eyes to the light.
Thus the child is born in the first line, "turns over" in the
second, "opens its eyes" in the third. The birth takes place
during the month of Makali'i, when the sun returns northward and the season of growth begins.

I am not sure whether Pokini would push the symbolism
back to an Adamic birth, origin of the race, or give it a more
immediate reference to the birth of the child for whom the
chant was first composed, whether Keawe's or another. If
she would actually refer it to the time now lost to memory

when the first Lono was born as a taboo chief on earth, the
lines might be paraphrased something like this:

The time of the birth of the taboo chief,
The time when the Heavenly One pushed his way out,
The time when the bright one first saw the light,
At first faintly like the light of the moon,
At the season of Makali'i in the far past.
From the slime of the mother the stock began,
Began in the spirit world,
Began in the time of the gods in a world of gods,
In the far distant past lost in remoteness;
Long ago was the coming of the bright one into the world of the
    gods,
  A world still peopled by gods alone.

CHAPTER NINE

The Refrain of Generation

THE Kumulipo chant opens with four sections or odes of identical pattern, each heralding the birth of a special class within the animal and vegetable world. Each class is governed by a parent-pair passing progressively from darkness toward the light, Kumulipo and Po'ele for the first class, Pouliuli and Powehiwehi for the second, Po'ele'ele and Pohaha for the third, Popanopano and Polalowehi for the fourth. Each ode opens with a poetic passage naming these generative agents, male and female, and setting the key word for the development of the pattern within each class. Each closes with an epilogue composed in similar cryptic style, generally descriptive of the world into which the new forms are born. Except for these two poetic passages, the ode consists in an enumeration of species paired one with another in monotonous sequence, tiresome in text translation but no doubt as pleasing in chanted recitation as our own memory tests in popular game formulas.

The pairing of species matching parent and child, plant and animal, or land and sea forms has no apparent rational basis but rather depends upon word-play between names. These names are not invented for mere rhyme value. Most were promptly identified with known species by one or another of my native informants or by Dr. Edmonson, zoölogist on the Museum staff, and Miss Neal in charge of plant collections. The punning names have in some cases a practical magical function. For example, in plant medicine the first food to be taken after dosing with a special medicinal herb is the sea-grown thing whose name matches with it. Thus, after dosing with the mint called *'ala'alawainui,* the *Plectranthus australis* of herbariums, the Hawaiian herb doctor prescribes the edible seaweed *'a'ala'ula* known to science as *Codium tomentosum* or *adherens* and still to be had in Honolulu fish markets. Such is the nature of the language that these lists may be extended indefinitely. Kukahi omits a number of pairs given in the Kalakaua text, and this suggests that the series may be used competitively like our own parlor games to test a knowledge of names within a given class, in our case generally arranged on an alphabetic basis rather than upon internal rhyming.

In each of the first four odes this simple listing of pairs is followed by their even more monotonous grouping within a six-line stanza, each introduced and concluded with an identical refrain, one line opening and three closing the couplet. This refrain gives the impression of a traditional formula and is undoubtedly old. No adequate interpretation has been offered for the lines as a whole, and a variation in the Kalakaua text from the manuscript form adds to the uncertainty. A typical stanza reads:

40. O kane ia Wai'ololi, o ka wahine ia Wai'olola
     Hanau ka 'Aki'aki noho i kai
     Kia'i ia e ka Manienie-'aki'aki noho i uka
     He po uhe'e i ka wawa
     He nuku, he wai ka 'ai a ka la'au
45. O ke Akua ke komo, 'a'oe komo kanaka

The words *Wai'ololi* and *Wai'olola* are applied in everyday speech to a narrow entrance through which water passes with force and a wide one which receives them without a struggle. Thus Pokini says the first term is given to a narrow bay along the coast where the water carries the fish in with a rush, the second to a wide shore line where the surf rolls in without breaking. "The names of the waters that were applied to a male and a female," writes Poepoe, and adds a familiar saying, *Ke uli mai nei, ke ola mai nei ka wai o ka hua,*

translated "The water in the gourd goes gurgle-i, gurgle-a."
Kawena Pukui remembers a similar saying applied to sounds
issuing from ventholes at the volcano: *Ke uli, ola* (or *uhi,
oha*) *mai nei o Pele.* Kupihea illustrated by the gurgling
sounds made in emptying a gourd filled with water according to the size of the aperture at its mouth, sounds which the
pupil in the art of chanting was taught to imitate in order to
gain control of the long vibration upon open or closed vowel
sounds at the end of a phrase, an achievement considered the
high point in a professional reciter's technique; but I do not
know whether this is a universal practice. The line is certainly correctly referred to the parts played by the male
(*kane*) and female (*wahine*) in the generative process. Bastian was no doubt well informed when he wrote, as translated by Rock,

> And the male strong in generative power
> And the female acquiescent.

This is a birth chant, and procreation is its theme. My informants read,

> Man born for the narrow stream, woman for the broad stream.

The reference in this first line of the refrain is thus to the
generation of life along shore as the waters meet the line of
rising land.

The last line is an equally clear reference to the office of
gods rather than man in the fertilizing process—

> The god enters, man cannot enter—

hence the reverence with which Hawaiians approach nature,
both animate and inanimate, filled as it is with powers beyond their control.

> The way to the po for the god (*Te ara ki te po no te atua*)
> The way to the ao for the man (*Te ara ki te ao no te tangata*)

is the Tuamotuan saying. In these different ways is expressed
the separation between man and the natural world, for

whose fructifying, so essential to the life of mankind, man must nevertheless wait upon the gods.[1]

For the third and fourth verses of the stanza as written in the Kalakaua text I have arrived at no satisfactory translation. Bastian, who had only the manuscript before him, which reads *He pou he'e i ka wawa*, refers the word *he'e* to the octopus and soliloquizes: "During this period of creation of the lowest forms of animal life ... the octopus is present as observer of the process described ...", but, since my purpose is to interpret Kalakaua's text, unless clearly bungled, I follow Ho'olapa's doubtful rendering: "Darkness slips into light," where *wawa* is perhaps a misprint for *waka*, "a flash of light," rather than the "tumult" of the literal translation. In the second line of the couplet the word *nuku* is the difficulty. One would read "nest," others a "splash" or a "quarrel," still others take *nuku* for a diminutive and, ignoring the comma, translate "A little water [*wai*] is food [*'ai*] for the tree [*la'au*]." Emory proposes "earth" as the Polynesian opposite for "sky," correctly written in Hawaiian as *nu'u* and *lani*. This suggestion, although far from satisfactory, I have adopted as perhaps what the Kalakaua text was intended to convey, since in later sections where birds and reptiles are in question the words change to *hua* ("fruit") and *'i'o* ("flesh"). The typical stanza pairing the tough edible seaweed called *'aki'aki*, "living in the sea," with the tough-stemmed *manienie* grass, "living on land," may thus be read,

> Man for the narrow stream, woman for the broad stream,
> Born is the 'Aki'aki seaweed living in the sea,
> Guarded by the Manienie-'aki'aki grass living on land,
> (Darkness slips into light,
> Earth and water are the food of the tree,) [?]
> The god enters, man can not enter.

1. Henry, pp. 347–49, *Journal of the Polynesian Society*, XII, 223, ll. 5, 9, 10; 232, ll. 60, 61. Cf. Smith, *Lore of the Whare-wananga*, pp. 138, 139; White, I, 138, 142, 143.

I believe, however, that the manuscript gives the true form, shifted in the Kalakaua text either deliberately or through ignorance of the meaning. Firth finds in Polynesian Tikopia the word *nuku* used in erotic verse for the "place of particular sex interest" in the female.[2] If *pou*, meaning "pillar," refers by analogy to the male generative organ, the two lines would agree in symbolism with the first and last lines of the stanza. The word *wawa* might then be an elision for *wa-(oei)wa*, defined like *wao* as "a place of the gods." Together the whole would refer specifically to the process of fertilization and growth in the natural world of the *po* controlled by the gods. But, since I have no Hawaiian confirmation for this interpretation, I use the vaguer symbolism proposed by Ho'olapa. Such a birth chant with its refrain of generation carried through the first four odes of the Kumulipo seems to link together the whole series in a kind of magical incantation to promote fertility in plant and animal forms necessary to man but over whose procreation he has no control.

2. Firth, *Work of the Gods in Tikopia*, p. 260.

CHAPTER TEN

Birth of Sea and Land Life

THE Prologue for the first section, if read literally, seems to picture the rising of land out of the fathomless depths of ocean. Along its shores the lower forms of life begin to gather, and these are arranged as births from parent to child. Poepoe calls this a device "used by the composer of the chant in order to get a source of reproduction as we see it in life," that is, he does not expect the poet to be taken literally. He writes:

Kumulipo was the husband, Po'ele the wife. To them was born Pouliuli. This was the beginning of the earth. The coral was the first stone in the foundation of the earth mentioned in the chant. It was the insect that made the coral and all things in the sea. This was the beginning of the period called the first interval of time. During this time grew the coral, the shellfish (such as the sea cucumber, the small sea urchin, the flat sea urchin, tiny mussels, the oysterlike mussels, the mussels of the sea, the clam, the barnacle, the dark sea snail, the cowry, and so forth). In this interval of time grew the moss and the little plants on land. It was still dark. The water was made to be a nest that gave birth and bore all things in the womb of the deep.

Poepoe knows that the coral polyp builds up the coral and that the shellfish makes its own shell—"it was an insect that made the coral and all things," says Poepoe. But was this known to the poet? The selection of hard-coated creatures as the first forms of life on earth harmonizes with the idea of reproductive power inherent in a stone into which a god enters, an idea fundamental to Polynesian thought about the structure of the world. According to a Tahitian chant of creation, the building-up of land during the "chaotic period" is due to "affinity" between rocks of opposite character that "meet and unite."[1] Pairs of rocks suggesting in shape male and female sex organs were worshipped as ancestral gods in old Hawaii, and fertility fish gods in the shape of stones occur in pairs in old fishponds. Even today the popular belief lingers. "Where else did all the stones come from?" asked a child from a well-educated family; and he brought me a box of so-called "breeding stones," which he assured me would produce young. But his elders must have interfered; the box disappeared before the test was completed.[2]

Following a series of stanzas pairing land and sea forms comes a ten-line epilogue, carrying on the idea of a world in its first stages of fecundity, stimulated to growth by the generative powers at work during this embryo period of its history. Soft-bodied shellfish have emerged out of the hard bed of ocean; along the just-risen shore line, sea plants float in the wash of the waves; delicate land growths stand rooted in the soil, their slender bodies swaying with the currents of air. The birth of the climbing pandanus vine, worshiped as a god of forest growth because of its spike of red at the fruiting point, symbol of fertility, leads directly to the advent of "the man with the water gourd," who is "Kane of the generative water," Kane-i-ka-wai-ola, represented, says Kupihea, in gushing spring water.

"The man with the water gourd, that is a god," begins the passage, and there follows the softening-up of earth and the increase of plant growth. The withering vine (*kalina*) is revivified (*ho'oulu*). Propagation (*ka huli*) causes growth (*ho'oka[u]wowo*). Rootlets (*paia['a]*) carry water to bathe and soften the developing tuber. Earth is pregnant (*piha*) with growth. Earth props up the sky, or, as Kupihea would read the symbol, commoners (*honua*) serve as staff (*ko'o*)

1. Henry, p. 340.
2. Beckwith, *Hawaiian Mythology*, pp. 88–90.

to support (*pa'a*) the chiefs (*lani*). May not the familiar Polynesian myth of the sky pushed apart from earth to let in the light of day, often forced upward upon the leaves of a growing plant, refer similarly in a figure to the rise of the chief class in distinction from that of the commoners? The whole passage, thinks Kupihea, here refers, not to the spread of vegetation but to the multiplication of a people through the procreative function symbolized in the "man with the water gourd," Kane-i-ka-wai-ola.

The concluding line, "O lewa ke au, ia Kumulipo ka po," with the reiterated "Po—no" ("Still it is night"), serves to balance the preceding "O he'e au loloa ka po," where the word *he'e*, I think, refers rather to the waving, twisting motion of sea growths, "sliding" (*he'e*) about through the water and of land plants swaying in the currents of air than to the squid in particular or to sliding sports, both of which derived ideas have obsessed translators of this passage. The word *au*, carried over in the first instance from the *auau* of the line before, may refer to a period of "time" in this unfolding world of the *po*, perhaps to its "length" (*loloa*) in the first instance, to Kumulipo as its generative agent in the second. At least, any translation I have seen of this passage has been so incredibly hopeless that an attempt to do justice to the poet's conception will not, I trust, be taken as an indignity to native genius.

Pokini Robinson sees, I think quite justly, in this image of an infant world with creatures floating in the wash of the waves or swayed by currents of air a symbol of the uncertain movements of the young child whose development she considers to be the subject of the whole chant. The rootlets (*paia*['*a*]) bathing the *manawa* she would refer to the veins carrying nourishment to the child through the fontanel (*manawa*) from which the unborn child is supposed to receive food from the parent and may still draw nourishment after birth if the mother's milk fails.

CHANT ONE

1. At the time when the earth became hot
At the time when the heavens turned about
At the time when the sun was darkened
To cause the moon to shine
5. The time of the rise of the Pleiades
The slime, this was the source of the earth
The source of the darkness that made darkness
The source of the night that made night
The intense darkness, the deep darkness
10. Darkness of the sun, darkness of the night
   Nothing but night.

The night gave birth
Born was Kumulipo in the night, a male
Born was Po'ele in the night, a female
15. Born was the coral polyp, born was the coral, came forth
Born was the grub that digs and heaps up the earth, came
   forth
Born was his [child] an earthworm, came forth
Born was the starfish, his child the small starfish came forth
Born was the sea cucumber, his child the small sea cucumber
   came forth
20. Born was the sea urchin, the sea urchin [tribe]
Born was the short-spiked sea urchin, came forth
Born was the smooth sea urchin, his child the long-spiked
   came forth
Born was the ring-shaped sea urchin, his child the thin-spiked
   came forth
Born was the barnacle, his child the pearl oyster came forth
25. Born was the mother-of-pearl, his child the oyster came forth
Born was the mussel, his child the hermit crab came forth
Born was the big limpet, his child the small limpet came forth
Born was the cowry, his child the small cowry came forth
Born was the naka shellfish, the rock oyster his child came
   forth
30. Born was the drupa shellfish, his child the bitter white shellfish came forth
Born was the conch shell, his child the small conch shell came
   forth

Born was the nerita shellfish, the sand-burrowing shellfish his
child came forth
Born was the fresh water shellfish, his child the small fresh
water shellfish came forth
Born was man for the narrow stream, the woman for the
broad stream
35. Born was the Ekaha moss living in the sea
Guarded by the Ekahakaha fern living on land
Darkness slips into light
Earth and water are the food of the plant
The god enters, man can not enter
40. Man for the narrow stream, woman for the broad stream
Born was the touch seagrass living in the sea
Guarded by the tough landgrass living on land

Refrain

46. Man for the narrow stream, woman for the broad stream
Born was the 'A'ala moss living in the sea
Guarded by the 'Ala'ala mint living on land

Refrain

52. Man for the narrow stream, woman for the broad stream
Born was the Manauea moss living in the sea
Guarded by the Manauea taro plant living on land

Refrain

58. Man for the narrow stream, woman for the broad stream
Born was the Ko'ele seaweed living in the sea
Guarded by the long-jointed sugarcane, the *ko 'ele'ele*, living
on land

Refrain

64. Man for the narrow stream, woman for the broad stream
Born was the Puaki seaweed living in the sea
Guarded by the Akiaki rush living on land

Refrain

70. Man for the narrow stream, woman for the broad stream
Born was the Kakalamoa living in the sea
Guarded by the moamoa plant living on land

Refrain

76. Man for the narrow stream, woman for the broad stream
Born was the Kele seaweed living in the sea
Guarded by the Ekele plant living on land

Refrain

82. Man for the narrow stream, woman for the broad stream
Born was the Kala seaweed living in the sea
Guarded by the 'Akala vine living on land

Refrain

88. Man for the narrow stream, woman for the broad stream
Born was the Lipu'upu'u living in the sea
Guarded by the Lipu'u living on land

Refrain

94. Man for the narrow stream, woman for the broad stream
Born was the Long-one living at sea
Guarded by the Long-torch living on land

Refrain

100. Man for the narrow stream, woman for the broad stream
Born was the Ne seaweed living in the sea
Guarded by the Neneleau [sumach] living on land

Refrain

106. Man for the narrow stream, woman for the broad stream
Born was the hairy seaweed living in the sea
Guarded by the hairy pandanus vine living on land
Darkness slips into light
Earth and water are the food of the plant
The god enters, man can not enter

112. The man with the water gourd, he is a god
Water that causes the withered vine to flourish
Causes the plant top to develop freely
115. Multiplying in the passing time
The long night slips along
Fruitful, very fruitful
Spreading here, spreading there
Spreading this way, spreading that way
120. Propping up earth, holding up the sky
The time passes, this night of Kumulipo
Still it is night

CHAPTER ELEVEN

The World of Infancy

THE chant of the second section celebrates the appearance of fish in the sea and forest growth on land under control of the generating agents Pouliuli and Powehiwehi. The word *uliuli* is applied to the color of deep ocean in comparison to the lighter shade of shallower waters near shore, *wehiwehi* to the shade under thick leafage where some light filters in; hence "Deep-profound-darkness" and "Darkness-streaked-with-glimmers-of-light" as this next stage in the development of life on earth advances toward the light, or, as Pokini would put it, as the newborn infant begins to show consciousness of the world about him.

The Prologue introduces the birth of a wonder child in the shape of a "*hilu* fish" as the theme for the listing of sea life to follow. Two species of this fish, *Anampses cuvier* and *Juli eydouxii*, are among the most brilliant in coloring found in Hawaiian waters, hence the name *hilu*, "elegant." The lines make sense only when applied to a human child in babyhood. In old days the first solid food given a child was thought to influence its afterlife. The red-eyed *kole* fish would give the child a rosy tinge, the "sticking" gobey fish would cause good luck to "stick" to him, the *hilu* fish would insure good looks. A discreet form of compliment in praising a pretty infant, since open admiration was not only in bad taste but might bring bad luck, was to call him a *hilu* fish. "Aren't you a *hilu* fish!" (*He hilu no paha oe!*) or "What a pretty fish the *hilu* is!" (*Ke hilu he i' a no'i-no'i!*) was the proper phrase. Similarly, the difficult second line may be referred to a lullaby that Kawena Pukui remembers her grandmother singing,

Toss, toss, hush	Ho'ole'ile'i, ho'onana
Hush my child.	Ho'onana ana i ku'u kama.

The early movements of an active youngster are, furthermore, exactly conveyed in the words "wrestler" and "pusher" also suggested by Kawena for the enigmatic line that follows. There comes next a passage explained by Pokini Robinson as applied to the freedom of a child in obeying the calls of nature. "Ta! Poho-mi-lua-mea!" cries an elder when the odor proclaims that a child has messed himself. The makeup of the word, from *poholua* for the hollow of the anus and *mi* for passing urine, is sufficient to indicate the relevance of the expression, and the lines that follow complete the incident.

The epilogue similarly plays between the underwater world, where swims the brilliantly colored fish, and the secluded valley, home of the gods in ancient times, where a chief's son was taken to be reared as a sacred child in order to preserve his high taboo rank as he grew to adolescence. In the sea world bright-colored *opule* fish play, "the sea is thick with them." Their persistent gulping and swallowing (*monimoni*) when at the surface links with the words *kolomio* and *miomio* for their disappearance under sea in a swift dive. From the "coral ridges" among which the little ones play, they "seek the dark currents" and slip away from land to the darkness that covers them.

To the symbolic sea world in which the child plays in infancy, allusion to the mythical Pimoe, Polikua, and Paliuli lend a playful note of mystery as well as of learning. They satisfy an imperative law of poetic composition common to Hawaiian as to early Greek song masters, where witness the reproach leveled at Pindar by his lady critic for omitting such allusions from his first eulogistic verses and her later sharp warning, upon his attempting to correct this fault, "to sow with the hand, not with the bag." Pimoe is a shape-shifting being of uncertain sex, for whom in her feminine form legendary heroes go fishing. Some call her "caretaker" of Kane's-hidden-island, a land "beyond the horizon." Poli-kua, from *poli*, "concave," and *kua*, "back," is the dip at the horizon beyond which the eye cannot reach, also personified in the playful saying of one who has been in the land of dreams that he has been "flirting with Polikua."

Paliuli names an ever verdant land of the gods where abundant food grows without labor.[1] The name is given to fertile spots in deep mountain valleys where in old days children of high chiefs were taken to be reared. These spots seem to be recognized as former homes of the gods by the abundance of wild growth, perhaps of wild fruits such as banana and breadfruit. Kupihea named one such spot in the mountains back of the Kamehameha girls' school on Oahu, another near Nahiku on Maui in the Keanae region, one above Halawa on Molokai where Kamehameha is said to have been brought up, and one on Lanai at Kumoku. Some say that each district had its Paliuli. Perhaps the name was given to whatever secluded spot was chosen in the district for the rearing of taboo chiefs from infancy without any form of labor on their own part. The poet here seems to compare the coral ridges of the sea where fishes play with the green heights where the little human "*hilu* fish" passes his childhood. Since the material world is linked so closely in Hawaiian thought with the psychical, it may be that the underwater world where the *hilu* fish moves is to be under-stood as symbol of the infant's first contact with the world of fluctuating realities into which he is so early plunged.

CHANT TWO

Born is a child to Po-wehiwehi
Cradled in the arms of Po-uliuli[?]

1. Beckwith, *Hawaiian Mythology*, chap. vi.

125. A wrestler, a pusher, [?]
    Dweller in the land of Poho-mi-luamea
    The sacred scent from the gourd stem proclaims [itself]
    The stench breaks forth in the time of infancy
    He is doubtful and stands swelling
130. He crooks himself and straddles
    The seven waters just float
    Born is the child of the *hilu* fish ånd swims
    The *hilu* fish rests with spreading tail-fin
    A child of renown for Po-uliuli
135. A little one for Po-wehiwehi
    Po-uliuli the male
    Po-wehiwehi the female
    Born is the I'a [fish], born the Nai'a [porpoise] in the sea
        there swimming
    Born is the Mano [shark], born the Moano [goatfish] in the
        sea there swimming
140. Born is the Mau, born the Maumau in the sea there swimming
    Born is the Nana, born the Mana fish in the sea there swim-
        ming
    Born is the Nake, born the Make in the sea there swimming
    Born is the Napa, born the Nala in the sea there swimming
    Born is the Pala, born the Kala [sturgeon ?] in the sea there
        swimming
145. Born is the Paka eel, born is the Papa [crab] in the sea there
        swimming
    Born is the Kalakala, born the Huluhulu [sea slug] in the
        sea there swimming
    Born is the Halahala, born the Palapala in the sea there swim-
        ming
    Born is the Pe'a [octopus], born is the Lupe [sting ray] in the
        sea there swimming
    Born is the Ao, born is the 'Awa [milkfish] in the sea there
        swimming
150. Born is the Aku [bonito], born the Ahi [albacore] in the sea
        there swimming
    Born is the Opelu [mackerel], born the Akule fish in the sea
        there swimming
    Born is the 'Ama'ama [mullet], born the 'Anae [adult mullet]
        in the sea there swimming

Born is the Ehu, born the Nehu fish in the sea there swimming

Born is the 'Ino, born the 'Ao'ao in the sea there swimming

155. Born is the 'Ono fish, born the Omo in the sea there swimming

Born is the Pahau, born is the Lauhau in the sea there swimming

Born is the Moi [threadfin], born the Lo'ilo'i in the sea there swimming

Born is the Mao, born is the Maomao in the sea there swimming

Born is the Kaku, born the A'ua'u in the sea there swimming

160. Born is the Kupou, born the Kupoupou in the sea there swimming

Born is the Weke [mackerel ?], born the Lele in the sea there swimming

Born is the Palani [sturgeon], born the Nukumoni [cavalla] in the sea there swimming

Born is the Ulua fish, born the Hahalua [devilfish] in the sea there swimming

Born is the 'Ao'aonui, born the Paku'iku'i fish in the sea there swimming

165. Born is the Ma'i'i'i fish, born the Ala'ihi fish in the sea there swimming

Born is the 'O'o, born the 'Akilolo fish in the sea there swimming

Born is man for the narrow stream, the woman for the broad stream

Born is the Nenue [pickerel] living in the sea

Guarded by the Lauhue [gourd plant] living on land

Refrain

172. Man for the narrow stream, woman for the broad stream
Born is the Pahaha [young mullet] living in the sea
Guarded by the Puhala [pandanus] living on land

Refrain

178. Man for the narrow stream, woman for the broad stream
Born is the Pahau living in the sea
Guarded by the Hau tree [hibiscus] living on land

Refrain

184. Man for the narrow stream, woman for the broad stream
Born is the He'e [squid] living in the sea
Guarded by the Walahe'e [shrub] living on land

Refrain

190. Man for the narrow stream, woman for the broad stream
Born is the 'O'opu [gobey fish] living in the sea
Guarded by the 'O'opu [fish] living in fresh water

Refrain

196. Man for the narrow stream, woman for the broad stream
Born is the Kauila eel living in the sea
Guarded by the Kauila tree living on land

Refrain

202. Man for the narrow stream, woman for the broad stream
Born is the Umaumalei eel living in the sea
Guarded by the 'Ulei tree living on land

Refrain

208. Man for the narrow stream, woman for the broad stream
Born is the Paku'iku'i fish living in the sea
Guarded by the Kukui tree [candlenut] living on land

Refrain

214. Man for the narrow stream, woman for the broad stream
Born is the Laumilo eel living in the sea
Guarded by the Milo tree living on land

Refrain

220. Man for the narrow stream, woman for the broad stream
Born is the Kupoupou fish living in the sea
Guarded by the Kou tree living on land

Refrain

226. Man for the narrow stream, woman for the broad stream
Born is the Hauliuli [snake mackerel] living in the sea
Guarded by the Uhi yam living on land

Refrain

232. Man for the narrow stream, woman for the broad stream
Born is the Weke [mackerel] living in the sea
Guarded by the Wauke plant living on land

Refrain

238. Man for the narrow stream, woman for the broad stream
Born is the 'A'awa fish living in the sea
Guarded by the 'Awa plant living on land

Refrain

244. Man for the narrow stream, woman for the broad stream
Born is the Ulae [lizard fish] living in the sea
Guarded by the Mokae rush living on land

Refrain

250. Man for the narrow stream, woman for the broad stream
Born is the Palaoa [walrus] living in the sea [?]
Guarded by the Aoa [sandalwood] living on land

Refrain

256. The train of walruses passing by [?]
Milling about in the depths of the sea
The long lines of opule fish
The sea is thick with them
260. Crabs and hardshelled creatures
[They] go swallowing on the way
Rising and diving under swiftly and silently
Pimoe lurks behind the horizon
On the long waves, the crested waves
265. Innumerable the coral ridges
Low, heaped-up, jagged
The little ones seek the dark places
Very dark is the ocean and obscure
A sea of coral like the green heights of Paliuli
270. The land disappears into them
Covered by the darkness of night
Still it is night

CHAPTER TWELVE

Winged Life

THE second section told of the birth of sea life and forest growth, in the third come winged creatures; first insects, then birds of land and sea. In the manuscript the order is reversed, bird life illogically preceding fish and forest necessary for their food and nesting. The symbolism of the Prologue plays not upon this winged life but upon the sprouting of the *Haha*, as upon the *Hilu* of the last section. The whole passage is to be understood, says Kupihea, as referring to the rise of the chief class under the figure of the sprouting taro plant, although the dictionary gives no clue to this symbolic use of the word *haha*.

The generating agents Po-'ele'ele, "Dark-night," and Po-haha, "Night-just-breaking-into-dawn," again suggest the idea of a constant approach to "light" in successive stages of the world's growth. The name Po-haha, from the word *pohá*, "to break forth, to appear suddenly," continues the play on the key word. In common use are the sayings *Pohá mai ka la*, "the sun breaks forth," said of the first ray of the sun at dawn; *pohakea* for the place where it shows itself; *pohaha ka la*, said of its habitual rising; *poháhá ka lani*, said symbolically of the perpetuation of the intelligent class, perhaps originally of the chief class.

Kupihea believes that the phrases "dark leaf" (*lau pahiwa*), "leaf of high chiefs" (*lau palaili'i*), and "the sprout from the rootstalk" (*ka pua o ka Haha*) refer specifically to the Uli line from whom chiefs of the islands of Maui and Hawaii reckon descent. The Kumulipo chant clearly belongs to a family on this line, as proved by the fact that part

68

of the fifteenth and the whole sixteenth section are devoted
to the listing of the Maui branch of the Uli genealogy from
Ha-loa, "Long-stalk," ancestor of the Hawaiian people, to
the Lono-i-ka-makahiki called a child of Keawe. The "nine
leaves" (*na lau eiwa*) of the Haha, Kupihea further refers to
the "nine daughters of Wakea," from whom, if I understood
him correctly, sprang nine branches of taboo chiefs recognized in the college of chiefs in Hawaii. These he enumerated as follows, but probably as they occurred to him
rather than in order of rank: .

Naha, "an Oahu class originating from marriage between uncle and
    niece"
Io, "a Kauai class named from a little bird that lives on high lehua
    trees, the class to which Queen Kapi'olani (Kalakaua's consort)
    belonged"
Puaiwa, "the class to which Kalakaua's line belonged"
Papaua, "the kahuna (priestly) line, a line of high chiefs"
Poloa, . . .
Hiwa, "a line direct from Tahiti"
Papalua, "a Lanai class"
Popolo, "a Maui class"
Lanikaula, "a Molokai class"

It would be interesting to correlate these "nine daughters of
Wakea" with John White's "nine sisters" of Tini-rau, son
of Takaroa in Maori tradition, although I do not find his passage in the Maori text.[1]

Kupihea further believes that certain passages of the chant
have been inserted to boast of Kalakaua's own high lineage
and throw discredit upon contemporary detractors. As an
instance he cites the break at mention of the *Auku'u* or
Hawaiian heron to picture the coming of flocks of these
birds and their settling along shore. The Auku'u have been
compared to a company of plotters fearful of being over-
heard by chance listeners, this because of their habit of "hud-

1. White, I, 23.

dling together along a sandbank and glancing furtively, owl-like, this way and that."

> Me he auku'u la ke kau i ke ahua
> Alaalawa na maka he pueo la

is the saying quoted by Andrews. It was on the ground of inferiority in rank that many Hawaiians had opposed Kala-kaua's title to the throne and had pushed the claim of Queen Emma, consort of Kamehameha IV. But even if the allusion has contemporary significance, this would not prove it a fresh interpolation. Plotters in high places were doubtless present in Keawe's time and certainly later under Kameha-meha.

The epilogue contains allusion to the birds Halulu and Kiwa'a whose feathers, attached to images of the gods, are supposed to rise or fall to predict success or failure of a war party: "wonderful feathers made out of particles of water from the dazzling orb of the sun," writes Kamakau. The birds are played upon in story and popular saying. A famous legendary hero slays the man-eating bird Halulu and its mate Kiwa'a in a story of tests for a shape-shifting bride, a tale not unconnected with the ancient heiau of Halulu at Kaunolu on the island of Lanai. Old sayings call Halulu "the bird that cries over the long-house," *O ka manu kani halau;* or "the loud-voiced bird crying from the long-house to the taboo houses for women on the borders of Kahiki," *O Halu-lu, o ka manu leo nui e kani halau ana i na pe'a kapu o kukulu o Kahiki.* Kupihea attaches the name to "a chief from a distant land, brought to Hawaii by one of the chiefs," possibly the visitor who introduced the custom of consulting feathered images as oracles; but the saying itself may have originated otherwise. Of Halulu's mate Kiwa'a we hear less often. A pun upon the name as Kia'i-wa'a, "Canoe-guide," gives the name Ki-wa'a to the pilot bird that leads a flock of its kind. Since this pilot bird invariably seeks the same landing-place,

the fisherman sets up his canoe shed at such a spot and when
far out at sea during the migrating season is able to direct his
own homeward course by that marked out by "the bird that
cries over the long-house."

This fitting of images from nature or the habits of daily
life into the traditional history of the past, this play of mythical allusion, is what gives value to poetic composition, according to Hawaiian standards. If the image or allusion can
be so turned as to apply to a present situation, so much the
better. Back of each image lies an emotional context baffling
to the literal translator. In this epilogue, out of a world
crowded with bird life on sea and land, the poet seems to
reconstruct the migration period that brought successive
waves of settlement to Hawaii, a period ending hundreds of
years before. After the conventional introduction of mythical allusion, he goes back abruptly to the rootstalk, the
Haha that "passes into a hundred branches." And with this
"branching of the nightborn" the ode concludes:

> Nothing but darkness that,
> Nothing but darkness this,
> Darkness alone for Po'ele'ele,
> A time of dawn indeed for Pohaha,
> Still it is night.

CHANT THREE

A male this, the female that
A male born in the time of black darkness
275. The female born in the time of groping in the darkness
Overshadowed was the sea, overshadowed the land
Overshadowed the streams, overshadowed the mountains
Overshadowed the dimly brightening night
The rootstalk grew forming nine leaves
280. Upright it grew with dark leaves
The sprout that shot forth leaves of high chiefs
Born was Po'ele'ele the male
Lived with Pohaha a female
The rootstalk sprouted
    The taro stalk grew

285. Born was the Wood borer, a parent
  Out came its child a flying thing, and flew
  Born was the Caterpillar, the parent
  Out came its child a Moth, and flew
  Born was the Ant, the parent
290. Out came its child a Dragonfly, and flew
  Born was the Grub, the parent
  Out came its child the Grasshopper, and flew
  Born was the Pinworm, the parent
  Out came its child a Fly, and flew
295. Born was the egg [?], the parent
  Out came its child a bird, and flew
  Born was the Snipe, the parent
  Out came its child a Plover, and flew
  Born was the A'o bird, the parent
300. Out came its child an A'u bird, and flew
  Born was the Turnstone, the parent
  Out came its child a Fly-catcher, and flew
  Born was the Mudhen, the parent
  Out came its child an Apapane bird, and flew
305. Born was the Crow, the parent
  Out came its child an Alawi bird, and flew
  Born was the 'E'ea bird, the parent
  Out came its child an Alaaiaha bird, and flew
  Born was the Mamo honey-sucker, the parent
310. Out came its child an 'O'o bird, and flew
  Born was the Rail, the parent
  Out came its child a brown Albatross, and flew
  Born was the Akikiki creeper, the parent
  Out came its child an Ukihi bird, and flew
315. Born was the Curlew, the parent
  Out came its child a Stilt, and flew
  Born was the Frigate bird, the parent
  Out came its child a Tropic bird, and flew
  Born was the migrating gray-backed Tern, the parent
320. Out came its child a red-tailed Tropic-bird, and flew
  Born was the Unana bird, the parent
  Its offspring the Heron came out and flew
   Flew hither in flocks
   On the seashore in ranks

325. Settled down and covered the beach
Covered the land of Kane's-hidden-island
Land birds were born
Sea birds were born
329. Man born for the narrow stream, woman for the broad stream
Born was the Stingray, living in the sea
Guarded by the Stormy-petrel living on land

Refrain

335. Man for the narrow stream, woman for the broad stream
Born was the Sea-swallow, living at sea
Guarded by the Hawk living on land

Refrain

341. Man for the narrow stream, woman for the broad stream
Born was the Duck of the islands, living at sea
Guarded by the Wild-duck living on land

Refrain

347. Man for the narrow stream, woman for the broad stream
Born was the Hehe, living at sea
Guarded by the Nene [goose] living on land

Refrain

353. Man for the narrow stream, woman for the broad stream
Born was the Auku'u, living by the sea
Guarded by the Ekupu'u bird living on land

Refrain

359. Man for the narrow stream, woman for the broad stream
Born was the Noddy [*noio*], living at sea
Guarded by the Owl [*pueo*] living on land

Refrain

365. This is the flying place of the bird Halulu
Of Kiwa'a, the bird that cries over the canoe house
Birds that fly in a flock shutting out the sun
The earth is covered with the fledgelings of the night breaking into dawn
The time when the dawning light spreads abroad
370. The young weak 'ape plant rises

A tender plant with spreading leaves
A branching out of the nightborn
Nothing but darkness that
Nothing but darkness this
375. Darkness alone for Po'ele'ele
A time of dawn indeed for Pohaha
Still it is night

CHAPTER THIRTEEN

The Crawlers

IN THE fourth ode the birth of amphibious creatures is
celebrated as "those of the sea take to the land." Translators tend to read the lines according to their own theory of
the relation of the passage to the history of life on earth. The
queen and the translator for *Aloha* are faithful to a generalized picture of amphibious creatures swarming up along the
coast onto the land, prototype of the growth and spread of
man over earth as human history emerges out of the dim
past. Bastian sees these as a succession ascending in scale from
lower to higher in the animal and vegetable world. Kupihea
believes we should relate the series to specific families of settlers belonging to the migration period. Pokini refers them
to a stage in the life of a child as it begins to crawl about and
meet the rough and tumble of life. In every case it is the
particular interpretation each gives to the whole meaning of
the chant that has decided the value given to any doubtful
phrase. In general I have followed Kupihea's fairly coherent
interpretation because it seems to hang together, although
this is not essential to Hawaiian poetic art, and to leave to
each reader his own evaluation of the symbolism involved.
If actually intended as a portrayal of conditions under a
historic migration, it makes a pretty sorry indictment of
the past.

Pokini, on the other hand, would explain each name of the
species born under Popanopano, the male, and Polalowehi,
the female, generative agents at this stage of life, as a play
upon the characteristics of the developing infant. They
show him "clinging" (*pilipili*) to his parents and "roughly"

75

(*kalakala*) separated; "chidden" (*ka'uka'u*), "forgetful"
(*palaka*), gaining "independence" (*kaihukunini*), "fed"
(*kupelepele*), growing "plump" (*kele*). Under Pokini's interpretation the general condition of filth and sluggishness in
which the half-land, half-sea creatures of this new era live,
summed up in the concluding lines—

> Reeling they go
> Go in the land of crawlers
> Born is the family of crawlers in the dim past—

gives rather a humorous than a sordid turn to the whole
picture.

It is to be noticed that, although an internal rhyme scheme
links verses closely for sound effect, generally into couplets,
each verse is read as if complete in itself, the second verse of
the couplet a balance, not a completion, to the first. This
piling-up of suggestive observations appropriate to the theme
gives to the whole passage a cumulative effect rather than
one of connected sequences. Kupihea's free translation of the
Prologue shows what may be done to read into such poetic
word-play a sustained development of thought based upon
his idea of the inner meaning intended by the poet under
the figure of the "family of crawlers," in this case, according
to his version, a consistent description of a historic immigration.

The opening lines of the ode, which I have given literally
after the text, have been variously read. Translators generally refer the lines to the coming of La'a, presumably the
La'a-from-Kahiki of traditional fame.

> Build up the fire of La'a there
> The great chief from over the ocean

is the most picturesque rendering offered me, the "dusky
black 'ape plant" being thus with much probability referred
to a specific immigration, but I am unable to bring the fire
building into line with this reading. The queen writes vague-

ly: "Established in the dawn of La'a's light," but fails to make
use of the allusion. It would be interesting to connect the
ode with the introduction of the taboos, the crouching, or
even the "burning taboo."

It has seemed worth while to dwell at this point once
more upon the possibility of variations in translation based
upon the text itself, in order to drive home the ease with
which the language of poetry may be twisted to fit a particular interpretation, and hence the caution with which any
such reading is to be accepted without certain knowledge of
the composer's original intention. Only a contemporary
audience acquainted with the facts in each case can be sure
of this, nor can one be certain that the meaning for Kalakaua's day was the same as that at the time of composition, or
that Kalakaua or another has not manipulated the text to suit
his own purposes, as Kupihea thinks; or, even so, just what
he and not Kupihea has read into particular passages.

CHANT FOUR

Plant the 'ahi'a and cause it to propagate [?]
The dusky black 'ape plant
380. The sea creeps up to the land
Creeps backward, creeps forward
Producing the family of crawlers
Crawling behind, crawling in front
Advancing the front, settling down at the back
385. The front of my cherished one [?]
He is dark, splendid,
Popanopano is born as a male [?]
Popanopano, the male
Po-lalo-wehi, the female
390. Gave birth to those who produce eggs
Produce and multiply in the passing night
Here they are laid
Here they roll about
The children roll about, play in the sand
395. Child of the night of black darkness is born
The night gives birth

The night gives birth to prolific ones
The night is swollen with plump creatures
The night gives birth to rough-backed turtles
400. The night produces horn-billed turtles
The night gives birth to dark-red turtles
The night is pregnant with the small lobster
The night gives birth to sluggish-moving geckos
Slippery is the night with sleek-skinned geckos
405. The night gives birth to clinging creatures
The night proclaims rough ones
The night gives birth to deliberate creatures
The night shrinks from the ineffective
The night gives birth to sharp-nosed creatures
410. Hollowed is the night for great fat ones
The night gives birth to mud dwellers
The night lingers for track leavers
413. Born is the male for the narrow stream, the female for the
broad stream
Born is the turtle [*Honu*] living in the sea
Guarded by the *Maile* seedling [*Kuhonua*] living on land

Refrain

419. Man for the narrow stream, woman for the broad stream
Born is the sea-borer [*Wili*] living in the sea
Guarded by the Wiliwili tree living on land

Refrain

425. Man for the narrow stream, woman for the broad stream
Born is the sea-worm living in the sea
Guarded by the bastard-sandalwood living on land

Refrain

431. Man for the narrow stream, woman for the broad stream
Born is the Okea living in the sea
Guarded by the Ahakea tree living on land

Refrain

437. Man for the narrow stream, woman for the broad stream
Born is the sea-urchin [*Wana*] living in the sea
Guarded by the thorny Wanawana plant living on land

Refrain

443. Man for the narrow stream, woman for the broad stream
Born is the Nene shellfish living in the sea
Guarded by the Manene grass living on land

Refrain

449. Man for the narrow stream, woman for the broad stream
Born is the Liko living in the sea
Guarded by the Piko tree living on land

Refrain

455. Man for the narrow stream, woman for the broad stream
Born is the Opeope jellyfish living in the sea
Guarded by the Oheohe [bamboo] living on land

Refrain

461. Man for the narrow stream, woman for the broad stream
Born is the Nanana [sea spider] living in the sea
Guarded by the Nonanona living on land

Refrain

467. With a dancing motion they go creeping and crawling
The tail swinging its length
Sullenly, sullenly

470. They go poking about the dunghill
Filth is their food, they devour it
Eat and rest, eat and belch it up
Eating like common people
Distressful is their eating

475. They move about and become heated
Act as if exhausted
They stagger as they go
Go in the land of crawlers
The family of crawlers born in the night

480.   Still it is night

CHAPTER FOURTEEN

The Night-Digger

IN THE fifth chant of the Night World, shore life is exchanged for the cultivation of food plants inland, and
the rooting pig is used, on the one hand, as symbol of the
planter who prepares the soil for the food crop, on the other,
as an erotic symbol for the function of the male in the founding of a new family branch upon the old stock.

According to Kupihea, the "new generation" (*makamaka
hou*) of "high chief rank" (*uli iliuli*) celebrated in the chant
is again the Uli line to which belongs the "pig-child" Kamapua'a whose exploits play so large a part in popular storytelling.[1] Half-man, half-god, and born in the shape of a pig,
this ravisher of ladies and superhuman warrior in battle has
left his trace upon many a rock formation, misshapen frag-
ment of earth, or mountain ravine made sacred by such association. He was by all odds the favorite figure of local
legend throughout the group, during the last fifty years, in
dramatic recital leading to high comedy that left nothing of
detail unsaid.

There is strong probability that Kamapua'a belonged to
the cult of Lono, god of fertility, to whose priesthood the
Kumulipo chant seems to have belonged. Possibly this new
branch upon the family line introduced taro culture.[2] Certainly whoever brought the black pig to Hawaii must have
stood good chance of candidacy to godhead. The black pig
was the most sacred sacrifice to be offered to the high gods
alone. The feeding of pork to Cook and his companion cli-

1. Beckwith, *Hawaiian Mythology*, chap. xiv.
2. Kepelino, pp. 152–56, 157; Handy and Pukui, *Hawaiian Planter*, pp. 6 ff.

maxed the honors paid to the bewildered captain in his apotheosis as god of fertility. Today a feast of pork is the ultimate word in gustatory satisfaction, a privilege from which women in old days were excluded under rigid taboo. The pig is the household favorite. No one who has picnicked on the black sands of Kalapana can forget the sociable assembling of sharp-backed "porkers of the night" that nuzzle against visitors like a brood of privileged puppies.

I am indebted especially to Kupihea for the identification of classes represented in the births of this period. Kawena Pukui has also furnished particular clarifications. Bastian saw in the pig birth "a wave of sensual passion" and, in the series following, the "beginning of reason and judgment resulting in the development of crafts." Pokini refers the first half-dozen names to the practice of shaping the head (po'o) by manipulation in infancy to conform to the family branch to which the child belonged. Thus the head might be elongated (po'owa'awa'a), angular (po'okihikihi), square (po'omahakea), round (po'omeumeu), with retreating forehead (po'oapahu), and so forth. In the whole series she sees pictured the arrival of a train of followers of a chief bearing gifts to lay before the first-born child upon the occasion of his presentation to the family clan.

Pokini's vivid and insistent identification of the scene is by no means contradictory to Kupihea's more generalized explanation. He attaches to each name the descriptive term characterizing different classes—social, occupational, or military—belonging to a chief's followers, carried over from a time even before that of Kamehameha and it may be much older. Of four terms naming varieties of taro, two are given to certain lower classes, one to the chief's favorites, a fourth distinguishes the lowest slave class. A fifth taro name, Pi'iali'i, was locally applied on Kauai to a class of men who trimmed their hair pompadour and held it up with a comb of shell. The Hulupi'i had kinky hair, cropped to stand up and col-

ored with lime. The *Pi'ipi'i* were picked men of Kalaniopu'u's army, said to stand "seven feet six inches" in height,
the same who were caught in ambush at the battle of the
sandhills at the time of the invasion of Maui from Hawaii.
"They wore small helmets and short capes and were great
fighters." The *Huelo-maewa* ("Wagging-tails") were "dogs
turned human beings," a class of shape-shifters belonging
primarily to the island of Maui. The *Hululiha*, also called
Hulumanu, were "retainers of the king who fought with
him," hence a kind of bodyguard.

The ode concludes with a paean of praise for the blossom-
ing period of the virgin land under the hand of the ancient
planter of taro-patch (*lo'i*) fame, Lo'iloa. The "walling up at
the back" and "in front" in an earlier line, Pokini referred to
old methods of potato planting.[3] The word *mohala* here applied to the land "is often used in the best poetry for the time
of maturity in the virgin"; hence it is here applied to the
flowering period of land made productive through cultivation. *Oma* is a name for a chief's leading official, here assigned
to the Night-digger, Po-kanokano. Under this symbol of the
fruitful earth lies the inner theme or *kaona*, picturing the rise
of a fertile new branch on the family line multiplying over
the land.

CHANT FIVE

The time arrives for Po-kanokano
To increase the progeny of Po-lalo-uli
Dark is the skin of the new generation
Black is the skin of the beloved Po-lalo-uli
485. Who sleeps as a wife to the Night-digger
The beaked nose that digs the earth is erected
Let it dig at the land, increase it, heap it up
Walling it up at the back
Walling it up in front
490. The pig child is born
Lodges inland in the bush

3. Kepelino, pp. 156, 157, Handy and Pukui, *Hawaiian Planter*, pp. 131 ff.

    Cultivates the water taro patches of Lo'iloa
    Tenfold is the increase of the island
    Tenfold the increase of the land
495. The land where the Night-digger dwelt
    Long is the line of his ancestry
    The ancient line of the pig of chief blood
    The pig of highest rank born in the time
    The time when the Night-digger lived
500. And slept with Po-lalo-uli
      The night gave birth
    Born were the peaked-heads, they were clumsy ones
    Born were the flat-heads, they were braggarts
    Born were the angular-heads, they were esteemed
505. Born were the fair-haired, they were strangers
    Born were the blonds, their skin was white
    Born were those with retreating foreheads, they were bushy-
      haired
    Born were the blunt-heads, their heads were round
    Born were the dark-heads, they were dark
510. Born were the common class, they were unsettled
    Born were the working class, they were workers
    Born were the favorites, they were courted
    Born were the slave class, and wild was their nature
    Born were the cropped-haired, they were the picked men
515. Born were the song chanters, they were indolent [?]
    Born were the big bellies, big eaters were they
    Born were the timid ones, bashful were they
    Born were the messengers, they were sent here and there
    Born were the slothful, they were lazy
520. Born were the stingy, they were sour
    Born were the puny, they were feeble ones
    Born were the thickset, they were stalwart
   Born were the broad-chested, broad was their badge in battle
    Born were the family men, they were home lovers
525. Born were the mixed breeds, they had no fixed line of descent
    Born were the lousy-headed, they were lice infested
    Born were the war leaders, men followed after them
    Born were the high chiefs, they were ruddy
    Born were the stragglers, they were dispersed
530. Scattered here and there
    The children of Lo'iloa multiplied

The virgin land sprang into bloom
The gourd of desire was loosened
With desire to extend the family line
535. To carry on the fruit of Oma's descendants,
The generations from the Night-digger
In that period of the past
  Still it is night

CHAPTER FIFTEEN

The Nibblers

THE sixth chant describes in a mood of whimsical humor the depredations of the rat tribe upon the vegetable food crop celebrated in the last chant. Although rat shooting with bow and arrow was a favorite pastime of chiefs and comparison to a rat an unlucky sign in word magic, the rat family were nevertheless in line of descent from gods of the Po and might appear on earth in offspring endowed with spirit power. Stories make the rat form to be a stage in the reshaping into human bodies of those returned to life from the spirit world, a belief not inconsistent with Hindoo religious philosophy. A Kauai conqueror has a brother born in the form of a rat. Priests catch and work over the spirit body of a dead child until he comes to life in a ratlike body. The exploits of the rat child Piko'i recall the tall tales of our own storytellers.[1] On the other hand, a native kahuna recéntly condemned a new-built house to vacancy by calling the shape devised for the doorway a "rat's nest," and the ancient priest Paao again and again refuses fish caught for sacrifice on the basis of the same ominous analogy.[2]

Today the native rat, *Rattus hawaiiensis,* no longer lives save on small islets cut off from the main land. His relatives from foreign lands have taken over the wider ranges. But in old days time was reckoned by the migration of rats to the shore when wild food plants failed in the uplands, thus "telling the seasons" to the lowland planter by the depredations

1. Beckwith, *Hawaiian Mythology,* pp. 424–27, 411, 480.
2. Malo, p. 333.

upon his crop; "nothing in the plains is safe from the rats, everything is burrowed out by them," complains Kepelino.[3]

The relation of the first four lines of the chant serving as a prologue to what follows is highly debatable. Kua-ka-mano, "Chief-over-thousands," is reputed to be "a great chief of old" and Kupu-kapu, "Taboo-sprout," to be similarly the name of the splendid feather-bound staff or brush, called *kahili*, carried before him as a sign of rank. All chiefs in old times had such symbols of office, and each had its distinguishing name of honor. Possibly there is meant here a sly analogy between the quivering whiskers preceding the approach of a rat and the stiff feather frill (*kuku*) proclaiming that of the equally predatory taboo chief.

But Kupihea is probably right in interpreting the spread of the rat family from upland to shore and their nibbling habits as symbolic of the rise of new lines of chiefs under whom taboos multiplied. Especially it refers perhaps to the dividing up of the land to landlords and these again to subordinate overseers, each taking toll from the crop of the next lower and all expected to contribute to the head chief, the *haku* or "lord," to whom all land was handed down by inheritance from his predecessor.[4] This idea as the *kaona* or theme of the chant I have tried to bring out in following, generally, Kupihea's translation. The trouble lies in the interplay of rhetorical devices such as linked rhymes, so that sound obscures sense. I infer that the multiplication of overseers went hand in hand with the development of cultivation of the soil for food crops, perhaps primarily with the introduction of wet taro culture as described in the chant of the rooting pig. The word *hili* means "to deviate from the path," hence, according to Parker, "from a settled line of conduct," and may well apply to social innovations. The word *mahimahi* looks like a reduplication of the word *mahi*,

3. Kepelino, pp. 86, 87.
4. *Ibid.*, pp. 146-51.

"to dig." *Linalina* is a word applied to wet clayey soil, *holi ana* means "sprouting," the whole couplet thus agreeing with the idea of preparation of abundance of vegetable food (*'ai*) with which the line concludes. But the "diggers" and "scratchers" may be the rats themselves.

Certainly the rodent family is on the surface the direct subject of the remainder of the chant, with an eye probably to its analogue within the social structure. Such lines as

> There in hollow places the parents dwell
> There huddle together the little rats,

to quote the queen's rendering, are distinctly so directed. The "lashes (whiskers?) upstanding," the "trace of the nibbling of these reddish ones," the "mark left upon the rind" of the so-called "mountain apple" or *'ohi'a* from a tree whose upland variety bears no fruit, all these passages bring the rat tribe itself clearly before the eye. The name Po-hiolo for the male parent may be a play upon Poho-'iole, "Rat-hole," and Po-ne'e-aku, for the female, upon the hitching motion, *ne'ene'e*, of the rat as it turns now this way, now that; a word applied also to the position in which the common people were obliged to approach the chiefs, crawling on hands and knees. Possibly the whole is also a play upon a child's pilfering habits as it begins to creep about, as Pokini would interpret it.

CHANT SIX

Many new lines of chiefs spring up
540. Cultivation arises, full of taboos
     [They go about scratching at the wet lands
     It sprouts, the first blades appear, the food is ready] [?]
     Food grown by the water courses
     Food grown by the sea
545. Plentiful and heaped up
     The parent rats dwell in holes
     The little rats huddle together
     Those who mark the seasons
     Little tolls from the land

550. Little tolls from the water courses
     Trace of the nibblings of these brown-coated ones
     With whiskers upstanding
     They hide here and there   .
     A rat in the upland, a rat by the sea
555. A rat running beside the wave
     Born to the two, child of the Night-falling-away
     Born to the two, child of the Night-creeping-away
     The little child creeps as it moves
     The little child moves with a spring
560. Pilfering at the rind
     Rind of the 'ohi'a fruit, not a fruit of the upland
     A tiny child born as the darkness falls away
     A springing child born as the darkness creeps away
     Child of the dark and child in the night now here
565.   Still it is night

CHAPTER SIXTEEN

The Dog Child

THE mystery of spirit life born into the body of a dog belongs to the breed described in this chant as dark red ('*i'i*), brindled ('*a'a*), and hairless ('*olohe*). The hairless 'Olohe people with whom the brindled dog is associated are believed to be dog men with the mystical shape-shifting powers of the demigods.[1] They lived in caves dug into the sandhills, where they are said to have been first discovered and used by Kahekili in the eighteenth century as a division of his army. Living witnesses today report men with dogs' heads marching in the ghostly processions of dead warriors returned to revisit their old haunts on earth, whose apparition is not uncommon among Hawaiians or is even reported by foreign-born mystics. Their relation is not clear with a class of powerful wrestlers, also called 'Olohe, who, contrary to the custom of the long-haired native warrior, cropped their hair and oiled the body to escape the clutch of an opponent and would lie in wait at strategic points along a trail to attack unwary travelers. The brindled dog associated in the chant with the dog-headed 'Olohe was supposed to have been born into the family of the volcano goddess and to be under her protection. Although ordinary dog meat was a favorite dish among Hawaiians and allowed also to women, one would hesitate to cook such a dog for fear of divine vengeance.[2]

In this seventh chant the half-jesting, even sneering, mood of the sixth gives way to a sense of awe and mystery. The

1. Beckwith, *Hawaiian Mythology*, pp. 343–51.
2. Green, *Folk-Tales*, p. 48; Green and Pukui, *Legend of Kawelo*, p. 178.

opening key word is *ano,* a word for "sudden fear," here
used in duplicate as *anoano* in the first five lines. There is
"fear of the mountain top," the *kualono* where gods assem-
ble; fear of the receding and advancing night, the Po-ne'e-
aku and Po-ne'e-mai, who are the generating agents of the
new birth; fear of "the pregnant night"; fear of a "breach
of the law," the *ha'iha'i,* whose penalty is death. The reference is to the priestly taboos against leaving any morsel un-
consumed of a sacrificial feast or bones and refuse exposed
to be trodden upon, and against approach to any sacred place
by the "narrow trail" used by a member of the priesthood
alone.

Fear changes to the more violent emotion of dread, *he
weliweli,* and finally to an awesome sense of reverence, *he
['ili]'ilihia,* toward the dog child, the *'ilio kama,* born to
Po-ne'e-aku and Po-ne'e-mai:

> A dark red dog, a brindled dog
> A hairless dog of the hairless ones
> A dog as an offering for the oven.

Kupihea was told by his grandfather, who served in a temple
on Hawaii, that dogs were not used for sacrifice until Kalaniopu'u's time, but this may not hold true for other islands.
In the passage following, the "dog as an offering for the
oven," literally "fire-pit," *'a'alua,* seems to serve as symbol
of the terrible *tapu wela,* the right given to high taboo chiefs
of burning the bodies of trespassers against their taboos, this
as a kind of propitiation for the god who had been offended
by the disrespect paid him in the person of his divine spokes-
man on earth. Pokini would doubtless refer the passage to
the bestowal of the burning taboo upon Keawe's first-born
at the time when he was officially introduced by name in the
heiau to the rank of a high taboo chief.

The line of thought seems to be next deflected to the journey of the disembodied dead, perhaps of one who has been

condemned under the taboo, as it flees, "pitiful without a garment," to join its companions at the gathering place of the dead, where lies on the coast an entrance or "leaping place" into the underworld.[3] "To Malama," says the chant, and Ho'olapa explained that Malama "is the place people go when they die," and Hula-ka-Makani, "the wind that blows at Malama." One such place he said lay "in Puna district on the island of Hawaii on the Pohoiki side of Kalapana," but I failed to learn from Ho'olapa whether all gathering places of the soul in other districts of Hawaii or on other islands are called "Malama" or whether, for all, the Hula (dance) wind blows. Hawaiians believe that dangers beset the soul's passage to this rendezvous lest it lose its way or be attacked by some unfriendly spirit unless guided by the guardian god of the family, to whom it has paid respect during life. For example, the barren sandy isthmus between East and West Maui, which must be crossed by the dead in order to reach the "leaping place of souls" on the west coast of the island, was said to be a haunt of such lost and spiteful spirits, to be avoided by the living at night.

The Hawaiian genius for quick transition of thought, piling up suggested images without compulsion of persistency to any one of them, makes it difficult to translate consistently, or, indeed, with any conviction, the three troublesome lines following the reference to the flight of the soul to the assembly place of the dead at Malama. Mrs. Pukui would render the lines thus:

> The nights grow less for the children
> From the head (of time) until the end
> From the biting (night) until the silence,

where the poet seems to pause for a general reflection about death as the universal fate of mankind, although, logically, we are still in the period of the Po, before the birth of human

3. Beckwith, *Hawaiian Mythology*, pp. 154–56.

life. The word *welewele*, however, like *welawela*, conveys
an idea of heat, whether physical or mental. The thought
may even carry back through the "spreading out of hot
stones" (*uluulu*), followed by "burning heat" (*welewele*),
to the "oven" of line 579. Another suggested rendering
would translate *mai* as a negative particle and conceive the
soul taking its way to "Malama"

> Without haste or grudging,
> Without gnashing or groping (as in death).

But the word *nenehe* conveys the idea of sound and motion,
rather than of "silence," and especially of a low, even sound
like that of moving feet, a rustling sound, certainly a neat
transition to the sound of shuffling feet as the soul's passage
ends in the companionship of the dance before taking its
leap into some other world of the spirit. Indeed, Hawaiian
stories telling of a visit to the assembly of the dead picture
them so engaged.

Abruptly follows the conclusion. Out of the slime fresh
rootlets spring. They branch and grow and young growth
spreads anew. The approaching night gives birth.

CHANT ›SEVEN

Fear falls upon me on the mountain top
Fear of the passing night
Fear of the night approaching
Fear of the pregnant night
570. Fear of the breach of the law
Dread of the place of offering and the narrow trail
Dread of the food and the waste part remaining
Dread of the receding night
Awe of the night approaching
575. Awe of the dog child of the Night-creeping-away
A dog child of the Night-creeping-hither
A dark red dog, a brindled dog
A hairless dog of the hairless ones
A dog as an offering for the oven
580. Palatable is the sacrifice for supplication [?]

Pitiful in the cold without covering
Pitiful in the heat without a garment
He goes naked on the way to Malama
[Where] the night ends for the children [of night] [?]
585. From the growth and the parching [?]
From the cutting off and the quiet [?]
The driving Hula wind his companion
Younger brother of the naked ones, the 'Olohe
Out from the slime come rootlets
590. Out from the slime comes young growth
Out from the slime come branching leaves
Out from the slime comes outgrowth
Born in the time when men came from afar
    Still it is night

CHAPTER SEVENTEEN

The Dawn of Day

WITH the eighth chant begins the period of living men called the "Day" or *Ao*. There appears now the "well-formed child" in the "time when men multiplied" and the "time when men came from afar," as the Po-kinikini and Po-he'enalu-mamao, generative agents of the period, have been paraphrased. Men multiply "by hundreds," and the function of sex is once more emphasized in the familiar antithesis

> Man born for the narrow stream
> Woman for the broad stream.

The time of the gods, *po akua*, is here; a time long ago, *po mamao*. Wave after wave come the new race, one following after another, the "gods" distinguished by ruddy faces and "white chins" or beards, the men of undetermined ancestry, the *kanaka*, dark in color.

There follows a play upon the words *ho'omalino* and *ho'ola'ila'i*, the word *malino* synonymous with *malie* meaning "peaceful," used here with *la'ila'i*, "calm, still," to express the moment of suspense in nature preceding the birth of gods and men. The juxtaposition of the two words has passed into classic use. An old mele ascribed to the wife of Kalaniopu'u begins

> O Kona kai opua i ka la'i
> O pua hinano i ka malie
>
> Kona of tranquil seas
> Pandanus blossom in the calm,

where the flower named, the pungent-scented pandanus

blossom regarded by Hawaiians as an aphrodisiac, gives an erotic turn to the couplet. Compare the similar pause in nature preliminary to a new birth reported from New Zealand at the moment when the Wide Sky above, Rangi-nui, seeks Earth in the person of Papa-tu-a-nuku: "In that period the amount of light was nil; absolute and complete darkness (po-kutikuti kakarauri) prevailed; there was no sun, no moon, no stars, no clouds, no light, no mist—no ripples stirred the surface of the ocean; no breath of air, a complete and absolute stillness." There follows the "planting" (*hikaia*) of land growths corresponding to the "births" recorded in the first seven chants of the Kumulipo.[1]

In the Kumulipo this stillness in nature prepares for the emergence of gods and men. There are born the woman La'ila'i and three males, Ki'i a man, Kane a god, Kanaloa "the hot-striking octopus." With them comes Day, the *Ao*. There follow a trio of more generalized concepts. "The wombs [?] give birth." "Ocean-edge" (Moana-liha) and "The-damp-forest" (Ka-wao-ma'aukele) possibly refer to the land and sea forms born into the night world in the preceding sections but more naturally to the economic divisions based upon the two sources of food supply, fish and vegetable food, *i'a* and *'ai*, upon which life was regulated for island dwellers. Last, in the lines sometimes paraphrased

> The first chief of the dim past dwelling in cold uplands
> The man of long life and hundreds upon hundreds of chiefs

is summed up the whole generation of the earliest stock from the beginning, whose genealogy, set down as man and wife in the eleventh section, occupies about one-third of the whole Kumulipo chant.

The lines undoubtedly have historical significance. We know from old sources that remote valleys inland were the preferred homes of the ancient chief stock. The gods Kane

1. Smith, *Lore of the Whare-wananga*, p. 117.

and Kanaloa are associated in chant and story with such habitations. Homes "in the heavens" may denote other islands left behind in migration. At some time the old line was superseded by a new branch who became the chief stock on the family genealogy. There came a split between gods and men, and this split is laid at the door of the woman La'ila'i who left her divine husband in the sacred place of the gods to live "as a woman" (*i kanaka*) and people the earth with mankind. "The woman sat sideways" is an old saying for a wife who takes another husband; *keke'e ka noho a ka wahine*, says the text.

The affair took place at a time of unfathomable antiquity, referred to in the two phrases *ka po he'e mamao* and *ka po kinikini; Kanaka mai ka po mai*, that is, "from the far past," is the modern expression. It took place in "the land of Lua." The word means "cave" or "pit," and we at once connect the place with stories of the 'Olohe or pit-dwellers already alluded to. Pokini Robinson knew of a place on the island of Oahu, "a little pool up somewhere in Wahiawa" called "Ka lua a Ahu," of which the native-born say, "If you bathe in that pool you have seen Oahu."[2] The three children born of this adventure are named in the text according to some obscure connection with the dim story of the past. "Clothed-in-leaves," *Lo-palapala*, is a name given today to a class of chiefs who, owing to some unlucky turn of fortune, are obliged to retire to the back country and live obscurely until fortune favors them once more, often in the shape of a child who gives promise of superior qualities. This last birth is thus definitely connected with the half-mythical 'Olohe people. Their pairing as male and female in the lines following plays once more upon the dominant theme of sex. The story seems to point to a debasement of rank through intermarriage of the "gods" with an inferior stock. But whether the newcomers or the old were the "gods" is not

2. Beckwith, *Hawaiian Mythology*, pp. 287–88.

made clear. Nor is it clear whether the part played in the spread of mankind over earth in line 635 is to be referred to La'ila'i herself or to the daughter Maila ("Beautiful"), as some would amend the text *Noho mai la*. The series of births which follow, after the first, which seems to be suggested as a play upon the name of the mother, must be taken as a purely figurative approach to the coming of Day and is not to be found listed among the genealogies of the Kamokuiki book, as is ,that born to La'ila'i in a later chant, assigned by Kamokuiki to the man Ki'i. A new race spreads over the land as a result of La'ila'i's affair in the land of the pit-dwellers. They cover earth like the creeping *ti* plant, the *Cordyline terminalis* of the botanist, to be found everywhere in damp growth of the low uplands. The night world presses on toward the dawn until day finally comes forth, "opening wide."

CHANT EIGHT

595. Well-formed is the child, well-formed now
Child in the time when men multiplied
Child in the time when men came from afar
Born were men by the hundreds
Born was man for the narrow stream
600. Born was woman for the broad stream
Born the night of the gods
Men stood together
Men slept together
They two slept together in the time long ago
605. Wave after wave of men moving in company
Ruddy the forehead of the god
Dark that of man
White-[bearded] the chin
Tranquil was the time when men multiplied
610. Calm like the time when men came from afar
It was called Calmness [La'ila'i] then
Born was La'ila'i a woman
Born was Ki'i a man
Born was Kane a god

615. Born was Kanaloa the hot-striking octopus
       It was day
     The wombs gave birth [?]
     Ocean-edge
     The-damp-forest, latter of the two
     The first chief of the dim past dwelling in cold uplands, their
       younger
620. The man of long life and hundreds upon hundreds of chiefs
     Scoop out, scoop out,
     Hollow out, hollow out, keep hollowing
     Hollow out, hollow out, "the woman sat sideways"
     La'ila'i, a woman in the time when men came from afar
625. La'ila'i, a woman in the time when men multiplied
     Lived as a woman of the time when men multiplied
     Born was Groping-one [Hahapo'ele], a girl
     Born was Dim-sighted [Ha-popo], a girl
     Born was Beautiful [Maila] called Clothed-in-leaves [Lopala-
       pala]
630. Naked ['Olohe] was another name
     [She] lived in the land of Lua [pit]
     [At] that place called "pit of the 'Olohe"
     Naked was man born in the day
     Naked the woman born in the upland
     [She] lived here with man [?]
     Born was Creeping-ti-plant [La'i'olo] to man
     Born was Expected-day [Kapopo], a female
     Born was Midnight [Po'ele-i], born First-light [Po'ele-a]
     Opening-wide [Wehi-loa] was their youngest
     These were those who gave birth
     The little ones, the older ones
     Ever increasing in number
     Man spread abroad, man was here now
       It was Day

CHAPTER EIGHTEEN

The Woman Who Sat Sideways

IN THIS second half of the Kumulipo chant, called the Ao, the period of living men, three myths of parenthood of mankind from the gods are blended. The first is the myth of La'ila'i who became mother of gods and men through her relations with the god Kane and the man Ki'i. The second is the myth of Haumea and the god Kanaloa, of Haumea's children born "from the brain" and her strange renewals of youth to become mother and wife of children and grandchildren. The third is the myth of Papa and Wakea; of Wakea's affair with his daughter and the consequent quarrel with Papa; of his fishing up an underseas woman, from whom sea creatures are born, a woman whose son usurps the normal succession upon the family line. In many ways these stories overlap as if they were variants from a common source. It is possible that they represent the way in which different branches on the family line have inherited from their masters of song the story of beginning traditional with their stock.

The first four sections of the Ao period tell the story of La'ila'i's relations with Kane the god and Ki'i the man. Kane is the word used for "man" in his procreative function, equivalent to our word "male"; Ki'i means "image." So in the Hebrew Scriptures man was created in the "image" of God. Kanaloa, listed as third in the trio of males born with the woman La'ila'i at the dawn of human life, disappears from the action altogether after his birth in the body of an octopus is anonunced in the eighth ode. This eighth section must be regarded as a kind of synopsis of the next three, although the harmonizing of the four is so extremely uncertain as to be best left to the intuition of the reader in the light of whatever information or suggestion can be gleaned further from native sources to clarify particular obscurities.

In the ninth chant La'ila'i seems to live successively with Kane and with Ki'i. A period of intermarriage follows among her posterity: literally, they increase "by forty thousand and by four thousand" (*he kini, he mano*) corresponding to the sacred numbering of the lesser gods invoked in temple prayers. The chant closes with the birth of the same three offspring of La'ila'i as were named in the eighth ode when she lived "as a woman" in the land of Lua, here called "part of the family of that woman mentioned above" (*la*). The gist of the story seems to be that the woman left the land of "the gods in the heavens" and life with her legitimate mate to wed a mere mortal on earth, whose offspring, half-god, half-man, are known as the ruddy-faced, bearded stock traditionally known as "children of Ki'i" and today connected with the family of the volcano goddess Pele, who thus becomes a fourth in the variations upon the part played by mother Eve in the Hawaiian genesis drama.

Two aphorisms used in this chant to describe the part played here by the "woman who sat sideways" of the eighth chant clearly refer, the one to the function of sex to insure family survival, the other to the freedom of woman in sex matters. The line reading *No ka aunaki kuku ahi kanaka* is an allusion to the common method of starting a fire by means of two firesticks. One, the hard-grained *aulima*, is held upright in the hand (*lima*) and rubbed back and forth upon the hollowed surface of the other, the softer *aunaki*, to produce the spark, the action being a perfectly understood sex symbol among Hawaiians. Hence the line is to be literally translated, "From the female firestick comes the fire that makes man." In other words, woman, impregnated by the male, nurses the spark of life that develops into a living man.

The second aphorism reads *I hohole pahiwa ka lau koa* and is rendered by Kawena: "She stripped the dark leaves of the koa tree." The allusion is to the branch of the forest *koa* tree, the native acacia set up on the altar in a school of the hula dance as a prayer for "courage" (*koa*). The symbolism depends upon word·play. *Koa* is the Hawaiian word for a soldier, used with the same intent. Call him that and he will be courageous; upon this principle a belief in word magic works. Courage in a woman depends upon her meeting successfully the challenge of sex relations, and it was hence the power to excite erotic emotion that marked the triumph of a hula dancer. Kawena Pukui recalls an old custom in Ka-u district of forbidding a dancer to refuse a kiss at the close of a hula performance, however distasteful the person offering the tribute—doubtless a survival of more intimate advances once encouraged in the name of the lustful divinity supposed to be directly inspiring the successful dancer.[1] It was this element in the hula tradition that shocked even a foreigner like Vancouver and made the hula dance a taboo pastime under missionary influence. With the revival today of the art, the aim is to merge the erotic element in the aesthetic.

Translation of the tenth chant is involved in considerable difficulty. Pokini Robinson interpreted it as a prayer for the building of the house in which a young couple were to start housekeeping together, and this seems plausible, although the exact bearing of each line upon this general background is not always evident. According to Pokini, Hawaiians call the prayer used at each stage of a house-building the *Pokini-kini*, the name here given to the parent of Kane in his reproductive energy, Kane of the Night-of-multitudes. The three children born to La'ila'i by Kane in the lines following, whose names appear also on the Kamokuiki genealogy, are invoked, says Pokini, as protectors in applying the thatch-

1. Pukui, *California Folklore Quarterly,* II, 219.

grass to complete the house. Kawena translates the names by such suggestively amorous terms for the girls as "Co-quette" and "Fondly-recalled," with "Fair-haired" for the male of the family.

On this basis, the doubtful opening lines take on a clearer meaning. As written in the text they name Maila, born to La'ila'i when she lived as a woman in the land of Lua; but, if read *O mai la*, where *O* replaces the regular *e* before an imperative, they would summon to a place in the interior of the new home the gods of procreation, the god Kane of the Night-of-multitudes and La'ila'i, the goddess who "sat sideways" to become mother of mankind. This would be in keeping with Polynesian thought, although we have no con-firmation of such an idea in Hawaii. Firth tells us that in Tikopia "structural members of a building" are regarded as "actual embodiments of deity"—hence the fixed positions in the house which were assigned to members of the household. At the house post sits the male head of the house with his sons and male guests whom he would honor, since the god is considered to be actually present in the stone upon which the post rests, while the women range along the opposite wall.[2] If this is true for Hawaii, where is the place of *Ki'i ka mahu* in the structural setup? The word *mahú* with the ac-cent on the last syllable is applied to a hermaphrodite; it is also given the sense of "quiet." Firth tells us that the Ti-kopians had gods regarded as double-sexed, not in the physi-cal sense but in the sense that, like the Indian god Siva, they were able to show themselves in either a male or a female body. A curious Tahitian chant gives to the god 'Atea such a shift of sex, a shift that would, if accepted in Hawaii, explain how Wakea, further on in the Kumulipo chant, lures a water maiden to shore by setting up images (*ki'i*), or why the god Kauakahi, in a folktale from Hilo district on Hawaii, is de-

2. Firth, *Work of the Gods in Tikopia*, p. 64.

scribed as hiding behind an image of a girl until the unsus-
pecting water nymph of whom he is amorous comes within
his grasp.[3] It is possible that Ki'i, as "image" of the god, has
the power of appearing in either sex, but I am without
evidence that Hawaiians regarded Ki'i as double-sexed or
whether, if they did so regard him, they would give the
name *mahu* to such an attribute. The queen's translation,

> Maila, with Lailai for protection
> And Kane of Kapokinikini was support, Kii was helpless,

seems to imply that Ki'i, perhaps representing the danger to
a young wife of a misalliance, is one of the evil spirits to be
conjured into helplessness. On the other hand, the word
mahu, unaccented, may apply to a smoldering fire and it
would then be possible to think of Ki'i as personifying the
fire of sexual passion, with a place in the interior of the
house at the oven kept smoldering for quick rekindling,
were it not for the fact that Hawaiians built their ovens
out of doors and had no need of house fires for heating. The
problem hence remains for further investigators, and I take
refuge in the more general of the suggested readings.

After the birth of offspring "at Kapapa," La'ila'i returns
to Kane the god and bears to him the three deities who guard
the thatching of the house. The last half of the chant takes
up the quarrel for the succession. Kamaha'ina, "First-born"
on earth, will take precedence over Hakea born in the
heavens. Ki'i the man, through this first-born, will establish
the long line of chiefs of the forest uplands enumerated in
chant eleven. Again comes the problem whether La'ila'i herself or the daughter Maila is involved in the scandal. The
phrase *lae punia* at line 698 is said to apply to a father-
daughter union like the traditional Wakea-Papa affair, and
the *'ape* which La'ila'i gives to Ki'i rather than to Kane, to

3. Firth, *We the Tikopia*, p. 470, Henry, p. 372; Beckwith, *Hawaiian Mythology*, pp. 540–41.

refer to the young daughter rather than to the mother. There is no doubt a historical allusion that escapes us.

Certainly the gossips are set in motion. If all the world loves a lover, all the world and their wives love a scandal, and a Hawaiian audience is particularly susceptible to this form of erotic titillation. The reaction upon outsiders and then that upon the injured husband is indicated by playing first upon the *k* sound to express precise forms of inarticulate disapproval in the head-shaking and kluck-klucking of the court gossips, then upon sounds in *m* combined with *u* to give the mood of sulky silence preserved at first by the husband when he begins to suspect the truth of the matter. The passage is impossible to render in English, certainly not literally. The fact seems to be that children are born but by whom Kane is ignorant. He suspects the woman of giving "the sacred *'apé*" to Ki'i, an expression equivalent to Eve's forbidden apple and here perhaps symbolizing the importance placed upon virginity for the wife of a taboo chief whose child is to become his heir.

As a matter of fact, the quarrel turns, not upon the proper jealousy of a husband for the honor of his wife, a quite unusual situation it would seem in Hawaiian court life, but upon this question of primogeniture. Kane sees that his own son will serve the son of Ki'i:

> His descendants will hence belong to the younger line,
> The children of the elder will be lord [?].

Thus the house-building prayer lays final stress upon a rule of utmost importance to family standing and to political security, the rule that gives precedence to a wife's first-born. The story of the "woman who sat sideways" may have been told at this point as a warning to the young wife not to lose for her offspring the rank she might preserve for them, but to give her first-born to the husband with whom she has been properly mated. It is altogether possible, however, that

the symbolism here has been deflected to this practical conclusion from an originally more mythical ending.

CHANT NINE

Still, trembling stands earth
645. Hot, rumbling, split is the heaven
This woman ascends to heaven, ascends right up to heaven
Ascends up toward the forest
Tries to touch the earth and the earth splits up
Children of Ki'i sprung from the brain
650. Came out, flew, flew also to the heavens
Showed the sign, the ruddy tint by which they were known
Showed the fine reddish hair at puberty [?]
Showed on the chin a reddish beard
The offspring of that mysterious woman
655. The woman of 'Iliponi, of within 'I'ipakalani
"From the female firestick comes the fire that makes men"
That woman dwelt in Nu'umealani
Land where the gods dwelt
"She stripped the dark leaves of the koa tree"
660. A woman of mysterious body was this
She lived with Ki'i, she lived with Kane
She lived with Kane of the time when men multiplied
Forgotten is the time of this multitude
A multitude the posterity of the time of child-bearing
665. She returned again upward
Dwelt in the sacred forest of the gods in Nu'umealani
Was pregnant there, the earth broke open
Born was the woman Groping-one [Haha-po'ele]
Born was Dim-sighted [Hapopo], a woman
670. Last born was Naked-one, 'Olohelohe
Part of the posterity of that woman
    It was Day

CHANT TEN

Come hither, La'ila'i [to] the wall [?]
Kane of Kapokinikini [to] the post; Ki'i be quiet [?]
675. Born was La'i'olo'olo and lived at Kapapa
Born was Kamaha'ina the first-born, a male
Born was Kamamule, a male
Kamakalua the second child was a girl
Came the child Po'ele-i [Midnight]

680. Came the child Po'ele-a [First-light]
Wehi-wela-wehi-loa [Opening-to-the heat, opening wide]
La'ila'i returned and lived with Kane
Born was Ha'i, a girl
Born was Hali'a, a girl
685. Born was Hakea, Fair-haired, a male
There was whispering, lip-smacking and clucking
Smacking, tut-tutting, head-shaking
Sulking, sullenness, silence
Kane kept silence, refused to speak
690. Sullen, angry, resentful
With the woman for her progeny
Hidden was the man by whom she had children [?]
[The man] to whom her children were born [?]
The chiefess refused him the youngest [?]
695. Gave the sacred 'ape to Ki'i
She slept with Ki'i
Kane suspected the first-born, became jealous
Suspected Ki'i and La'ila'i of a secret union [?]
They pelted Kane with stones
700. Hurled a spear; he shouted aloud
"This is fallen to my lot, for the younger [line]" [?]
Kane was angry and jealous because he slept last with her
His descendants would hence belong to the younger line
The children of the elder would be lord
705. First through La'ila'i, first through Ki'i
Child of the two born in the heavens there
    Came forth

CHAPTER NINETEEN

The Flood

IN THE eleventh section a poetical prologue repeats the theme of the last three chants. The marriage union most approved in Hawaiian taboo chief families was that between brother and sister, called a *pi'o* or "arching over." The child of such a union had the highest possible rank, that of a "god," *akua*. The opening lines of the eleventh chant show La'ila'i "living among chiefs and married to her brother" (*noho lani a Pi'olani no*). From her high position she comes "bending down over Ki'i," that is, she takes a mere man as a husband, and from this union mankind is born, "the earth swarms with her offspring." The enumeration of some eight hundred pairs, man and wife, descended from Kamaha'ina, "first-born" son of La'ila'i and Ki'i, and Hali'a, La'ila'i's daughter by Kane, sufficiently testifies to the fertility of the match.

At the close of the genealogical listing comes an eloquent passage depicting, on the face of it, a flood of waters rising silently over the land to the inhabited places. These lines offer an excellent and thoroughly characteristic example of poetic symbolism. "The whole means that Ki'i slept with her," summarized Ho'olapa, thus bringing the entire declamatory effusion down to a most explicit conclusion. Expressions such as *Kaui-ka-wa*, explained as the position of the legs in a bow as in swimming, *Lele ka ihe* and *Kaui-ka-hoe*, whose exact meaning Ho'olapa passed over, are recognized terms for positions taken in the act of mating, hence are capitalized in the text.

There follows a reference to "the cock born on the back

of Wakea," an event which spells the end of the genealogy of the long-lived man of the eighth chant. His genealogy becomes extinct with the name of Po-la'a, "Sacred-night." The allusion to the "cock," to be met more than once in the course of the Kumulipo chant, is to a great chief born into the family from an alien source, whose branch becomes itself the main stock from which subsequent ruling chiefs on the family line count descent. Further trace of the old stock who count descent from the "first chief dwelling in cold uplands" is lost, "vanished into the passing night."

The translation of the poetic passages in this section must necessarily be idiomatic. *Noho lani* means "living among chiefs," as *noho kanaka* implies "living as a woman" among the people. Legend is full of such romantic situations enjoyed by both chiefs and chiefesses when the restrictions of court life became irksome. The closing lines are particularly difficult; some must go untranslated as I was unable to keep the flood motive, where double meanings were involved, consistent with the text. Bastian (p. 154) struggled with the same difficulty, although probably unaware of the inner meaning. The *kua* is the woman's house of a family setup. *Naueue* may imply "withdrawing to a private place." Both *konikoni* and *hi'a* refer to "ardent desire" as applied to the emotions, and *hi'a* to the art of fire-making, a well-known sex symbol.

CHANT ELEVEN

She was a woman living among chiefs and married to her
   brother
She was a restless woman living among chiefs
710. She lived above and came bending down over Ki'i
The earth swarmed with her offspring
Born was Kamaha'ina [First-born], a male
Born was Kamamule, her younger born
Born was Kamamainau, her middle one
715. Born was Kamakulua her little one, a girl
Kamaha'ina lived as husband to Hali['a]

. . . .

[There follow some four hundred pairs, man and wife, to lines 1332–33, where a pair of brothers are named, Ali'iho-nupu'u the elder, Opu'upu'u the younger. They seem to have a common wife named Ka-ea-honu, a name connecting her with the species of turtle from which the precious tortoise shell for ornament is obtained. From this point four hundred more pairs carry the genealogy of the elder line to Po-la'a. That of the younger appears in the next section.]

1530. Born was Pola'a
    Born was rough weather, born the current
    Born the booming of the sea, the breaking of foam
    Born the roaring, advancing, and receding of waves, the
        rumbling sound, the earthquake
    The sea rages, rises over the beach
1534. Rises silently to the inhabited places [?]
    Rises gradually up over the land .   .   .

  . `. .   .   .   .
  . . . .
    Born is Po-elua [Second-night] on the lineage of Wakea
1540. Born is the stormy night
    Born the night of plenty
    Born is the cock on the back of Wakea
    Ended is [the line of] the first chief of the dim past dwelling
        in cold uplands
    Dead is the current sweeping in from the navel of the earth:
        that was a warrior wave
1545. Many who came vanished, lost in the passing night

CHAPTER TWENTY

The Woman Who Bore Children through the Brain

THE long-lived man's genealogy ends with the eleventh section of the Kumulipo chant as we have it today. The twelfth takes up the genealogy of a younger branch from Opu'upu'u and continues from another younger brother called 'Ololo, "Brain." The thirteenth opens with a genealogy from the elder Paliku branch. This section introduces the figure of the mysterious form-changing goddess Haumea by whom are "born from the brain" a brood of offspring, first to the god Kanaloa and then to her own descendants, a story returned to in still more detail in the poetical prologue introducing the genealogy of the fifteenth section. Here, "jealous of her husband's second mate," Haumea "becomes a woman," takes a husband among men, and lives up Kalihi valley in the northern range of mountains on the island of Oahu, finally using her power as a goddess to disappear into a breadfruit tree: "A breadfruit body, trunk and leaves she had," says the chant.

The name Ha(na)u-mea, "Sacred-birth," is perhaps derived from the strange births "from the brain" with which the chant credits her or from the different forms she takes to "sleep" with children and grandchildren. It does not appear in any other Hawaiian genealogy so far as I know, in spite of the important part played by the goddess Haumea today in folk belief. Haumea is goddess of childbirth and in the Hawaiian "Book of Medicine" is credited with having saved a chief's daughter of Oahu from a Caesarean operation by giving her an herb medicine to produce natural birth. In view of the reference in a variant story to a bamboo tree worshiped in her name in connection with this achievement and the ingenious instruments of bamboo used in old days for procuring abortion,[1] it seems to me likely that her services in connection with birth were of this nature rather than the other. Possibly it was she who introduced the custom. The story written into the medicine book may have been a modern attempt to whitewash the character of the goddess of birth in the light of Christian mores.

However this may be, Haumea's children are described not only as "born from the brain" (*ma ka lolo*) but as "drivelers." "*Ha'ae wale ka hanauna lolo*," says the chant, and today Hawaiians call children who drivel at the mouth "Haumea's children from the brain." The soft spot on an infant's head, called *manawa*, they derive from Haumea's form of giving birth: "*Oia wahine hanau manawa i na keiki*," as the chant puts it. Even today, if a mother lacks milk for her infant, a mash of sweet potato bound over the fontanel is supposed to supply nourishment. Popular legend has localized the life of Haumea up Kalihi Valley and added details to the story. The old heiau of Kai'ele in Kalihi is sometimes pointed to as the place where she changed her shape from age to youth. The spot on the Nu'uanu stream is well known where grew the breadfruit tree into which she vanished with her husband to escape those about to put him to death for trespassing upon the chief's taboo plantings. Another legend makes Haumea controller of wild vegetable food on Oahu. From her home on the mountain ridges she sends a drought. Men seek food from other lands and food plants are introduced. Haumea is, further, a goddess of underground heat, and some call her mother of the Pele fam-

1. Ellis, IV, 327; Beckwith, *Hawaiian Mythology*, chap. xix.

ily at the volcano, each member born from a different part
of her body, Pele alone from between her thighs. In her
character as goddess of heat she may become a possessing
spirit (*akua noho*).[2] Says Ho'olapa, "Taro greens placed on
the back of a person Haumea has entered will cook there,"
and he adds, "I have eaten such *luau* and it was really
cooked."

In spite of all these uncouth elements in the Haumea
story, its likeness to that of La'ila'i, notwithstanding its less
aristocratic setting, can scarcely be dismissed as coincidental.
La'ila'i is also a shape-shifting (*paha'oha'o*) woman. She
comes from 'Iliponi within 'I'ipakalani, as Haumea from
'I'ilipo, and both from the land of the gods called Nu'umealani, to which Papa also retires in one version of her story.
La'ila'i's children by Ki'i come, like Haumea's, "from the
brain." The heat of sexual passion ascribed to La'ila'i in
connection with the aphorism of the fire stick is attributed
to Haumea as an indwelling spirit, although not directly
noticed in the chant. La'ila'i's affair in the "land of Lua" is a
close parallel to Haumea's and must belong to a common
tradition, independently elaborated.

Just as Haumea in folk legend has a part in the Pele
myth, so La'ila'i's offspring by Ki'i closely resemble those
Hawaiians today called *'ehu* people, who are believed to
belong to the Pele family from the brown color of their
hair and the reddish tint in their skin. The chant of the
ninth section describes them as "ruddy" (*ke aka 'ula*) with
"fine reddish hair at puberty" (*he hua ulu 'i'i*) and red-
brown beard (*huluhulu 'a*) among a dark, black-haired,
smooth-faced people. They are aggressive and "leap to the
heavens" (*lele pu i ka lani*), meaning perhaps that they push
their claim to rank. "The Ki'i people give good jobs to their
children," says Ho'olapa. Their advent into the social order

2. Malo, pp. 155–57.

is accompanied by the "trembling of earth" (*ola'i ku honua*) and the "splitting open of the heavens" (*owa ka lani*), suggesting the commotion among an established theocracy at the rise of an upstart branch from an alien source.

The story of Haumea begins at line 1760 of the Paliku genealogy, where Mulinaha the husband takes to wife 'Ipo'i. The word *'ipo* means "sweetheart," and the intensive termination gives her first place of her kind, hence "Sweetheart-supreme." It is difficult to say whether the nine women named in the lines following with their respective husbands are supposed to have been born of these two. All are said to be Haumea herself in one of her manifold forms, five of them those in which she "lived with children and grandchildren." There is also some ground for identifying "Sweetheart-supreme" herself with Haumea, as the lines seem to read. At all events the break with Ki'o, "from whom spread the chiefs," may indicate a breakdown, under a new regime, of the social system set up under the Kanaloa priesthood. The whole treatment of Haumea as wife of the god Kanaloa in the two chants elaborating her story can hardly be anything but a symbolic retelling of some such event in the family history, to be discussed more in detail under the closing section of the chant. I can only add here a purely speculative suggestion that the curious birth "from the brain" (*ma ka lolo*) may derive from a play upon the 'Ololo ("Brain") branch and carry a hint of some liaison on the elder Paliku line with the younger branch, as of La'ila'i with Ki'i.

CHANT THIRTEEN
PART I

[At line 1710 of section twelve there are born Paliku and his younger brother 'Ololo. The genealogy of this section continues from 'Ololo to Wakea; that of the thirteenth opens at line 1735 with Paliku and his wife Paliha'i. From

this point man and wife listed on the Paliku branch lead to
Mulinaha and his wife, as below.]

1760. Mulinaha was the husband, 'Ipo'i the wife
    Born was Laumiha a woman, lived with Ku-ka-haku-a-lani
    ["Ku-the-lord-of-heaven"]
    Born was Kaha'ula a woman, lived with Ku-huli-honua
    ["Ku-overturning-earth"]
    Born was Kahakauakoko a woman, lived with Ku-lani-'ehu
    ["Ku-(the)-brown-haired-chief"]
    Born was Haumea a woman, lived with the god Kanaloa
1765. Born was Ku-kaua-kahi a male, lived with Kuaimehani
    Born was Kaua-huli-honua
    Born was Hina-mano-ulua'e ["Woman-of-abundance-of-
    food-plants"] a woman
    Born was Huhune ["Dainty"] a woman
    Born was Haunu'u a woman
1770. Born was Haulani a woman
    Born was Hikapuanaiea ["Sickly"] a woman; Haumea was
    recognized, this was Haumea
    Haumea of mysterious forms, Haumea of eightfold forms
    Haumea of four-hundred-thousand-fold forms, Haumea of
    four-thousand-fold forms
    With thousands upon thousands of forms
1775. With Hikapuanaiea the heavenly one became barren
    She lived like a dog, this woman of Nu'umea [?]
    Nu'umea the land, Nu'u-papa-kini the division
    Haumea spread through her grandchildren
    With Ki'o she became barren, ceased bearing children
1780. This woman bore children through the fontanel
    Her children came out from the brain
    She was a woman of 'I'ilipo in Nu'umea
    She lived with Mulinaha
    Born was Laumiha ["Intense-silence"] born from the brain
1785. Born was the woman Kaha'ula ["Erotic-dreams"] from the
    brain
    Born was Ka-haka-uakoko ["The-perch-of-the-low-lying-
    rainbow"] from the brain
    Haumea was this, that same woman
    She lived with the god Kanaloa
    The god Kaua-kahi ["First-strife"] was born from the brain

1790. Born from the brain were the offspring of that woman
Drivelers were the offspring from the brain

[There follows a peroration addressed to Papa as wife of Wakea, to be included with the chant of Wakea in the next chapter.]

CHANT FIFTEEN
PART I

1930. Haumea, woman of Nu'umea in Kukuiha'a
Of Mehani the impenetrable land of Kuaihealani in Paliuli
The beautiful, the dark [land], darkening the heavens
A solitude for the heavenly one, Kameha-'i-kaua [?]
Kameha-'i-kaua, The-secluded-one-supreme-in-war, god of
    Kauakahi

1935. At the parting of earth, at the parting of high heaven
Left the land, jealous of her husband's second mate
Came to the land of Lua, to 'Ahu of Lua, lived at Wawau
The goddess became the wife of Makea
Haumea became a woman of Kalihi in Ko'olau

1940. Lived in Kalihi on the edge of the cliff Laumiha
Entered a growing tree, she became a breadfruit tree
A breadfruit body, a trunk and leaves she had
Many forms had this woman Haumea
Great Haumea was mysterious

1945. Mysterious was Haumea in the way she lived
She lived with her grandchildren
She slept with her children
Slept with her child Kauakahi as [?] the wife Kuaimehani
Slept with her grandchild Kaua-huli-honua

1950. As [?] his wife Huli-honua
Slept with her grandchild Haloa
As [?] his wife Hinamano'ulua'e
Slept with her grandchild Waia as [?] his wife Huhune
Slept with her grandchild Hinanalo as [?] his wife Haunu'u

1955. Slept with her grandchild Nanakahili as [?] his wife Haulani
Slept with her grandchild Wailoa as [?] his wife Hikapua-
    neiea
Ki'o was born, Haumea was recognized
Haumea was seen to be shriveled
Cold and undesirable

1960. The woman was in fact gone sour
     Hard to deal with and crabbed
     Unsound, a fraud, half blind, a woman generations old
     Wrinkled behind, wrinkled before
     Bent and grey the breast, worthless was [the one of] Nu'u-
        mea [?]
1965. She lived licentiously, bore children like a dog
     With Ki'o came forth the chiefs
     He slept with Kamole, with the woman of the woodland
     Born was Ole, Ha'i was the wife

· · · · · · · · · · · · · · · ·

[The genealogical line follows from Ki'o seven generations to Ki'i at line 1974. To Ki'i is born by his wife Hinako'ula, a famous name in Hawaiian romance, the two sons
'Ulu and Nana'ulu, names common to other Polynesian
genealogies of chief line. To one or the other of these two
all Hawaiian chiefs trace their line of descent. The Kumulipo genealogy continues from 'Ulu. At line 1984 it introduces the parents of the Maui brothers, and the section concludes with the name song of the Maui born "on the back
of Wakea," presumably the same Maui who heads the closing genealogy of the sixteenth section.]

CHAPTER TWENTY-ONE

Papa and Wakea

WAKEA in the form of Atea or Vatea, replaced in New Zealand by Rangi (Lani) meaning "Sky," appears as a primary male generative force throughout eastern Polynesia, the name a symbol of the upper regions of air, whence descend sunshine and rain to fertilize earth. The wife Papa, a word applied in Hawaii to a flat surface or layer, symbolizes the warm upper layer of earth, where lies the fertilized seed awaiting the period of maturity to spring into life. But to the Polynesian these functions of sky and earth are themselves direct analogues of the process of human reproduction. Animate nature manifested in the physical universe is equally potent, if properly approached, to insure human fertility. Father Sky and Mother Earth are, the first parents of human life on earth as they are of plant life that springs living from earth under the influence of sun and rain from heaven and of animal life that feeds upon it.

At the time of foreign contact Hawaii, too, counted its stock from Wakea and Papa as the official parent-pair. Their names occur on the earliest genealogy of the race given out by Hawaiian students at the mission high school in 1838 and repeated forty years later by Judge Fornander in his *Account of the Polynesian Race*. They are quoted by Malo and incorporated into the report made in 1904 by a committee of native scholars appointed by the legislature to inquire into the true native tradition of "the beginning of the Hawaiian people."[1]

1. *Mo'olelo Hawaii*, p. 36; Fornander, *Polynesian Race*, I, 188-90; Malo, p. 311; Kepelino, Appendix, p. 182.

Equally on the common tongue, although stoutly repudiated by the *Mo'olelo Hawaii* and called "doubtful" by Malo, was the story of Wakea's desire for his youthful daughter, the plan to allay Papa's suspicions by instituting taboo nights when men should live apart from their wives, Papa's discovery, her repudiation of Wakea and her taking a mate in another land, finally her return to Wakea upon hearing that he, too, had solaced himself with another wife.[2] A famous chant of Kamehameha's day tells the story under the figure of the "birth of islands," symbolizing by means of the various alliances of the two parents in the myth the actual rise of ruling chief families on the islands of the Hawaiian group.[3] The sly sobriquet of "Wakea" said to have been attached to the Ka-'I-'i-mamao to whom the Kumulipo chant was allegedly dedicated, who took his own daughter to wife, further shows the myth to have been current at the time that the prose note to the Kumulipo was written down. More obscurely but with equal consistency was repeated the name of Haloa, the first living child born to Wakea, some said by his own daughter, and named from the "long-stalk" (*ha-loa*) of the taro plant that grew from the body of an earlier embryo child buried beside the house.[4]

Thus heading the genealogy of chiefs, their story woven into chant and applied to contemporary court life, Wakea and Papa seem to have been in historic times at least the officially accepted progenitors through Haloa of the Hawaiian people, if not of the whole race of humankind. The *Mo'olelo Hawaii* reads, "Wakea and Papa were the first ancestors of the Hawaiian people, both chiefs and common-

2. *Mo'olelo Hawaii*, pp. 37–40; Malo, pp. 314–15; Kepelino, pp. 62–67; Kamakau, *Ke Au Okoa*, October 14, 1869; Fornander, *Collection* ("Memoirs," No. 6), p. 250, Beckwith, *Hawaiian Mythology*, chap. xx.

3. Fornander, *Collection* ("Memoirs," No. 4), pp. 12–16, 17.

4. Malo, p. 320; Kepelino, Appendix, pp. 192–93; Fornander, *Collection* ("Memoirs," No. 6), p. 319.

ers." "This is the genealogy of the Hawaiian people; that is, from Kumulipo-ka-po to Wakea and Papa," concludes the committee report of 1904. Malo calls Haloa "progenitor of all the peoples of the earth." "Now you must understand that the children born from Haloa, these are yourselves," reads a passage from the manuscript notes kept by the Hawaiian Naua Society, organized during the period of the late monarchy. It is not difficult to see that by the name "Haloa" the Hawaiian genealogist is merely symbolizing the male sex organ. It is the genius of the storyteller, probably stimulated by the habit of concealing under cover of myth some court incident of his own day, that has woven so rich a background of fiction about these ancient impersonations of the sex function invoked to insure permanence in the family succession.

Important as the two seem to be as parent-pair in modern Hawaiian tradition, in the Kumulipo, Wakea and Papa play an apparently minor part. Always their names and story come at the end of a section as if possibly inserted as an afterthought or introduced late into the family tradition. Still less is the name of Haloa important. The Opu'upu'u branch of the twelfth section closes with his birth: "Wakea lived (noho) with Haumea, with Papa, with Haohokaka-lani [commonly written Ho'ohokukalani], Haloa was born," reads the passage. Only in a brief peroration to Papa at the close of the thirteenth section is the story noticed of Wakea's deception of Papa, the taboos imposed, and the birth of the embryo Long-stalk and the living son Haloa. At line 1951 Haloa's name is thrust into the list of grandchildren with whom Haumea "slept" (moe). Otherwise he has no important place upon the final genealogy leading to the chief stock with which the chant concludes. Papa and Wakea do not appear there at all. Papa's traditional life as a woman in the land of Lua is transferred to Haumea or perhaps originally told of La'ila'i. Altogether we must sup-

pose that Wakea and Papa as parent-pair responsible
through Haloa for the spread of mankind over earth had no
initial importance for the family whose divine ancestors
were commemorated in the Kumulipo prayer chant.

In the genealogy of the fourteenth section, certainly,
Wakea is rather fully represented, but here again his story
stands at the close rather than the beginning of the genealogical listing with which the chant opens. This breaks off
at line 1840 with the birth of Wakea under the name of
Pau-pani-a[wa]kea, "End-of-the-shutting-out-of-light."
Hawaiians call midday Awakea and the eulogistic title may
herald the light of the midday sun when no shadow is cast
and a magician's power is greatest. It further suggests the
myth so fully developed in Tahiti and New Zealand of the
separation of Sky Father and Earth Mother in order to give
light and space for life to expand on earth, or that told in
Mangaia of Vatea carried upward by the wind with his wife
Papa into the upper world of light.[5]

Born with Wakea are two others, Lehu'ula, generally
written Lihau'ula and sometimes identified with Kanaloa,
and Makulukulu. The three, according to a perhaps late
tradition, represent the ancestors of the three classes of
Hawaiian society: chiefs, priests, and commoners.[6] The
chiefs held the land under a single ruling chief who appor-
tioned it, and each farmed out his share to a succession of
overseers whose duty it was to see that a proportionate
share of the produce was brought in as tribute to his overlord.[7] Makulukulu in the trio I take to represent this function of the commoners, and the "stars hung in the heavens,"
enumerated at length in the lines following to symbolize the
"bundles" brought in as tribute at the Makahiki or some

5. Henry, pp. 405–7, 409–13; White, I, 161–62; Smith, pp. 121–22; Gill,
pp. 6–8.
6. Fornander, Polynesian Race, I, 112.
7. Malo, pp. 78–90, 96–101; Kepelino, pp. 140–51; Hobbs, chap. i.

other great festival of the clan, the whole representing, according to Pokini, the procession arriving with their gifts to lay before the young heir, made up into a pair of bundles and "swung" over a shoulder pole as was the customary way of carrying loads in Hawaii.

The Makahiki itself takes its name from the rising of the Pleiades, known throughout Polynesia as Makali'i, and Makulukulu may perhaps be a chant name for Makali'i. In the migration legend of the great fisherman Hawaii-loa, who discovers and renames the islands of the group, Makali'i is said to be navigator of the fleet and to become ancestor of commoners as Hawaii-loa is ancestor of a chief stock.[8] In fiction Makali'i is a popular character and always represented in connection with food supply. He is a chief living on the island of Kauai, or at South Cape on the island of Hawaii, or "in Kahiki," or in the upper heaven as seer and caretaker of the vegetable garden of the gods Kane and Kanaloa. His men have special arts in fishing. He controls vegetable food and is niggardly with it, "hangs it up in the heavens," as the saying is, when a drought burns up a crop. Always in the stories there is a thief who robs the patch or cuts the cords of the net in which his foodstuffs have been stored away. A string figure called "net of Makali'i" shows the net, its several divisions, and the exact point where, with a single cut, the whole figure falls to pieces. One of the ceremonies of the Makahiki festival was the shaking of a loose-meshed net filled with all kinds of vegetable foods in order to determine by the amount that fell through the meshes the success of the crop for the coming year.[9]

For the identification of stars named in the next fifty lines I am indebted to Dr. Maud Makemson, who obtained her information from living Hawaiians or from previously re-

8. Beckwith, *Hawaiian Mythology*, pp. 363–65.

9. Makemson, pp. 75–84, 129–32, Malo, pp. 197–98; Beckwith, *Hawaiian Mythology*, pp. 365–69, and see Index.

corded sources.[10] Their appearance in the heavens directly
after the birth of Wakea has ended the "shutting out of
light" agrees with the New Zealand myth, where the covering of the naked expanse of Sky with the heavenly bodies
and of Earth with vegetation follows the pushing upward
of the sky to let in the light. The list may further be regarded as a kind of genealogy, since Hawaiians claim that
stars are called after chiefs, although the exact connection
has never been fully explained. The genealogy of beginning quoted by the Committee of 1904 notes the birth of
"men" who "flew to heaven . . . after all of whom stars are
named." So in Tahiti an obscure passage in the story of the
"Birth of the Heavenly Bodies" tells how Ta'ura "The red
one," a name given to the star Sirius, took a wife of whom
"princes" were born, Matari'i (Makali'i) being one; then
were "created kings of the chiefs of earthly hosts on one
side, and of chiefs in the skies on the other side. All were
royal personages in Fa'ahiti . . . from the period of darkness
(Po) and they each had a star. They bore the names of
those stars, and those names have been perpetuated in their
temples in this world."[11]

Following the star lists comes a passage touching upon
the adventures of Wakea with a goddess celebrated in Hawaiian story as "Hina-of-the-moon," she who is known in
Tahiti as "Hina-who-stepped-into-the-moon," or, in Hawaii
again, as Lonomuku, "Maimed-Lono" because, if the myth
is correctly interpreted, when she fled to the moon from
her earthly companion she left in his hand as he grasped
after her one of her legs, from which grew the potato.
Directly after, Hina-kawe'o-a is named, but whether the
same Hina or another is not made clear. This Hina is certainly identical with "Hina-of-the-fire" who is mother of
Maui in the chant of the fifteenth section. A Fornander

10. Makemson, chap. vii.
11. Henry, p. 363.

genealogy gives Maui's mother the name of Kawea. The name of Hina-of-the-fire, Hina-a-ke-ahi, according to one old Hawaiian, is the fire goddess Pele's sacred name as controlling fire from the earth. In Tahiti Pere is called "goddess of the heat of the earth, a blond woman" (*atua vahine no te vera o te fenua, e vahine 'ehu*). The word *we'a* or its equivalent *we'o* is applied in Hawaii to a red coloring matter, but I take the name Kawe'oa to come directly from the Tahitian by elision *te-ve(r)a-(a te fenu)a*.[12] The whole treatment of the Wakea story here suggests a late handling influenced from Tahiti.[13]

The first Hina comes floating to Wakea in the form of a bailing gourd, a trick familiar in South Sea story but there, so far as I know, always employed by a male shape-shifter to secure passage in a canoe already refused him.[14] Taken into the canoe the bailer becomes a beautiful woman, hence called "Hina-the-bailer." When he takes her home and "sets her by the fire," a euphemism for the sex act, strange sea creatures are born. Next Hina-kawe'o-a "craves food," and Wakea sets up a row of images (*ki'i*), conceals himself in one of them, and from this union is born the same "cock on the back of Wakea" whose birth so radically upsets the established social order at the close of the eleventh section. This Hina is the "Underseas-woman" or "Woman-born-below" (Wahine-lalo-hana[u]) of myth, who nibbles the bait from a chief's fishhooks and is lured to shore by the same trick of the images; to whom her brother brings the stars and moon for food, or, in another version, whose family overwhelms the land with a flood to avenge her abduction.

12. *Ibid.*, p. 359.
13. *Ibid.*, p. 407; Beckwith, *Hawaiian Mythology*, pp. 241–44, and chap. xv; Fornander, *Collection* ("Memoirs," No. 5), pp. 266–69; ("Memoirs," No. 6), p. 318; Malo, pp. 307–10.
14. Thrum, *More Hawaiian Folk Tales*, p. 249; Beckwith, *Hawaiian Mythology*, pp. 449–51.

It is hardly necessary to repeat that both canoe and "image" (*ki'i*) are perfectly understood male sex symbols and are to be so understood in the folk-tale versions here noticed. The word *moa*, "cock," is used for a high chief, especially in connection with a struggle between competing aspirants, as witness the famous description of a cock fight in the chant describing Kamehameha's victorious campaign on the island of Hawaii.[15] Since it is death for an inferior to allow even his shadow to fall upon the sacred head of a taboo chief, the perch of the cock upon the ridgepole here means that the son claimed higher rank than that of his parent. The story seems to point to a union with some family of high rank, either after the migration to Hawaii or somewhere along the way, whereby an interloping branch gained the position of ruling stock on the family line. The name song of Hina's son Maui, born in the shape of a cock, as told in the chant of the next section, certainly represents such a struggle for position by one born of an alien strain. This "seed of the High One begotten in the heavens" shakes heaven and earth "even to the sacred places."

CHANT THIRTEEN
Part II

Papa-seeking-earth
Papa-seeking-heaven
Great-Papa-giving-birth-to-islands
1795. Papa lived with Wakea
Born was the woman Ha'alolo
Born was jealousy, anger
Papa was deceived by Wakea
He ordered the sun, the moon
1800. The night to Kane for the younger
The night to Hilo for the first-born
Taboo was the house platform, the place for sitting

15. Fornander, *Collection* ("Memoirs," No. 6), pp. 382–86; Beckwith, *Hawaiian Mythology*, pp. 427–29.

Taboo the house where Wakea lived
Taboo was intercourse with the divine parent
1805. Taboo the taro plant, the acrid one
Taboo the poisonous 'akia plant
Taboo the narcotic auhuhu plant
Taboo the medicinal uhaloa
Taboo the bitter part of the taro leaf
1810. Taboo the taro stalk that stood by the woman's taboo house
Haloa was buried [there], a long taro stalk grew
The offspring of Haloa [born] into the day
    Came forth

CHANT FOURTEEN

[The birth of Li'a-i-ku-honua at the "Appearing-of-heaven-and-earth," with whose name the genealogy opens, is mentioned at line 1754 of the preceding branch. The genealogy of that branch is continued through a younger brother, that of the fourteenth through the older. By his wife Ke-aka-huli-honua Li'a has a son Laka. Thirty pairs, husband and wife, precede the birth of Wakea.]

Born was Pau-pani-a[wa]kea
This was Wakea; [born was] Lehu'ula; [born was] Makulu-kulu-the-chief
Their youngest, a man of great bundles
Collected and placed with Makali'i; fixed fast
1850. Fixed are the stars suspended in the sky
[There] swings Ka'awela [Mercury], swings Kupoilaniua
Ha'i swings that way, Ha'i swings this way
Kaha'i swings, swings Kaha'iha'i [in the Milky Way]
Swings Kaua, the star cluster Wahilaninui
1855. Swings the flower of the heavens, Kaulua-i-ha'imoha'i
Puanene swings, the star that reveals a lord
Nu'u swings, Kaha'ilono swings
Wainaku [patron star of Hilo] swings, swings Ikapa'a
Swings Kiki'ula, swings Keho'oea
1860. Pouhanu'u swings, swings Ka-ili-'ula, The-red-skinned
Swings Kapakapaka, [and the morning star] Mananalo [Jupiter or Venus]
Swings Kona, swings Wailea [patron star of Maui]

Swings the Auhaku, swings the Eye-of-Unulau
Swings Hina-of-the-heavens, Hina-lani, swings Keoea
1865. Ka'aka'a swings, swings Polo'ula [star of Oahu]
Kanikania'ula swings, Kauamea swings
Swings Kalalani [of Lanai], swings [the astrologers' star]
Kekepue
Swings Ka'alolo [of Ni'ihau], swings the Resting-place-of-
the-sun [Kaulana-a-ka-la]
Hua swings, 'Au'a [Betelgeuse] swings
1870. Lena swings, swings Lanikuhana
Swings Ho'oleia, swings Makeaupe'a
Swings Kaniha'alilo, swings 'U'u
Swings 'A'a [Sirius], swings 'Ololu
Kamaio swings, swings Kaulu[a]lena
1875. Swings Peaked-nose, swings Chicken-nose
Swings Pipa, swings Ho'eu
Swings Malana, swings Kaka'e
Swings Mali'u, swings Kaulua
Lanakamalama swings, Naua swings
1880. Welo swings, swings Ikiiki
Ka'aona swings, swings Hinaia'ele'ele
Puanakau [Rigel] swings, swings Le'ale'a
Swings Hikikauelia [Sirius of navigators], swings Ka'elo
Swings Kapawa, swings Hikikaulonomeha [Sirius of astrolo-
gers]
1885. Swings Hoku'ula, swings Poloahilani
Swings Ka'awela, swings Hanakalanai
Uliuli swings, Melemele swings [two lands of old]
Swings the Pleiades, Makali'i, swings the Cluster, na Huihui
Swings Kokoiki [Kamehameha's star], swings Humu [Altair]
1890. Moha'i swings, swings Kaulu[a]okaoka
Kukui swings, swings Konamaukuku
Swings Kamalie, swings Kamalie the first
Swings Kamalie the last
Swings Hina-of-the-yellow-skies, Hina-o-na-leilena
1895. Swing the Seven, na Hiku [Big Dipper], swings the first of
the Seven
The second of the Seven, the third of the Seven
The fourth of the Seven, the fifth of the Seven
The sixth of the Seven, the last of the Seven
Swings Mahapili, swings the Cluster

1900. Swing the Darts [Kao] of Orion
     Sown was the seed of Makali'i, seed of the heavens
     Sown was the seed of the gods, the sun is a god
     Sown was the seed of Hina, an afterbirth of Lono-muku
     The food of Hina-ia-ka-malama as Waka [?]
1905. She was found by Wakea in the deep sea
     In a sea of coral, a turbulent sea
     Hina-ia-ka-malama floated as a bailing gourd
     Was hung up in the canoes, hence called Hina-the-bailer
     [-ke-ka]
     Taken ashore, set by the fire
1910. Born were corals, born the eels
     Born were the small sea urchins, the large sea urchins
     The blackstone was born, the volcanic stone was born
     Hence she was called Woman-from-whose-womb-come-var-
       ious-forms, Hinahalakoa
     Hina craved food, Wakea went to fetch it
1915. [He] set up images on the platform
     Set them up neatly in a row
     Wakea as Ki'i [image] slept with Hina-ka-we'o-a [?]
     Born was the cock, perched on Wakea's back
     The cock scratched the back of Wakea
1920. Wakea was jealous, tried to brush it away
     Wakea was jealous, vexed and annoyed
     Thrust away the cock and it flew to the ridgepole
     The cock was on the ridgepole
     The cock was lord
1925. This was the seed of The-high-one
     Begotten in the heavens
     The heavens shook
     The earth shook
     Even to the sacred places

CHAPTER TWENTY-TWO

Maui the Usurper

THE name song of Maui at the close of the fifteenth section of the Kumulipo chant tells the story of the struggle for power of a younger son born into the family through an alien alliance, one entitling him to a higher-ranking status than the natural heir. Maui is born to a god, as the phrase goes. His mother is Hina-of-the-fire, his grandparent Mahui'e is known throughout Polynesia as keeper of underground fire. His mother sends him back to her own (or his father's) family for a wife, and his posterity replace the old stock on the line of ruling chiefs who carry on the family descent.

Stories of the Maui brothers are by no means local to Hawaii alone, but the name Maui-of-the-loincloth for the trickster hero is used, so far as I know, only here and in New Zealand; Maui-tikitiki, -ti'iti'i, or -ki'iki'i he is commonly called. A story to justify the sobriquet is told in both areas. In the Hawaiian version told at the east end of the island of Maui, Hina, walking on the beach, picks up a man's loincloth and, girding herself with it, lies down to sleep. She conceives a child, and her husband, far from taking the affair badly as in the Wakea chant, recognizes the offspring of a god and rejoices to have "found our lord."[1] One recognizes here a euphemized variant of the subterfuge used by Tiki to gain access to his daughter by the sand woman as told in the Stimson manuscript from the Tuamotus. In the New Zealand account from Nga-i-tahu

1. Beckwith, *Hawaiian Mythology*, p. 229.

sources Hine bears an abortion and wrapping it in her
bloody "apron" (*maro*) casts it into the sea, or among
brambles in one version, whence it is rescued by ancestral
deities and shaped into a human being.[2] So in the Hawaiian
chant of the "Birth of Islands"—

> The afterbirth of the child was thrown away
> Into the rolling sea,
> The froth of the heaving sea
> Was found as a loincloth for the child,
> Molokini the island,
> This was an afterbirth.[3]

In New Zealand Maui makes himself known to his family
in human form. In the Kumulipo he is born in feathered
form as a *moa*, generally translated "cock." He makes a cry
not like a human being but "like an animal" as the word
Alala is defined. In the South Pacific the trickster Maui
shifts to the form of a pigeon, a *rupe*. It is in this form that
in New Zealand he visits his ancestors in the underworld.
Rupe in pigeon shape flies to the rescue of his sister in the
Hine-Tinirau tale. In Mangareva, Toa Rupe, daughter of
Te Rupe, is mother of the Maui brothers. Obviously the
Hawaiian *moa* should be a pigeon, but, since the pigeon was
not known to Hawaiians, the composer uses the fighting
cock as feathered symbol of the part the newborn infant is
to play in the world.[4] He is to be an *aiwaiwa* child, a word
denoting excellence as an expert but also used in a deroga-
tory sense as we use the word "notorious." Such double
intention in an epithet seems to us like a contradiction of
terms, but to the Polynesian it agrees with the opposition he
observes inherent in human judgments. The character Maui
plays in story cycles throughout the South Seas shifts like
his shape. Some make him a bungler, vainglorious and re-

2. White, II, 63, 65, 71, 79.
3. Fornander, *Collection* ("Memoirs," No. 4), pp. 4, 5; cf. Henry, p. 408.
4. White, II, 66–67, 72–73, 96–98; Buck, *Ethnology of Mangareva*, p. 310.

vengeful; others, a benevolent culture bringer, using his gifts of magic for the good of man.

Maui's exploits or *ua* in his struggle for power are listed by number. So White enumerates the "acts" of Maui under the term *patunga*.[5] The first contest is against his own kindred, those who seem to be guarding Hina's virginity. The word *ana* probably refers to the cave dwelling of Hina familiar to Maui stories; one such is still pointed out on the mountainside back of Waianae village on Oahu. The next five contests are directed toward the establishment of his claim to the privileges of high chief rank. Kava drink made of the black-stemmed variety is sacred to the "gods." The "bamboo" may be the knife used for the rite of incision, perhaps similarly limited to the chief class. The *paehumu*, if the corrected text is accepted, is the inclosure within the heiau set apart for images, to the right of which stood the prayer scaffold or *anu'u*. From both places all were excluded save those of high rank.

The struggle for the privileges of rank turns Maui's attention to the question of his parentage. His mother is evasive and puts him off with the story of the loincloth. Immediately after, she sends him to his "father" after "line and hook." Perhaps this is a parent on his mother's side. At all events the land-fishing expedition upon which she sends him is to be interpreted, not as so literally exploited in folk tale but as symbolizing a wooing expedition to win a wife by whom he may unite in their child the blood of close kin born in lands distant geographically but drawn together by this bond of family union. A fairy wife who sends her favorite son to seek a wife among her own kin in a land of deities is a popular theme in Hawaiian as well as South Sea family story cycles.

The seventh adventure in seizing the sister of Hina in the shape of a mudhen is the first step in this wooing. The folk

5. White, II, 72–73 (text), 79–80.

tale telling how Maui learned from the red-headed mud-
hens the secret of fire-making by the use of fire sticks is
conspicuously absent from the enumeration here ōf Maui's
exploits. The reason is obvious; it is not fire-making but the
secret of sex that Maui learns in preparation for "drawing
the islands together" by a propitious marriage. The fishhook Manai-a-ka-lani is equally a sex symbol. The word
manai is used for a sharp needle-like instrument used in
stringing flowers for wreath-making, and in wooing stories
the maiden courted is traditionally given a flower name.

The obscure treatment of the courting story is a good
illustration of poetic courtly style. Seeking a wife among
his close kin, he probably comes incognito and meets opposition in the form of the parent, who probably does not
recognize him, and only after defeating this obstacle does
he win the girl already destined to become his wife by
arrangement among their common parents. The struggle
with the sea monster here represents the obstructions put in
his way, sometimes by the girl herself as the theme is developed in popular romance. The whole courting episode is
here treated with lively humor. The phrase "to live through
the tail" (*Ola ... ma ka pewa* or *ma ka hi'u*) is used when
a slim chance of escape offers itself in a dangerous predica-
ment. Every Hawaiian knows the story of how, during the
great shark war, when the shark Mikololou was dragged
ashore and eaten "all but his tail," or his "tongue" in some
versions, a dog seized the remnant and leaped with it into
the sea, whereupon the shark, feeling itself in its native element, resumed its full form. "Mikololou died but lived
again through his tongue" is similarly said of one who talks
himself out of a dangerous situation.[6]

Maui eventually wins the lady Mahana-ulu-'ehu for
whom "love grew." Her name is paired with his on the

6. Pukui, *Ke Awa Lau o Pu'uloa*, pp. 58–59; Beckwith, *Hawaiian Mythology*, p. 139.

genealogy of the Kamokuiki book equivalent to that of the
sixteenth section of the Kumulipo chant, where Hina-ke-
aloha-ila is named as wife of Maui. The two names must
hence be pseudonyms for the same lady. Maui has now
concluded his ninth adventure, and from this point the
numbering becomes confused. The scratching-out of the
eyes of the eight-eyed Pe'ape'a who has abducted his
mother is declared to be his "last exploit." But there follows
the sun-snaring, introduced by the line "With Moemoe the
strife ended." The story is probably merely another version
of the abduction incident, so well known through popular
retelling as to be scarcely worth repeating. "Everybody
knows" is Ho'olapa's happy rendering of the Hawaiian
phrasing. As I heard it many years ago on the island of
Maui, the fight with Moemoe came as the final episode of
the sun-snaring. We were riding from Lahaina toward Ka-
hakaloa Point, where one strikes the trades across East
Maui, and came upon a huge pillar-like block of stone fallen
toward the sea. This was the "great black rock of Kaana-
pali" marking the prostrate form of the overthrown shape-
shifter who had taunted Maui, some say attempted to stay
him, when he set out from Lahaina to do battle with the
Sun. Maui promised to deal with him on his return, and,
with the silencing of the reviler, Maui's labors ceased.

The whole treatment of this name chant is an excellent
example of the song-master's art; whether it was in its present form originally a part of the prayer chant it would be
difficult to say. The lovemaking is developed as a comic
relief to the drama of strife against the gods, which is the
main theme of Maui's lawless career. Four times their
names occur as a refrain, first when Maui seizes the "bunch
of black-stemmed kava," again with the strife over the
"bamboo" of Kane and Kanaloa. With the hooking of the
great fish the two gods are "shaken from their foundation."
Finally, Maui drinks the "yellow water" of Kane and Kana-

loa, an adventure sometimes referred to as a quarrel over the right of participation in a kava-drinking ritual. The closing lines reciting the parentage, place of birth, and places of burial sacred to the memory of a family hero are in the true laconic style of the name song or *inoa*. At the close is summed up the essential character of the Maui figure in the terms *ho'upu'upu* and *ho'okala*, the last word more precisely rendered by "lawless" than by the more generally used "mischievous." In the final play upon the word *moku* there seems to be, as pointed out by Ho'olapa, a double application, on the one hand to the land itself, on the other to the lawless chief who overran it, "a chief indeed."

The Maui cycle as judged from its comparative uniformity of detail, in spite of individual variations over a wide geographical spread, must have developed in approximately its present essential form before or during the migration period. The various forms the story took throughout the Pacific are fully treated in Dr. Katherine Luomala's recent study of "Maui-of-a-thousand-tricks." I may be pardoned a digression here to bring out some of the modern folk tale variants told in the Hawaiian group that may cast light upon the Kumulipo rendering.

Fornander's version of Kaulu, who sacks the land of Kane and Kanaloa by means of superior magic and trickery, is an obvious retelling of the Maui story. Kaulu is "son of Ka-lana," youngest born of the family and "born in the shape of a rope," obviously an umbilical cord and probably that of the favorite brother, to rescue whom he seeks the land of Kane and Kanaloa, where his brother has been carried away to serve the gods. There he upsets the order of the gods, sharing their kava cup by a ruse, wrecking their vegetable garden, turning the land upside down, even carrying away "the rays of the sun" in his search for his brother, and finally tearing apart the jaws of the great shark in whose body the brother has been hidden. This "shark" must be the same as Maui's "fish" whose drawing ashore shook Kane and Kanaloa from their foundation. It appears in Tahiti as "the handsome blue shark of Ta'aroa" snatched up by the gods from those who would have destroyed it and placed in the Milky Way, the stream of the water of life (*vai ola*) in which the gods bathe to renew their youth, where it may be seen today as a dark patch against the bright belt of light whose diurnal pivoting as the earth revolves is spoken of in Hawaii as the "turning of the fish."[7]

Maui's fishing feat has its modern version in a tale of Red-Ku-of-the-sea told me not many years ago by the sheriff of Hana district, who pointed out on the beach an eel's head turned to stone with jaws apart, together with other material evidence of the factual character of the story.[8] The hero used, of course, the fishhook Manai-a-ka-lani, and the device my informant described for drawing the monster to land by means of ropes attached to the hook and pulling at an angle from two points on the beach must have been also Maui's procedure. Such a device was used in handling one of the huge kites of ancient days and I am told is employed today by fishermen off Lahaina to get a squid to shore too big to handle otherwise. The point of meeting at which the ropes are attached is called *hanai*, a word Ho'olapa seemed to connéct with the *manai* of Maui's hook. Rays of the afternoon sun glancing to the sea in the phenomenon we call "the sun drinking water" are known as "Maui's lassos" or "snaring ropes," with reference to the sun-snaring adventure. I think it likely that the fishing-up of islands, the hooking and drawing to shore of a sea monster, and the modern version of the sun-snaring myth are all variants from an older legend. Perhaps the myth of drawing the sun from its underworld hole in order to lighten a darkened world, told in Hawaii of the famous demigod Kana, was

7. Beckwith, *Hawaiian Mythology*, pp. 436–41; Henry, pp. 369, 403, 404.
8. Beckwith, *Hawaiian Mythology*, pp. 20–22.

the original and more elemental adventure upon which have
been imposed such embellishments as the search after fire,
the freeing of abducted ladies, the fishing after troublesome
sea monsters; or perhaps, on the other hand, the cosmic adventures have developed with a growing taste for symbolism out of a particular incident of human abduction.

CHANT FIFTEEN
PART II

Waolena was the man, Mahui'e the wife
Akalana was the man, Hina-of-the-fire the wife
1985. Born was Maui the first, born was Maui the middle one
Born was Maui-ki'iki'i, born was Maui of the loincloth
The loincloth with which Akalana girded his loins
Hina-of-the-fire conceived, a fowl was born
The child of Hina was delivered in the shape of an egg
1990. She had not slept with a fowl
But a fowl was born
The child chirped, Hina was puzzled
Not from sleeping with a man did this child come
It was a strange child for Hina-of-the-fire
1995. The two guards [?] were angry, the tall and the short one
The brothers of Hina
The two guards within the cave
Maui fought, those guards fell
Red blood flowed from the brow [?] of Maui
2000. That was Maui's first strife
He fetched the bunch of black kava of Kane and Kanaloa
That was the second strife of Maui
The third strife was the quarrel over the kava strainer
The fourth strife was for the bamboo of Kane and Kanaloa
2005. The fifth strife was over the temple inclosure for images [?]
The sixth strife was over the prayer tower in the heiau [?]
Maui reflected, asked who was his father
Hina denied: "You have no father
The loincloth of Kalana, that was your father"
2010. Hina-of-the-fire longed for fish
He learned to fish, Hina sent him
"Go get [it] of your parent

There is the line, the hook
Manai-a-ka-lani, that is the hook
2015. For drawing together the lands of old ocean"
He seized the great mudhen of Hina
The sister bird
That was the seventh strife of Maui
He hooked the mischievous shape-shifter
2020. The jaw of Pimoe as it snapped open
The lordly fish that shouts over the ocean
Pimoe crouched in the presence of Maui
Love grew for Mahana-ulu-'ehu
Child of Pimoe
2025. Maui drew them [?] ashore and ate all but the tailfin
Kane and Kanaloa were shaken from their foundation
By the ninth strife of Maui
Pimoe "lived through the tailfin"
Mahana-ulu-'ehu "lived through the tail"
2030. Hina-ke-ka was abducted by Pe'ape'a
Pe'ape'a, god of the octopus family
That was Maui's last strife
He scratched out the eyes of the eight-eyed Pe'ape'a
The strife ended with Moemoe
2035. Everyone knows about the battle of Maui with the sun
With the loop of Maui's snaring-rope
Winter [?] became the sun's
Summer became Maui's
He drank the yellow water to the dregs [?][9]
2040. Of Kane and Kanaloa
He strove with trickery
Around Hawaii, around Maui
Around Kauai, around Oahu
At Kahulu'u was the afterbirth [deposited], at Waikane the
    navel cord
2045. He died at Hakipu'u in Kualoa
Maui-of-the-loincloth
The lawless shape-shifter of the island
    A chief indeed

9. Titcomb, p. 156.

CHAPTER TWENTY-THREE

The Dedication

THE genealogy of the sixteenth section opens with the names of Maui and his wife Hina-of-the-love-mole, possibly the same who is called Mahana-ulu-'ehu in the song of Maui's fishing. The pairs, man and wife, continue down the line of high chiefs well known to tradition, who ruled successively on the island of Maui, to the famous name of Pi'ilani, whose daughter Pi'ikea became one of the wives of 'Umi, ruling chief on Hawaii. From a son of this union the powerful 'I family of Hilo district counted descent, and by a daughter of the 'I family there was born to Keawe the Lono-i-ka-makahiki to whom the Kumulipo chant was allegedly dedicated. The closing lines of the chant are hence devoted to the detailing of Pi'ikea's ancestry and the aggrandizement of her immediate posterity.

No more famous family in Hawaiian annals could a girl claim as her own than that of Pi'ilani, who succeeded to his father's lands as ruling chief on the eastern end of the island of Maui. His wife was daughter of a high taboo chief of Oahu by his father's sister Kelea, a girl whose dexterity in surfing won her the sobriquet of "fin-bearing" and whose romantic adventures were a favorite theme of courtly song and story.[1] Abducted while engaged in her favorite sport and carried away to the island of Oahu by an inland chief of inferior rank, Kelea wearied of life in the uplands and, leaving home to indulge her passion for surfing, was seen and taken to wife by the high chief of Ewa district. To him she bore the daughter La'ielohelohe, and the girl was

1. Fornander, *Polynesian Race*, II, 83–87.

137

brought up in strict seclusion as a sacred child. In time messengers came from Maui to ask for her in marriage to the son of her mother's brother. Again the court romancers found a theme to their liking in the ceremonies attending this wooing embassy. To Pi'ilani, La'ie bore the daughter Pi'ikea who became 'Umi's wife. Their grandchild obtained the rank of *wohi* with the right to the crouching taboo. The right claimed for his descendant 'I to offer human sacrifice and to cut down *'ohi'a* wood for images would imply that as ruling chief over the land section of Pakini, lying in Ka-'u district, he was entitled to erect a war *heiau*, a right denied to lesser chiefs.

Other famous names appear on this genealogy, some no less well known to Hawaiian romance than to that of southern groups, from which source they may well have been brought. One such noted cycle, intrenched at the east end of the island of Maui, is headed by Ai-kanaka and the stranger wife who fled back to the moon.[2] At line 2070 are born the sons of Palena and his wife Hikawainui, Hanala'a the great and Little Hanala'a, from whom important family lines branch on Hawaiian genealogies. The whole section may well have been added in Kalakaua's day to bring the chant up to date with his own family claim, but variations in the names prove an independent source from the Fornander genealogies of a slightly earlier period.[3]

CHANT SIXTEEN

2049. Maui-son-of-Kalana was the man, Hina-kealohaila the wife

. . . .

2055. Hulu-at-[the]-yellow-sky was the man, Hina-from-the-heavens the wife

Ai-kanaka was the man, Hina-of-the-moon the wife

Born was Puna-the-first, born was Hema, born was Puna-the-last

2. Thrum, *More Hawaiian Folk Tales*, pp. 69–72; Beckwith, *Hawaiian Mythology*, chaps. xvii, xviii.

3. Fornander, *Polynesian Race*, I, 191, 193.

Born was Kaha'i the great to Hema, Hina-ulu-'ohi'a was the
  wife

Hema went after the birthgifts for the wife [?]

2060. Wahieloa was the man, Ho'olaukahili the wife

Laka was the man, Hikawainui the wife

. . . .

2070. Palena was the man, Hikawainui the wife

Born was Hanala'a-nui, born was Hanala'a-iki

Hanala'aiki was the man . . .

. . . .

Kahekili [the first] was the man, Hauanuihoni'ala was the
  wife

2090. Born was Kawauka'ohele and [his sister] Kelea-nui-noho-
  ana-'api'api ["Kelea-swimming-like-a-fish"]

She [Kelea] lived as a wife to Kalamakua

Born was La'ie-lohelohe, [she] lived with Pi'ilani, Pi'ikea was
  born

Pi'ikea lived with 'Umi, Kumalae-nui-a-'Umi [was born]

His was the slave-destroying cliff

2095. Kumulae-nui-a-'Umi was the man, Kumu-nui-puawale the
  wife

Makua was the man, standing first of *wohi* rank on the island

Kapo-hele-mai was the wife, a taboo *wohi* chiefess, the
  sacred one

'I, to 'I is the chiefship, the right to offer human sacrifice

The ruler over the land section of Pakini

2100. With the right to cut down *'ohi'a* wood for images, the pro-
  tector of the island of Hawaii

To Ahu, Ahu son of 'I, to Lono

To Lono-i-ka-makahiki

CHAPTER TWENTY-FOUR

The Genealogies

U P TO a certain point names listed on this latest genealogical branch of the Kumulipo chant, begun in the fifteenth section and completed in the sixteenth, not only appear on accepted genealogies of Hawaiian chief families but bear a striking similarity to some of those reported from southern Polynesia. Fornander may be right when he argues that these likenesses are due to the introduction by a new immigrant stock of its own ancestral line from the south. He fixes upon the settling of Oahu by the powerful Maweke family from North Tahiti as the source of this displacement, since the similarities cease about the time that their names appear upon the Hawaiian genealogical line.[1]

One would like to explain upon this basis the curious introduction on the genealogy of the twelfth section, at lines 1713 to 1715, of a trio of males corresponding to that named in the eighth section at the opening of the period of the Ao. The trio in both cases includes the names of Kane and Kanaloa, in this second case listed as "twins," *mahoe*, and a third name, the man Ki'i in the eighth section, Ahuka'i, "much younger" (*muli loa*), in the twelfth, where the trio follow the name of Kumuhonua. In the Moikeha saga Kumuhonua is the eldest of three sons descended from the migrating Maweke family, who, at his father's death, inherits the family lands on Oahu. Olopana and Moikeha are his younger brothers. With the rise to power of the Moike-

1. Fornander, *Collection* ("Memoirs," No. 6), p. 250.

ha ruling line, that of Kumuhonua dies out.[2] The name of
Ahuka'i appears on the 'Ulu-Puna line as grandparent of
Moikeha's young relative La'a-mai-kahiki, whom he sum-
mons from Tahiti to look after his bones, hence supposedly
a relative of the migrating Maweke family.[3] According to
custom, a chief takes the name of a distinguished ancestor.

Ahuka'i, La'a, La'a-mai-kahiki, ke li'i

begins the young chief's name song. La'a's story has already
been told and the part he played in peopling the Hawaiian
group.

The Moikeha saga further states that the two younger
brothers live for a time at Waipi'o on the island of Hawaii
until they are driven out by a freshet and return to Tahiti.
There they quarrel over Olopana's wife Lu'ukia, and Moikeha sails back to Hawaii, and eventually his line succeeds to
the ruling power on the two islands of Kauai and Oahu. A
quite unrelated legend states that "the gods Kane and Kanaloa" accompanied by "Haumea" once came to Hawaii "in
the shape of human beings," landing first at Keei in South
Kona on the island of Hawaii and then living for a time at
Waipi'o, where Kanaloa is described as "tall and fair," Kane
as dark with thick lips and curly hair.[4] May not the brothers
Olopana and Moikeha, coming with their superior culture
to the simpler islanders on Hawaii, have been taken for the
gods Kane and Kanaloa as was Captain Cook for the god
Lono? The beneficent activities of the two gods, sung in
chant and told in story and commemorated in local legend,
may belong to this early period before the quarrel took
place which separated the two brothers, so that Olopana,
alias Kanaloa, remained in the south when Moikeha, or

2. Fornander, *Polynesian Race*, II, 48–58; Beckwith, *Hawaiian Mythology*, chap. xxv.

3. Fornander, *Polynesian Race*, I, 194.

4. Thrum, *More Hawaiian Folk Tales*, pp. 259–60, Lyons, *Journal of the
Polynesian Society*, II, 56; Kamakau, *Ke Au Okoa*, March 31, 1869.

Kane, returned and became a great chief in the Hawaiian group, dominating the western islands. Such a hypothesis would give meaning to the association of the name of Ahuka'i in the trio with Kane and Kanaloa and all three with that of Kumuhonua on the genealogy of the twelfth section.

Not that we should even attempt to identify historically the long lists of names that make up the genealogical portions of the Kumulipo. Such lists, paired as man and wife, cover approximately eleven hundred of the fourteen hundred lines that make up the second period of the chant. They pretend to trace the family genealogy from its beginning. They claim for it descent from a single stock represented by the approximately eight hundred pairs listed on the long-lived man's genealogy of the eleventh section and on the much shorter branches of succeeding sections stemming from it. How are we to interpret such an ancestral series handed down by word of mouth alone, even if carried back before the migration to Hawaii, as later genealogists declare? Are these actual genealogies in our sense of the term? Are they intended to represent direct descent from father to son?

Many have so regarded them. The Kamokuiki book arranges the names in genealogical succession as man, wife, and child, but this may be the late recorder's idea rather than that of the genealogist from whom he learned them. The length of time they would represent on this basis must strike even an enthusiast's mind as unthinkable. Allowing only half the usual twenty years to a generation, the eleventh section would reach back some eight thousand years. Thereafter comes "the cock on the back of Wakea" whose genealogy of the sixteenth section has some traditional authority.

Most explain the series as purely rhetorical, a mere stuffing of the past for the sake of family prestige. There is some evidence for such a conclusion. We know that such verbal feats of memory were a delight to both audience and reciter from the fact that the early missionaries were urged not to omit in the translation of the Hebrew Scriptures those genealogical portions over which the tongue might linger as a fresh incentive to rhythmic syllabication. Moreover, names on the last half of the eleventh section follow a pattern of repeated syllables making up the name of the long-lived man as it appears in the eighth section and again at the close of the eleventh. This must be essentially a mnemonic device and can hardly be other than artificial.[5]

Designed also it would seem as an aid to memory is the listing by numerical count of the first two sections into groups of four hundred. The eleventh section breaks into two parts of approximately four hundred pairs each. An even closer count to four hundred is to be had by adding to the hundred and eighty-eight pairs of the younger brother's branch listed in the twelfth section the two hundred and fifteen pairs in the eleventh before the twelfth branches from it. Thus, as the fingers of the reciter slipped over the knotted cord on which he kept the sacred count, he must have held his memory in check by means of the "count by four hundred" upon which was woven the ancestral pattern. The whole meticulous structure of these early genealogies must have served to elaborate the symbolism inherent in the content, that of the unbroken inheritance of an entire people from a common ancestral stock. This was the main idea, the *kaona* once more, of such a sacred intertwining of the lives of the living with the fabric of a long, deified past, with "the forty thousand gods, the four hundred thousand gods, the four thousand gods" of temple prayers.[6]

But I believe there was something more than mere inven-

5. Beckwith, *La'ieikawai*, pp. 313–14; Stokes, *Journal of the Polynesian Society*, XXXIX, 1 ff.

6. N. B. Emerson, *Unwritten Literature of Hawaii*, p. 24, note d.

tion as the basis of the listing. The first four hundred names
are short, often monosyllabic. So are, on the whole, the
names of the twelfth section. Even the second four hundred
of the eleventh, shorn of their word play, have monosyllabic values. This agrees with what is said today of the early
preference for short family names before elaborate compounds became the fashion. It is hence possible to read these
names, not as representing vertical descent in time from
father to son but as the horizontal spread, so to speak, of a
kinship group under a single ruling lord or his direct suc-
cessors, those heads of households whose reckoning would
be important for land distribution or conscription for war.
When Kepelino writes, "All the days of Kumuhonua's life
were almost four hundred *hanauna* or more," although he is
obviously under the influence of biblical phrasing and uses
the word as if in its ordinary sense of "generation," he probably thinks of it in its meaning of "kinsfolk," and the statement becomes literally acceptable. It is possible, that is, that
the lists once had relevance. When the line died out and a
new stock took its place, the ancient numbering became
memorialized among the deified dead, and their names were
passed down by oral transmission in behalf of the family
honor and glory by those who knew the "pathway of
chiefs."

Nevertheless, it is not to be denied that the case for a
straight genealogical descent from father to son for these
Kumulipo listings is strong. Hawaiians certainly consider
this their intent. The extremely tenacious memories of
trained reciters in Hawaii and their special fondness for
catalogues of names make a traditional record possible, even
though at some point along the line invention filled in the
numerical count. One must not forget the analogous testi-
mony of Herodotus, to whom the priests at Thebes declared
the count of 341 priest-kings who had succeeded from
father to son from the beginning of the race, to prove

which they showed him rows of wooden images of these kings coresponding in number to that claimed for them. It is true that the Egyptians were a literate people, but the fact remains that both peoples felt the importance of keep-ing a record of descent from the beginning—the Kumu-lipo of the race.

Another feature, common not only to the Kumulipo chant but to all similar prayer chants to the ancestral gods handed down from Hawaiian sources, is the variety of names used for these deities as expressive of their function in the process of generation, so that a single deity may ap-pear under different titles according to the particular aspect under which he or she is worshiped by a given family branch. "Each island had a separate tree," notes Fornan-der,[7] and the attempt to synchronize genealogies on a his-torical basis alone without reference to this possessive urge to poetic invention would be barren of results. Such names are preserved in a family as titles of honor. Thus the child of a chief owned a sacred name bestowed by a god in a dream and not to be revealed beyond the immediate family. He might also take the name of a famous ancestor. He was given nicknames to mark important events in his career or traits of character that he developed. How much more readily, then, might a common ancestral deity be marked off for worship under a particular attribute according to the function he was called upon to fulfil or the special relation that he held to the family of the petitioner.

The Kumulipo is full of such instances. The name Li'ai-kuhonua which opens the genealogy of the fourteenth sec-tion replaces that of Huli-honua in the more common ver-sion and explains a puzzling invocation quoted by Emerson, "E Ku, e Li," opening a prayer for fertility on land, in the sea, and in offspring to man, developed along quite similar lines to the Kumulipo and probably possessing, although in

7. *Collection* ("Memoirs," No. 4), p. 406.

little, like incantational value.[8] Li's wife Ke-aka-huli-honua;
on the other hand, may most certainly be equated with Ata-
(huli-ho)nua, wife of Tagaroa in Mangareva, and of 'Atea
in the Marquesas. Wela-ahi-lani, named just at the close of
the twelfth section with his wife Owe, a contraction of
Owehewehe meaning "to open," is Malo's W(ela-)ahi-lani
who "opens" the heavens and comes down to the beautiful
La'ila'i on earth,[9] she here synonomous with Owe and both
with Wakea and Papa under special family titles, perhaps
those played upon in the two opening lines of the ninth section. Again, 'Ipo'i, wife of Mulinaha on the genealogical
branch of the thirteenth section, just before the birth of
Haumea, may be identical with Uhiuhi-ka-'ipo-i-wai born
with the gods Kane, Lono, and Kanaloa in the "Genealogy
of the First from Intense Darkness" reported by the Committee of 1904, from whom, through her union with the
god Kanaloa, were descended "the generations of Hawaii
from the beginning of Heaven and Earth."[10] Such elabora-
tions upon the functions of a deity are honorific and no
more imply plurality than the epithets attached to the supreme deity of the Hebrews.

The unique place given to Haumea on the genealogy of
the fifteenth and sixteenth sections of the chant in place of
Papa, commonly named on the same genealogy, has already
been noticed. The birth from this union of the god Kauakahi, "First-strife," or Ku-kaua-kahi, "Arising-of-first-
strife," and of Kaua-huli-honua, "Strife-overturning-earth,"
seems to imply some kind of revolutionary movement as a
result of Haumea's match with Kanaloa. It is in Mangareva
alone that Haumea occupies the place of wife to Tagaroa
comparable to that given her here in the Hawaiian Kumu-

8. Fornander, *Polynesian Race*, I, 184; J. S. Emerson, *The Lesser Hawaiian Gods*, pp. 17-20.
9. Malo, p. 23.
10. Kepelino, Appendix, p. 182.

lipo. In Mangarevan myths of beginning Tagaroa holds the leading place among "primary gods without a known origin" belonging to "the long period of darkness." Some call him creator, "a god who made all the things in the world," but Dr. Buck, whose report on Mangarevan ethnology I am following, thinks this a late rationalization influenced from Tahiti.[11]

The Mangarevan myth gives to Haumea eight children by Tagaroa. Tu, the first-born, is god of breadfruit and "principal functioning god of Mangareva." She then leaves Tagaroa, and he takes to wife the daughter of the "fisherman" Tane. The girl hesitates to bear a child because it is the custom to cut open the mother at childbirth, but Tagaroa teaches her natural delivery. Haumea takes a husband named Pia and has eight more sons. Her story then turns upon the familiar theme of the cannibal wife. She becomes a maneater and attempts to kill Pia. Her sons flee with their father by boat, and when she follows they slay her and leave her body to be broken to pieces by the sea. Tagaroa desires her again and recovers her broken parts. Out of her body he forms "Atanua," who seems to be the same lady whom we have equated with Ke-aka-huli-honua, wife of Li'a-i-ku-honua of the Kumulipo. From the blood and afterbirth born of the union with the reincarnated goddess come the spawn of fish in March and the jellyfish of the sea. From members of her body he forms wives for other Tagaroa gods.

Several elements in this Mangarevan myth bear a striking likeness to the Kumulipo story. Not only is Haumea mated with Tagaroa, who is Kanaloa in Hawaii, and bears to him "Ku" as her eldest son, but she also leaves her husband to become mated with one who seems to be no god but a human being. In changed form she takes many husbands, in the Kumulipo by changing from age to youth, in Manga-

11. Buck, *Ethnology of Mangareva*, pp. 419-22, 508-9.

reva through the fertilizing power of the parts of her body; in both cases she becomes wife and mother to the family of the god. After the distribution of her fertile members, however, the likeness passes to the Wakea myth, where the parent of mankind, deserted by Papa, takes into his canoe the shape-shifting bailing gourd, and from the beautiful woman who emerges from it are born strange sea creatures. Certainly the composer of this portion of the Kumulipo chant and the Mangarevan mythmaker must have drawn from a common source.

There is no suggestion in the Mangarevan myth that the function of warrior was attached to Ku, god of breadfruit and child of Haumea, nor is Haumea concerned with a popular folk tale told in Hawaii of the god Ku's change into a breadfruit tree, although her own conversion into such a tree must not be forgotten. Ku-kauakahi as god of war has no place on other Hawaiian genealogies of beginning, nor is he named in either Malo's or Fornander's rather full description of ceremonies attending the consecration of a luakini or heiau erected to the war god Ku for the purpose of petitioning for success in war. His may have been a sacred name forbidden to common usage, hence replaced on the Hawaiian theocracy by the all-embracing Ku.

In popular romance, however, the name is kept alive in the person of the high taboo chief Kaua-kahi-ali'i ("Kaua-kahi-the-chief") who lives in a sacred pleasure garden of the gods on the island of Kauai high up near the source of the north fork of the Wailua River and lures to him by his pipe-playing a pretty chiefess from the seacoast. Complications follow, notably in some versions a fight with the girl's former suitor. The story has much in common with the Kumulipo theme of Wakea's affair with Hina-kawe'o-a, especially the euphemistic version told in a note to Malo of Kauakahi's wooing of a water maiden by means of an image of a girl behind which he hides, pretending it is she who invites companionship. After winning the water nymph's favor he disappears, and the girl is obliged to follow him to his home and pick out from a number of identical images (*ki'i*) the particular one in which he is hidden.[12]

Is Wakea an equivalent, then, not of Kanaloa but of Kauakahi, who introduces war through an alien alliance, or of Kaua-huli-honua, who overthrows an old divine hierarchy and sets up a new? The answer is that he is all three. I think the idea must be abandoned that these earlier genealogies represent a succession of generations rather than of events arranged under whatever symbolic titles belong by tradition to the family who are memorializing those events in the name of divinities believed concerned in their achievement. Names thus become interchangeable. Relationships disappear. Parents become telescoped into sons or brothers or into descendants, and each takes on any one of a number of honorific family titles appropriate to the place assigned in the succession. Especially in storytelling, deeds once related of a parent shift into the name song of son or grandson or are transferred to a popular figure belonging to a quite unrelated period. Historical accuracy just does not exist as we understand the term, and the painstaking toil of our own scholars in calculating dates far into the past from these oratorical recitations must certainly be abandoned as a case of virtue its own and only reward. It was enough that the family understood and applauded each allusion. Never may we outsiders rob them of their "sole treasure."

12. Malo, pp. 117–19; Beckwith, *Hawaiian Mythology*, pp. 538–42.

PART III

The Polynesian Chant of Creation

CHAPTER TWENTY-FIVE

Hawaiian Accounts of Creation

A FAMILY chant like the Kumulipo, passed down orally from one generation to the next without the stabilizing force of a written text, must have been constantly exposed to political changes within the family and to the urge felt by a new song-maker to revitalize the old memorial by giving it a fresh application to more recent family events. Although as a whole it preserves structural unity, the chant also gives evidence of a piecing-together of genealogies from different branches, together with the myths connected with them, and of changes in mere phrasing to give a different turn to the original design of a passage. Hawaiians themselves are cautious about accepting the Kalakaua text of the chant as the original form. Kupihea, as has been said, believes that Kalakaua took the opportunity to turn some of the enigmatic phrasing into a sneer at his detractors, as he most certainly intended glorification of his own dynasty by publication of the manuscript text. In Kalakaua's rendering some lines differ from this source, as other Kumulipo texts differ in minor details from the Kalakaua text. Poepoe puts it thus: "The writer [Poepoe himself] can not prove this to be the true form of the Kumulipo prayer chant as it was begun in ancient days. . . . It is also not clear to him that the form of the chant issued anew in Kamokuiki's book is the same as the original form . . . [but it contains] many difficult words . . . whose meaning can not be understood in these days. . . . It is [therefore] proper that this prayer chant of the Kumulipo be called 'The Genealogy of the Beginning of the People of Hawaii' (*Ku-*

auhau Ho'okumu Honua o Hawaii)." By the word *Honua*
I understand not the land itself but the people who inhabit
it, just as Hawaiian usage makes interchangeable the name
of a chief with the piece of land he occupies. The word
Ho'okumu, literally "causing to begin," may be better read
"founding" or "begining" than by the word "creation,"
which reflects biblical thought.

All evidence points to the general acceptance among Hawaiian scholars of Poepoe's cautious conclusion. From the
beginning of missionary interest in Hawaiian tradition, the
earliest informants have referred first to the authority of the
Kumulipo. Poepoe quotes the *Mo'olelo Hawaii* in these
words: "in this genealogy [the Kumulipo] it is said that the
earth was not born nor was it made by hand but just
grew."[1] David Malo writes, as translated by Emerson: "In
the genealogy called Kumulipo it is said that the first human
being was a woman named La'ila'i and that her ancestors
and parents were of the dim past [*he po wale no*], that she
was the progenitor of the human race." He goes on to tell
how "The-chief-who-broke-through-heaven" (Ke-ali'i-
wahi-lani) looked below and saw this beautiful woman
La'ila'i dwelling in Lalowaia and came down and made her
his wife, and "from the union of these two was begotten
one of the ancestors of this race." He imagines that these
persons originated outside Hawaii but that their names have
been preserved in Hawaiian genealogies.[2]

Kepelino, an early convert of the Roman Catholic mission and strongly influenced by the biblical story of creation, makes Kane the active agent in forming heaven and
earth. He writes: "In the Hawaiian account, darkness (*ka
po*) was the first thing and light (*malamalama*) followed.
And because Kane made the darkness he was called Kane-
in-the-Long-Night (*Po-loa*), because he alone dwelt at that

1. *Moolelo Hawaii,* p. 1.
2. Malo, pp. 23, 312.

time and he made it. . . . And he was called Kane-in-the-Light, meaning that he was the god that made light. And the light was called The-wide-light-made-by-Kane. . . . And so with the heaven (*ka lani*), it was called The-wide-heaven-made-by-Kane, because Kane made it."[3] Here, in spite of Christian coloring, the order of creation is like that suggested in the Prologue to the Kumulipo and similar phrases occur. There is first darkness, *po*, or deep darkness, *po-uli*, then light, *malamalama*. Later in the passage Kepelino tells how "muddy-earth" (*honua-kele*) is "drawn by Kane out of the ocean." Kane becomes "the chief who broke through heaven" of Malo's account, ancestor of the high taboo chiefs or *hoali'i* in distinction from the low-ranking, *na li'i noa*, who do not command the taboos of gods.

Other later Hawaiian accounts of beginnings include a memorandum of "The Board of Genealogists of the Chiefs of Hawaii" given before the legislature of 1884, which calls the Kumulipo chant "a setting in order of the beginning of the earth for this race of men," and the committee report of 1904 already quoted. Both are preserved in manuscript in the Bishop Museum, and the second is printed as an appendix to Kepelino.[4] It concludes, without mentioning the chant itself, "This is the genealogy of the Hawaiian people, that is, from Kumulipo-ka-po to Wakea and Papa."

Hawaiians generally represent *Po* as a period of darkness and give the word the meaning of night as opposed to day (*ao*). So my translator in a passage from Kepelino: "There was Deep-intense-night (*Po-nui-auwa'ea*), a period of time without heaven, without earth, without anything that is made. There was only darkness (*pouli*), therefore it was called Deep-intense-night and Long-night.

"The Deep-intense-night was the darkness out of which

3. Kepelino, pp. 14–16, 17.
4. Hoike Papa Kuauhau Ali'i, p. 15; Kepelino, pp. 180–82.

all created things (*na mea i hanaia*) issued (*i ho'opuka*). . . .
Only gods (*he mau akua wale*) lived at that time. . . ."[5] The
only attempt I have seen made to explain these two opposites, *Po* and *Ao*, on the basis of Hawaiian thought about the
relation between this material world and a corresponding
spirit world called the Po is to be found in Joseph Kukahi's
printed text of 1902. There he places the Kumulipo beside
other genealogies of beginning like that of Puanue, where
"the pillars of earth and the pillars of heaven" (*na kukulu o
ka honua a me na kukulu o ka lani*) are said to have been
"born" to Paia-ka-lani and his wife Kumu-kane-ke-ka'a; or
that of Wakea, where Papa gave birth to "this group of
islands"; or the statement of others that it "was really made
by the hands of Kane" (?), although "in the genealogy of
Kumulipo, it is said that the Po gave birth to all things and
established (*pa'a*) the heavens, the earth, and all things
therein."

Kukahi goes on to explain the *Po* as a time of nonhumans
when there were no "souls" (*'uhane*) of men living in the
flesh but only strange fairy-like beings called *'e'epa* and
many-bodied beings called *laumanamana*. He expounds the
meaning of the saying "the first people of Hawaii were
born of the *Po*" in connection with the structure of the
Kumulipo. He writes:

> Like the first seven divisions in the first period of the world in
> the genealogical account of the Kumulipo night followed night and
> there lived gods alone [?]. During those intervals night reproduced
> night by living as man and wife and producing many gods often
> spoken of by the people of Hawaii as "the forty thousand gods, four
> thousand gods, four hundred thousand gods," and in the eighth in-
> terval birth changed to that of human beings; that is, to La'ila'i and
> all those born with her. . . .
> Laying aside the teachings and beliefs of this people (Hawaiians)
> in this new time, let our thoughts go back to where the very begin-
> ning was thought to be of the growing up of the generations of

5. Kepelino, pp. 8, 9.

these islands, to the actual birth of the first person and those born
with her out of the enclosures biting hard so as to be felt of the Po
(*paia 'a'aki konouli o ka Po*).

The ancients believed that Po was divided into classes similar to
the divisions among men. There is a head and there are head gods
(*Po'o-akua*) who dwell in power over Po; below them are gov-
erners (*Kuhina*), the executioner (*Ilamuku*), messengers (*Alele*),
guards (*Kia'i*), down to the lower grades of gods who are commoners among the gods.

The head gods have great power (*mana*) in heaven and on earth.
The generations descended from them are their direct heirs from
the Po and they received power in Po. The *Kuhina* and *Ilamuku*
continue to carry out their power in Po. They have power (*mana*)
over great things and small in Po. Their descendants have like *mana*
to the *Kuhina* and *Ilamuku* [of the Po]. From the messengers and
guards down to the commoners among the gods come the innumerable hosts of night. They reproduced, separated, and spread
throughout Po. It was said that in this life in Po some people were
born without bones (*'alu'alu*) and from that time birth began to
change in Po until human bodies came into being. These changes
are shown in the genealogical history of the Kumulipo.

From the leading gods, the *Kuhina* and *Ilamuku*, descended the
classes of chiefs and the priests. They had great power over the
lives of people in ancient days and to them were given signs and
mysterious omens not forgotten by the people of this race. At the
time when the mother gives birth, those of the Po show the signs
of a chief. These are made visible in the arching of the rainbow,
the flash of lightning, the vibrating roll of thunder, the spread of a
low-lying rainbow, and in other signs common to this race. Men of
other races . . . have been puzzled . . . by these signs peculiar to
this people. There is no other explanation except the memory of
the old faith held by this race that the chiefs are offspring and descendants of the ruling gods of Po, those who have power over the
heavens and the earth.

In the night was Mary's son born from the womb of his human
mother in the place where animals were fed in the town of Bethlehem. The Magi were startled by a strange light. As they watched
closely they saw a bright star over the land to the east and believed
and knew that a great person from Po had come to dwell with man.

On the same night while the shepherds were absorbed in watch-
ing their lambs outside the town of Bethlehem, they were startled

by the shouts of thousands and thousands of armies of Po announc-
ing in a genealogical chant,

> "Glory to god
> In the highest heaven
> Peace on earth
> Good will to men."

This is an event handed down by the descendants of the inhabitants of the land of Canaan and they fully believed that this was a
seed conceived by the *'uhane* (Po) and born to a human being. The
people of these islands were accustomed to such things and firmly
believed that they were the people whom Po caused to be conceived and born here, that they were the *Iku ha'i* (*Ali'i* or *Mo'i*)
and the *Ikialealea* (*Ali'i papa* [class of chiefs], *pua li'i* [descendants
of chiefs]) of the *Nu'upule* (*Noho-ali'i*) referring to the lesser
chiefs.

It cannot be argued that ideas of an educated Hawaiian,
however steeped in old tradition, can today, after more
than a century of foreign contact, fully or even necessarily
correctly interpret priestly teaching in the days before foreign infiltration. Certainly Kukahi does little to clarify the
Kumulipo idea of night following night and, "by living as
man and wife," producing the little gods represented, I suppose, by the varieties of plant and animal species which
become their bodies in the material world, and later as be-
getting gods and men in bodily form. This is scarcely
straight personification but rather a doctrine of souls corresponding to and animating material bodies and grouped in
succession in time as a means of reaching a system of classi-
fication corresponding to the Hawaiian approach to the
universe and to society as a whole. He draws a literal picture of the spirit world much as our ancestors took heaven
and hell on their face value, but I think his idea of it as a
duplicate of this world we live in is a genuine native concept, and certainly the chiefs' authority and grading were
upheld by this doctrine alone of birth from the gods, than
which no Mohammedan or Christian teaching of predesti-

nation could lay better claim to an invulnerable basis. For his belief, he points to the connection of the spirit world with outward signs in the heavens at the time of a chief's birth and refers to the star over Bethlehem so dear to Christian story, and to the conception of the son of God in the womb of Mary. However primitive may seem to us the premise, granted this, the conclusions drawn are not those of a people lacking in quickness of mind or in mental intelligence.

CHAPTER TWENTY-SIX

Other Polynesian Accounts of Creation

THE last chapter has made it clear that Hawaiians informed in the old culture believed the Kumulipo chant
to be certainly at base a genuine native prayer of beginnings
handed down from ancient times. Is such a chant unique to
Hawaiian culture, or do a similar cosmic philosophy and
similar traditions of beginning prove for it a common Polynesian heritage? Since there is general agreement that there
was intercommunication with Tahiti during the migration
period, we may look first to Tahitian chants for such likenesses. Tahitian texts recorded by John Orsmond before
1848 and edited by his daughter Teuira Henry for the Bishop Museum publications do contain quite similar concepts
based upon a like nature philosophy in their treatment of
cosmic forces. From a creation story given to Orsmond in
1822 and repeated later by another reciter with but slight
variation I quote from Miss Henry's translation:

Ta'aroa was the ancestor of all the gods; he made everything. . . .
He was his own parent, having no father or mother. . . .
Ta'aroa sat in his shell (*pa'a*) in darkness (*te po*) for millions of
ages. . . .
The shell was like an egg revolving in endless space, with no sky,
no land, no sea, no moon, no sun, no stars.
All was darkness, it was continuous thick darkness (*po tinitini ia
e te ta'ota'o*). . . .
But at last Ta'aroa gave his shell a filip which caused a crack re-
sembling an opening for ants. Then he slipped out and stood upon
his shell . . . he took his new shell for the great foundation of the
world, for stratum rock and for soil for the world. And the shell
. . . that he opened first, became his house, the dome of the god's

sky, which was a confined sky, enclosing the world (*ao*) then forming. . . .

Ta'aroa made the great foundation of the earth (*te tumu nui o te fenua*) to be the husband, and the stratum rock (*te papa fenua*) to be the wife . . . and he put his spirit into it, which was the essence of himself, and named it Ta'aroa-nui-tumu-tahi, Great-Ta'aroa-the-first-beginning.

Ta'aroa dwelt on for ages within the close sky . . . he conjured forth (*rahu*) gods (*atua*), and they were born to him in darkness (*i fanau i te po*). . . .

. . . It was much later that man (*ta'ata*) was conjured [forth] when Tu was with him.[1]

Another chant given to Orsmond in 1822 in Borabora and again in Tahiti describes a "chaotic period" after a condition of nothingness in which all was originally confined in a state of balance between such opposites as darkness (*po*) and light (*ao*), rapid and slow movement (*huru maumau, huru mahaha*), thinness (*tahi rairai*) and thickness (*tahi a'ana*). Pairs of rocks having "affinity between them" (*e tau'a ta raua*) are the first elements of growth. Tu ("Stability") is conjured forth as artisan. "Roots (*a'a*) were born for growth in the world." Ta'aroa fixes the dome of the earth upon pillars (*pou*) brought forth by Tumu-nui as male, Papa-raharaha as female parent. This allows widening of the sky "upon the pillars of the land of Havai'i." The *po* is extended, mountains grow, water rushes forth, ocean grows, rocks increase, skies increase to ten in number, rain falls, moss and slime appear, forests, food, the paper mulberry plant, creeping plants, weeds, all living things. Atea is above in space—"Earth had become land and it was filled with living creatures. Fresh water flowed throughout the land, sea filled the ocean, and they [land and ocean] were filled with living creatures. But still all was in thick darkness (*poiri ta'ota'o*). . . ." All this is still taking place within

1. Henry, pp. 336–38, see also Emory, *Journal of the Polynesian Society*, XLVII, 52–63.

the original shell (*'apu*) out of which Great Ta'aroa had
formed the sky of the gods, the shell called *Rumia*, translated "upset" in the text.[2]

Compare these Tahitian chants with the Kumulipo. The
idea of a first cause in the person of an anthropomorphic
deity presiding over creation is absent from the Hawaiian
story. In the Tahitian the concept is quite fully developed.
Ta'aroa (Kanaloa in Hawaii) "gives a filip and cracks the
shell" in which he is confined. He crawls out and stands
upon its outer edge. He grows to be a lad, still within the
"shell" out of which he has formed a sky for the new land.
Ta'aroa feels weariness and delight. At one time he is a con-
juror molding earth in his hands or uttering an incantation
to stabilize the forms he has molded, at another time a god
sending his essence into the rock Tumu-nui that it may
unite with Papa-raharaha and upset the condition of equi-
librium that has prevented growth and change. Everything
is Ta'aroa's. He has created everything. All this is foreign to
the Kumulipo. But the Tahitian chants stress, like the Hawaiian Kumulipo, the idea of affinity (*tau'a*) between pairs
of natural forms. They stress the period of darkness during
which the shaping of earth and sea took place and their filling with living forms before man appeared.

In Maori myth one cosmogonic account takes the form
of a family group like that in the Hawaiian "Chief-who-
opened-heaven" to come down to earth and make the beautiful La'ila'i his wife. Here it is the Wide-sky itself, Rangi-
nui, who takes Papa-tu-a-nuku to wife, "sets" (*hikaia*) vegetation to cover her and "places" (*makaia*) small creatures
"to animate the earth and the waters thereof." Gods are
created, seventy of whom are named. All are confined
within the embrace of their parents, unable to move or
stand upright. A glimmer of light shows and gradually they
come forth into the outer world. Eventually they separate

2. Henry, pp. 340–44.

their parents to enlarge space for living, and raise the sky upward, a story fully elaborated also in Tahiti but hardly recognized in the Kumulipo. The New Zealand teaching goes on to organize the world, giving to each god his special function and classifying forms according to their order of creation as in Tahiti; first ocean out of which grew land, then small plants, trees, reptiles and insects, animals, birds, the heavenly bodies; finally woman, "from whom mankind in this world sprang," an arrangement scarcely differing from that of the Kumulipo except for its neglect of sea life, so important in the structural plan of the Hawaiian creation chant.[3]

In Mangaia, myths collected by the missionary W. Wyatt Gill describe under a different symbol the change from life within the Po to that of the world of the Ao, the world of living men on this earth. One myth tells how the primal generator, the female spirit Vari-ma-te-takere, dwells in darkness at the base of the dark underworld of Avaiki, "the Mangaian equivalent of Po." Avaiki is conceived like the inside of a coconut shell. It is divided into spaces or lands to each of which one of Vari's children is assigned. Buck thinks such a structural conception is foreign to the Polynesian mind and was probably suggested by the questioner, but such imaginary divisions are applied by Hawaiians to the arch of the sky as it rises from the horizon, and to the spaces of air as one looks toward the zenith—certainly not a foreign interpolation.[4] Uppermost, in the thin land next to the outer shell, dwells Vatea, the Wakea or 'Atea or Rangi of other groups. He climbs into the light and lures "Papa" to him. Gods are born of the two, and eventually Mangaia is pulled up from the depths and peopled by men,

3. Smith, *The Lore of the Whare-wananga,* pp. 117–22, 136–37; Grey, pp. 1–3; White, Vol. I, chaps. ii, ix–xi; Henry, pp. 409–13.
4. Malo, pp. 30–31.

offspring of the primal gods. Stories of chiefs succeed those of primal gods.[5]

Here again the poet shapes his story of beginnings upon similar basic conceptions. In a line from a song dated about 1790 the primal goddess Vari-ma-te-takere is addressed as "a goddess feeding on raw taro" (*E tuarangi kai taro mata*), a reference recalling the children of Haloa born on the Hawaiian genealogy to Wakea and Papa. The word *wari* (*wali*) occurs in various Polynesian groups and always with reference to a softened substance: "mud" or "muddy" in Tahiti and Rarotonga; "pulp" or "pap" in Mangareva; "a marsh" in the Tuamotus; "potato grown watery with age" in New Zealand. It is equivalent to the *walewale* out of which life springs in the first lines of the Kumulipo. The epithet *ma-te-takere* is translated "at-the-beginning." *Takere* is applied ordinarily in Polynesia to the keel of a canoe, in Maori to "the bottom of deep water." Perhaps just "at the bottom" would be a fair rendering as applied to Vari. The taro plant propagated by budding, sending up stalk and leaf into the light out of the mud of its underwater or underground rooting, may well be the symbolic form in which the poet of Mangaia, where taro culture is, as in Hawaii, the basic vegetable food, conceives the story of the parent-stock of mankind.

From the Takaroa atoll of the Tuamotus Dr. Kenneth Emory of the Bishop Museum collected a cosmic chant in which "the earth's origins" or "roots," as Gessler reads *te tumu henua*, are similarly compared to the growth of a plant. Emory translates as follows:

> Life appears in the world,
> Life springs up in Havaiki.
> The Source-of-night sleeps below
>   in the void of the world,
>   in the taking form of the world,

5. Gill, chap. i.

in the growth of the world,
the life of the world,
the leafing of the world,
the unfolding of the world,
the darkening of the world,
the branching of the world,
the bending down of the world.[6]

Hawaiians use a similar incantation in approaching certain forms of plant life imagined to have originated in the underworld of the Po or 'Avaiki, referred to here as "Kahiki," whose spirits are supposed to show themselves on earth in the body of the plant. A species of kava plant called *'ava nene* is prescribed to quiet a fretting (*nene*) child, and Kawena Pukui gives the following invocation to be used in its plucking:

O great kava that sprouted in Kahiki
    grew taproot in Kahiki
    spread rootlets in Kahiki
    grew stalk in Kahiki
    branched in Kahiki
    leafed in Kahiki
    blossomed in Kahiki
    bore leafbuds in Kahiki
I have come to get your leafbuds
    for medicine for ——
    for long life for ——

In a "family story" from the same informant a similar chant is addressed to an ancestral coconut called upon to provide a bridge for passing over seas. Here the lines conclude with the maturing of the plant which has

fruited in Kahiki,
ripened in Kahiki,

and the coconut sprouts above ground, puts forth leaves and fruit and shoots upward as in all good fairy stories. The coconut tree is, of course, to be understood here as a phallic

6. *Journal of the Polynesian Society*, XLVII, 50.

symbol of generation from a single stock which allows the
young adventurer to approach his kin over seas.[7]

The process of creation as Emory finds it described in the
Tuamotus reads much like the Hawaiian.[8] Development
proceeds by "pairing of matter, phenomena of nature, or of
abstractions such as 'source of Night' ...," and Emory calls
this "a wide-spread and ancient Tuamotuan teaching ...
confirmed by cosmogonic genealogies and chants which
have survived" and not the result of "missionary teaching."
In schematic charts illustrating the progress of development
of the world in its making, a primal pair represented by
male and female phallic symbols lies at the base of the egg-
shaped shell out of which, as in Mangaia and Tahiti, life is
thought of as emerging. These are named on the chart Te
Tumu and Te Papa. They are the source of generation.
Above them lies the land of Tumu-po:

> Tumu-Po, source of the night world
>   sleeps below in the non-existence of the earth,
>   the slime of the earth
>   the limpidity of the earth, etc. . . . .
> Source whence human beings spring,
> Source whence 'Atea sprang.

The shell representing the night world, the Po, is divided
in the chart into layers filled with easily recognizable outlines of plants, animals, and men, these last in prostrate position. Above each layer arches a sky; to the summit of the
highest sky reaches a ladder of men, one on the shoulder of
another. The men seem to be climbing out of the underworld of the Po into a succession of outer worlds, taking
with them the plants and animals of the night world as they
go. The drawing looks like an adaptation to a migration
legend rather than to one of development culminating in
the intellectual faculties of adulthood such as some see in

7. Green and Pukui, *Legend of Kawelo*, p. 180.
8. *Journal of the Polynesian Society*, XLVIII, 1–29.

the Kumulipo. As in the Kumulipo, there is no single presiding deity. Birth proceeds by the pairing of earth, the female, with sky, the male. Above the first land, Tumu-Po, arches Tumu-Ao; above the last land, Fakahotu-henua, arches the sky 'Atea. The two are translated by Emory, "Fruitfulness-of-earth" and "Space." They are the parents of mankind:

> 'Atea produces above,
> Fakahotu produces below.

There is much in common here with other creation stories, both Tahitian and Hawaiian. In Tahiti Ta'aroa made "the great foundation of the earth" (*te tumu nui o te fenua*) to be the husband and "the stratum rock" (*te papa fenua*) to be the wife. Although the generation of rocks does not enter into the Kumulipo story as we have it, rocks of phallic shape are worshiped in Hawaii as ancestral fertility gods. Tumu-po as source of the night world is no other than Kumu-([u]li-)po of the Hawaiian prayer chant. "This is the genealogy of the Hawaiian people, from Kumu-lipo-ka-po to Wakea and Papa," concludes the report of the Committee of 1904. Both areas represent a succession of generative pairs, in the Tuamotus of "lands" and "skies," in Hawaii of "nights" (*Po*) advancing toward day (*Ao*), with some identical names between the two. Both lead up to 'Atea (Wakea), parent of mankind and apex of the arching spaces of sky.

Emory sees a tendency to multiplication of these divisions in the Tuamotus, and this may well have happened also in Hawaii. Original drawings show but three instead of ten, and an early Tuamotuan text reads:

The universe was [first] like an egg. . . . It at last burst and produced three layers superimposed one below propping two above.

This threefold pattern is perhaps reflected in the trio of males regularly named on Hawaiian genealogies of begin-

ning and active in creation stories relating to the ordering of
the universe and the origin of mankind. The appearance of
this pattern in Hawaii is generally laid to missionary influence. Although the Christian trinitarian doctrine may have
strengthened its use, I see no reason for supposing it to have
originated under missionary teaching.

The gods Kane and Kanaloa are rather regularly named
in this trio with a third figure representing man. Ki'i as this
third member occurs but once, and that quite naturally at
the moment of dawning from the night world, the Po, into
the light of day, the Ao. Similarly a Tahitian chant called
"Creation of Man" given to Orsmond by three different reciters between 1822 and 1833 shows Ta'aroa, after land, sky,
and ocean have been filled with living things, consulting
"Tu, the sacred one, Tu, the great artisan of Ta'aroa," about
filling "the room for man." He "conjures up from below"
(*rahu ra i raro*) the man Ti'i. Ti'i takes to wife the "Woman
who ate before and behind," and between the two the different classes emerge: "the high chiefs of the royal girdle"
(*ari'i nui maro 'ura*) begotten of the first pair; the lesser
nobility (*hu'i ra'atira* and *ari'iri'i*) from the union of these
with their inferiors; the commoners (*te ta'ata ri'i* and *te
manahune*) who are not "born" (*fanau*) but "conjured
forth" (*i rahua*) by Ti'i and his wife.[9]

Ti'i, Tiki, or Ki'i, traditional first man throughout eastern
Polynesia, thus personifies the procreative power of mankind or specifically the male sex organ. In New Zealand
the progenitor of man is Tane (Kane) son of the sky god,
hence called Tane-nui-a-Rangi. To him is attached the story,
absent in Tahiti but present in fringing groups of the eastern
Pacific, of the father-daughter marriage ascribed to Tiki in

9. Henry, pp. 402-3.

Mangareva and the Tuamotus, in Hawaii to Wakea.[10] Allowing a shift from Tu to Kane in Hawaii, both gods of artisans in Tahiti, the Tahitian story of man's origin corresponds in time, place, and function with the first Kumulipo trilogy. Three males join in the task of peopling earth with mankind, Ta'aroa, Tu, Ti'i in Tahiti and an equivalent trio of Kane, Kanaloa, and Ki'i in Hawaii. The "Woman who ate before and behind" in Tahiti becomes La'ila'i, the "Woman who sat sideways" of the Kumulipo.

Another common element with South Sea mythical conceptions in the Kumulipo trio is the octopus form taken by Kanaloa in this chant of the first dawn of day. Exactly in agreement is the Tahitian myth of the cutting away of the arms of the octopus Tumu-ra'i-fenua, "Beginning-of-Heaven-and-Earth," into which Ta'aroa has placed his essence, and the consequent dawn of light (ao) after "the long wearisome night" (po).[11] Hitherto gods have been called into being in darkness; now light dawns over earth. In the Kumulipo, spirits of darkness have generated animal and plant life of land and sea; now, generations of mankind people the land. In the Kumulipo manuscript the first line of the refrain accompanying the births of the first four sections reads, not Ka po uhe'e i ka wawa with its suggestion of the "slipping away" (uhe'e) of night, but Ka pou he'e i ka wawa, thus picturing the god in the form of an octopus (he'e) supporting (pou) in darkness the first heaven and earth exactly as in the Tahitian chant. This is not darkness in the physical sense but applies to the supremacy of the spirit world, the Po, as compared with the world of living men, the Ao.

The eight-armed octopus, called in the Kumulipo the

10. Smith, *The Lore of the Whare-wananga*, pp. 138–43, 144–45; Buck, *Ethnology of Mangareva*, pp. 307–10; White, I, 130–64; J. Frank Stimson, "Legend of Tiki." MS in Bishop Museum, Beckwith, *Hawaiian Mythology*, pp. 294, 296–98.

11. Henry, pp. 338, 356, 390, 404–12.

"hot-striking" (*hauna-wela*), is the manifestation or body
in which Kanaloa may appear in some Polynesian groups
as god of the sea and sea creatures in contrast to Kane, god
of land forms. In Hawaii, a prayer at the launching of a
canoe names both gods, Kane as god of the forest from
which the tree was cut, Kanaloa as god of the element over
which the canoe must travel. A sorcerer's prayer for the
healing of the sick invokes Kanaloa "god of the octopus"—
ke akua o ka he'e.[12] The Samoan demigod Tae-o-Tagaloa is
born of a woman part human and part *fe'e* ("octopus"),
hence he is part god and part human.[13] Magic connected
with the number eight throughout southern Polynesia may
derive from the eight-armed octopus. The Maui figure,
sometimes represented as a son of the Tagaroa family, is
"eight-headed" in Tahiti, "eighth born" in Samoa.[14] In the
Marquesas, according to Handy, "an octopus, or if one
could not be obtained, a taro root with eight rootlets was
used ceremonially in certain rites."

A further factor entering into the position of Kanaloa in
Hawaiian accounts of creation, but not apparent in the
Kumulipo, shows strife to have arisen at some time either
before or after the migration into the Hawaiian group between followers of the Kanaloa priesthood and that of
Kane, with Kane eventually triumphant, Kanaloa repudiated, and god Ku set up in his stead as agent with Kane
in the creation story. Fornander notes:

"In the mo'olelo of Moi the prophet . . . of Molokai; in the
prophecies and sayings of Nuakea, the prophetess . . . ; of Maihea
and Naulu-a-Maihea, the prophet race of Oahu . . . ; of the prophet
Hua of Maui—in all these prophesies—it is said that the gods (*na
akua*) created heaven and earth. The gods who created heaven and
earth were three, Kane, Ku, and Lono. Kanaloa was a great enemy
of these three gods. Before this creation of heaven and earth, etc.,

12. Malo, pp. 171–73, 149–50.
13. Kramer, I, 45, 392–93, 409.
14. Beckwith, *Hawaiian Mythology*, pp. 209–10; Krämer, I, 393, note.

everything was shaky, trembling and destitute, bare (*naka*, '*olohe-lohe*); nothing could be distinguished, everything was tossing about, and the spirits of the gods were fixed to no bodies, only the three above gods had power to create heaven and earth. Of these three Kane was the greatest in power, and Ku and Lono were inferior to him. The powers of the three joined together were sufficient to create and fix heaven and earth [from *Ke Au Okoa*, October 14, 1869].[15]

Since neither Ku nor Lono is named in the Kumulipo chant, it looks as if the displacement of Kanaloa in national worship took place after its composition. Certainly by the time of the American mission in 1820 the idea prevailed that Kanaloa was rebellious against Kane and worked against him. The missionaries compared Kanaloa with the biblical Satan. Best says, quoting Fornander, "Kanaloa is in Hawaii . . . a personified spirit of evil, the origin of death, the prince of Po . . . a revolted, disobedient spirit who was conquered and punished by Kane (Tane). . . ."

A similar character is given to Tangaroa in the Tuamotus. There a Tangaroa god "who delighted in doing evil" set fire in the highest heaven "seeking thus to destroy everything." "Tangaroa-i-te-po" he is called and "supreme ruler of the underworld."[16] In New Zealand a quarrel is said to have arisen between Tane and Tangaroa when reptiles took to the land and Tangaroa resented this encroachment upon his preserves.[17] In the Tahitian octopus myth it is Tane who cuts away the clinging arms of the octopus body of Ta'aroa and fills earth and sky with beauty. Again, in a composition called "Strife and reconciliation between heaven and earth," Tumu-nui, the rock foundation in which Ta'aroa has placed his essence, is pitted against Tane, the two plying their enchantments: Tumu-nui sending heavy mists and rain, fam-

15. From Kamakau in Fornander, *Collection* ("Memoirs," No. 6), pp. 322–23.
16. Emory, *Journal of the Polynesian Society*, XLVIII, 12, 13.
17. Grey, pp. 4–5.

ine, night; Tane matching him with clear weather, abundance, the sun by day.[18]

In Hawaii, a contest over the right of the kava drink seems to be connected with Kanaloa's overthrow. In the prayer quoted above he is distinguished as "Kanaloa the kava drinker" (*inu 'awa*). It is as if an upstart priesthood had overthrown the exclusive prerogative of a ruling priesthood to the kava bowl.[19] The situation may reflect a historic conflict. A Fornander note equates Lihau'ula, "a priest of greater renown than any other," with Kanaloa. Tradition tells also of war between Lihau'ula the elder and Wakea the younger son, after the death of their father has left Wakea landless, and of the eventual success of the younger.[20]

But may not the idea of opposition between the gods depend upon a more basic symbolism in the universal facts of human birth? The embryo lying surrounded by the sac of fluid within the mother's womb belongs to the spirit world, to Kanaloa; with birth it emerges into the world of living men and becomes the child of Kane. Again, Kanaloa, god of darkness and the underworld, takes over man at death. The father-daughter marriage is in some groups said to usher in man's mortality. In New Zealand it is Tane son of Rangi by Papa-tu-a-nuku, originally Tangaroa's wife, who takes his own daughter to wife, and it is she who, learning of her relationship to him, escapes to the lower world "to drag our offspring down." "And now," says one version of the tale, "from this time onward the flow of the 'current of death' of mankind to the 'everlasting night' became permanent."[21] In Mangaia Tangaroa is the first-born son of 'Atea and Papa, but Rongo (Lono) not only secures for himself the main food supply but also takes Tangaroa's

18. Henry, pp. 353–54.
19. Fornander, *Collection* ("Memoirs," No. 6), p. 268.
20. *Ibid.*, p. 272, Malo, pp. 312–13.
21. White, I, 131–32, 144–46, Smith, *The Lore of the Whare-wananga*, pp. 144–45.

wife Taka and has by her a daughter Tavake by whom he has children, and "with the birth of Tavake's children the lineage of the main stock of Mangaia became definitely human."[22] In Hawaii a story tells how the two gods each make a figure of a man and Kanaloa's dies while Kane's lives. Perhaps because Kanaloa made his figure first, all men must eventually die. That is the way the mind works under a deterministic priesthood: "In Adam's fall, We sinned all." It may be that death became inevitable when the first child born to Wakea by his daughter came into the world a foetus. The gods are immortal, renewing their youth as a crab its skin. Once man had this power, say old Hawaiians, and a number of stories are told throughout the Pacific of some trivial failure of the culture-bringer that determined death for mankind.[23] If the connection with man's ultimate fate suggested above for the drawing contest between Kanaloa and Kane is correct, is it possible that late reciters of the Kumulipo chant have obscured the part played by Kanaloa in the story of Ki'i and La'ila'i, and "Ki'i the man" was originally Kanaloa's figure drawn after the form of god Kane, into which Kanaloa has "placed his essence" to deceive the woman, just as Wakea in the later story enters the image (ki'i) set up to lure Ka-we'o-a? It may be that the quarrel over the precedence of the first-born to Ki'i rather than to Kane had originally for the priestly composer an eschatological rather than a political implication.

Changes and substitutions in cult practice must lie back of these variations upon the common theme of world beginnings. Adaptation of traditional elements depends in each case upon the special migration history of the group, its fresh contacts and their resulting influence upon family and cult history. We cannot tell whether a historical strug-

22. Buck, *Mangaian Society*, pp. 17–18.
23. Kepelino, p. 48, Beckwith, *Journal of the Polynesian Society*, LV, 191–92.

gle between leaders of different factions with their rival
deities has given rise to the symbolism of conflict in creation stories or whether the cosmic conflict was itself a
symbol of the universal facts of birth and death. Certainly
fancy personifies and plays with such cosmic elements. The
hero's search after the sun hidden by a god in the underworld or to recover a bright lady from an underseas ravisher, and his famous fishing after a robber sea god, are all
variations upon the theme of daybreak translated into popular fiction. On the other hand, the cosmic story is itself
a symbol of the coming into life, out of the sea of water
within the mother's womb, of the child born, as we say, "to
the purple," or as the Hawaiian puts it, "hot with fiercest
taboo," the child who must, however, eventually die because of some misdoing of the primary deity from whom
man sprang.

CHAPTER TWENTY-SEVEN

Ceremonial Birth Chants in Polynesia

IN THE preceding chapters evidence has been brought to show that the Kumulipo chant was accepted as a genuine tradition of beginning for the Hawaiian people and that corresponding traditions from southern groups prove its composers to have drawn from common Polynesian sources. It is possible to go farther and to show that the recitation of similar genealogical prayer chants carrying the family stock back to the gods and connecting it with the beginning of life on earth played a part in other Polynesian groups in ceremonies held at the birth of a chief's son.

Word of such ceremonial functions has as yet come from but two sources, from the Marquesas, reported by Handy, and from the Tuamotus, by Percy Smith.[1] In the Marquesas there are held, says Handy, "Great chanting festivals . . . intoned with accompanying rites . . . celebrated for various purposes by family groups, or, in the case of chiefs' families, by the tribe." One such occasion is at "the arrival of a first-born heir." The "central feature" is the chanting of the creation chants, *vavana* and *pu'e*. Recitation of genealogies is also a feature of the occasion, participated in by representatives of the different branches of the family line. A single chanter opened the recitation. "When he came to a certain point in his chant he would stop and a representative of some branch of the family would continue with the reci-

---

1. Handy, *Marquesan Native Culture*, pp. 314–30, Smith, *Journal of the Polynesian Society*, XII, 221–42.

tation of the genealogy of his branch." This went on until all branches had been represented.

The creation story recounting the impregnation of One-u'i (the sand woman) by 'Atea (Wakea) is the subject of the *pu'e* chants. It is said to be taboo to teach these to women and women are excluded from the audience when these are recited. The *vavana* have to do with the development of the child and their recitation is open to all. To quote Handy's summary of their content:

> The words [of the *vavana*] recapitulate the conception, birth, growth, and so on of the child, linking these with the mythical birth of the gods from the level above (*papa una*) and the level below (*papa a'o*). In subsequent sections the chants refer to the making of ornaments, weapons, and utensils for the child, to his canoe, to his sacred house and to various practices such as bathing, making cloth, etc., connected with it . . . connecting all with mythological references to gods and ancient lands. In parts various gods are summoned to assist in the rite. The chant is very long, containing more than ten thousand words. There is much repetition of phrases—some of them meaningless. . . . Throughout there is mingling of narrative referring to incidents connected with the child, mythological references, and these meaningless phrases.

There is no reason to suppose that Hawaiian chants of beginning would follow the exact pattern in content and meaning laid down by the Marquesan. In fact these chants differed among Marquesans themselves: "Every tribe had its own rendition of these sacred chants," says Handy. Nevertheless the description of style fits the Hawaiian to the letter and that of the content supplies a strong argument for Pokini Robinson's view of the Kumulipo as based upon the progress of a child from birth to maturity. That part of the chant, too, which "recounts the basic stages of growth of the world" by naming the various plants as "births" by One-u'i after impregnation by 'Atea in order to provide materials needed for the child's activities after birth may give a clue to the meaning of the sea and land births listed in the Hawaiian Kumulipo. In the Marquesan chant the "mothers of various kinds of material" are invoked to furnish these for the construction of the house of the first parents, 'Atea and One-u'i. The introduction here of "various kinds of fish in the sea" as "wives of 'Atea," which puzzles Handy, must have a similar significance. Thus the gods favorable to mankind are shown preparing upon earth and in the sea provision for the livelihood of that child who is to be their direct offspring, descent from whom down the generations is claimed for the first-born of each family of the tribe through the recitation of *vavana* and *pu'e*.

Some twenty years earlier than Handy's report on the Marquesan ceremony, S. Percy Smith had published in the *Journal of the Polynesian Society* the text and translation of two Tuamotuan chants "sung at the birth of a high chief." These have, so far as I know, attracted no attention from scholars in this area. The translation is the work of "a Tahitian gentleman," with some corrections by Smith himself in line with Maori usage, who discovered in the text "many identical phrases to be found in Maori *karakias*." These identities he unfortunately does not quote. To Maori influence also he ascribes the prominence of the god Tane and the little importance attached to Tangaroa in the chants. Of their general contents he writes: "In the usual cryptic manner of these compositions, they go back to the beginning of all things, and then trace the origin of the new born to the gods and thence through ancestors to the migration."

In form and spirit as well as in content the chants resemble those of the Kumulipo. There is a like emphasis upon opposites, upon mythological allusions, upon refrain. In the first chant the word *tumu* serves as keynote as the chanter welcomes the generating pair Tane and Hine, "source" or "cause" or "origin" of all things; hails the rainbow, sign of the birth of a chief, and wishes long life to the child under the name of Rongo, a name identical with the invocations to "Rono" at the ceremony for Captain Cook's deification in Hawaii as the god Lono and highly suggestive in view of the dedication of the Kumulipo to "Lono of the Makahiki." In the second stanza "thought" (*manava*) expands in various directions, all propitious to the new-born "Rongo." Word is brought and the drum beaten for the chief Rongo. Next a search is declared for the "cause," the "origin," and the child is found to be born from the "stem," from the "seed" spread by 'Atea, Fakahotu, and Rongo, the repeated word *tumu* in the text being given a variety of meanings in the English translation. A couplet follows voicing an aphorism consistent with Kukahi's distinction between the separate worlds for gods and men:

> The way [*te ara*] for the god [*no te atua*] is below [*ki te po*];
> The way for man [*te tangata*] is above [*ki te ao*].

There follows a series of three-line stanzas, each concluding with a refrain proclaiming the "growth" (*tupuranga*) of lesser gods (*Vaitu*) and of men.

The next stanzaic-like verses are recited in turn by representatives from the assembled company, as explained by the translator: ". . . when the subjects of a king went to congratulate him on the birth of a child or other important event, they assembled at the court or *mahora*, and before commencing their speeches, the one about to commence stamped with his foot to indicate that he asked permission to speak. As soon as he had caught the king's eye, he knelt, and with the preamble '*maeva te ariki*' commenced his speech of homage. Having concluded, he arose and gave place to the next."

The second chant opens with a comparison of the family stock, not to a "pathway" but to "a small tree shooting out its roots and becoming widespread like the Kofai." The reference is to a tree bearing red and yellow flowers, colors sacred to chiefs throughout Polynesia and hence an appropriate symbol for the royal lineage. A kind of migration story follows with an enumeration of well-known lands of the Pacific. Succeeding stanzas having to do with the birth of gods are too obscurely phrased for me to attempt analysis. To the god Tane is ascribed power to cause the growth of vegetation. The earth is "broken up," mankind "came forth," and the rainbow is hailed.

In this part of the chant "speakers" from every quarter bring their "orations," which consist in a listing of place names. The word *vananga* so translated is identical with the Marquesan *vanana*, and this identity marks a close connection between the function of such ceremonial chants in the two areas. Possibly the Hawaiian word *hanauna* for "a circle of relatives of one family" is its Hawaiian equivalent. At least it seems to me that Smith's translation of the word *vananga* in this connection by "oration" does not give the full implication. The whole development of the Kumulipo is based upon the idea of blood descent from a single stock established from the beginning of the race and derived from primary gods. It is fair to conclude from Handy's excellent but all too limited report upon Marquesan ceremonies for a first-born that interest centers here also, not upon any speculative philosophy about how the world came to be so ordered, but upon the immediate effect of the chant upon the child to whom the family must look for its perpetuation on earth. As Handy puts it, "The chants really amount to elaborate causative spells."

Just how far the idea of magic versus religious worship is involved in any ceremonial act is an individual question, not one possible of verifying as a general conclusion. My own observation of the attitude of Hawaiians toward even their minor deities, derived, however, entirely during post-Christian times, leads me to believe that the majority endowed their gods with the passions of men just as they gave their chiefs the honors of gods during life, and after death set them up as gods. Certainly they looked upon these dwellers in the spirit world as capable of manifesting themselves not only in material forms and forces of nature but also in the bodies of human beings living on earth among men. Chants and stories of the gods are so handled. The whole material world is thus the product of deity made manifest. The newborn child of high chief rank is himself quite literally born a god. The recitation of the genealogical prayer chant not only honors the long line of ancestral gods with whom he claims kinship but reminds them of their responsibility to this new offspring in the family descent, hence claiming for him as for a child of beloved parents those benefits of fertility in plant and animal life and of success along the pathway of human life necessary for his well being and within the power of gods alone to provide.

Conclusion

THE Kumulipo chant in its present form is evidently a composite, recast from time to time as intermarriage brought in new branches and a fresh traditional heritage. It seems to have belonged in Keawe's time to the Lono priesthood, perhaps brought from Oahu, where Lono worship was particularly active, to Maui, the genealogy of whose ruling chiefs down to Pi'ilani occupies the last section; thence brought into the island of Hawaii through the marriage of Pi'ilani's daughter Pi'ikea with 'Umi, usurping chief over that island after Liloa, with which marriage and its offspring the reckoning ends.

We have no proof that, as in the Marquesas and the Tuamotus, the birth of a son and heir to the ruling chief was celebrated in Hawaii by the recitation of the story of creation together with genealogies and songs of honor belonging to different branches along the family line, and that the Kumulipo chant served this function within the family to whom it belonged. Hawaiian accounts of ceremonies at the birth of a royal child do not mention the chanting of a Kumulipo at a great tribal gathering as part of the rites on such an occasion, nor does the prose note offer evidence of such a recitation. But from its likeness to chants so used in the Tuamotus and the Marquesas and the queen's association of its composition with the birth of Keawe's firstborn son, we may perhaps infer some connection with the ceremony.

Every birth of a *niaupi'o* child was in fact regarded as a repetition of the first human birth, that of the son Ha-loa to Wakea through his own daughter, from whom the whole race counted descent. So the Hawaiian *Naua Society* writes,

181

after telling the story of the "Lauloa taro" that grew from the buried foetus of Wakea's first child, after which the living child was named: "Now you must understand that the children born to Haloa these are yourselves. . . ." Every first-born of a ruling chief took, to quote Fornander, the name Wakea: *O Wakea ka inoa, o ke kumu ali'i keia o Waloa*, reads the text.[1] The word *Wa-loa* I take to be a contraction of *Wa'a-loa*, "Long-canoe," and the whole phrase, left untranslated in Fornander, to mean that he is "a male of the chief stock." The canoe is, like the plant-stalk, a symbol in riddling speech of the male procreative organ. The epithet "long" in both cases emphasizes by means of a concrete symbol the long continuance of the stock down the ages from the first divine procreator, here memorialized under the name Wakea. In the child is born again an image of the divine parent, to insure continuance of the family line.

Not that the cosmic conception has no place in the poet's imagery. The rebirth of light each day, the annual return of the sun from the south to revivify earth, serve not only as symbols of this human birth but as that birth's direct pattern or even its determining factor in the perpetuation of the race. The priest celebrates the rebirth of day, the Ao, with the story of the emergence of plant and animal forms in perpetual continuity, calling each by name. He celebrates the birth of man with the history of the lineage of which the child is offshoot, rehearsing the names of ancestors by whom the perpetuation of the family line has been secured. The dawn of day, the annual turn of the sun, are not only symbols but the event itself to which the birth of mankind succeeds and upon the acknowledgment of which man depends for his own high claim to ancestry from the gods. As Wakea, the sky world, bursts the bonds of night and rises out of the womb of waters where it has lain in

1. Fornander, *Collection* ("Memoirs," No. 6), p. 5.

darkness, so the child bursts the sheath where it lay within its mother's womb and emerges into the light of reasoning human life.

Kupihea reasoned from the flow of water preceding childbirth that water must be the medium through which the god of generation "works." Whether this idea of water as the original fructifying element was traditional or was Kupihea's own idea I do not know. It is, however, clear that his thinking started with observed facts of human birth and proceeded by analogy to cosmic beginnings. In the same way the Polynesian creation story as a successive appearance of plant and animal forms leading up to man must be referred to some such factual observation. This was easily to be found in the life of the embryo from conception up to the time of birth, a course of development which must have been perfectly known to a people skilled in agriculture, expert also in the art of abortion, upon which also depend so many beliefs and practices connected with embryonic deities in animal form, and out of which the picture of an evolving cosmos might easily serve as prototype. The poet gave it expression in the two worlds of the Po and the Ao. Hawaiian tradition passed down the teaching in the story of the buried foetus out of which sprang the taro plant, to be followed by the birth of mankind, to whose genealogy is thus attached the creature world born not to man but to the gods, whose spirits inhabit the Po and manifest themselves on earth for man's harm or protection. "To what shall I apply my procreative power?" asks the first parent in a Maori birth chant. It was not by the dawn of light that the generative god made himself known but by the organ of procreation itself, through which was intrusted to the newborn male the preservation of the family stock on earth and its continued functioning in the spirit world of the gods. Not speculative philosophy about how the world came to be must have inspired the poetic symbolism, but care for the sacred spark in man from its inception to its maturity into a divinity born as a human being on earth to carry on the family ruling line. The cosmos is thus the symbol, the sexual life and its fulfilment in the child the inner meaning, the *kaona*, of the Hawaiian creation chant.

We must read this ancient prayer chant in the light of Polynesian thought. Certainly it includes much that is ancient and pre-Christian. Additions may have been made from time to time, even up to that of its late transcription. Parts are undoubtedly omitted or altered from their original form. Old symbols may be applied in new directions. Such changes however cannot destroy the value of the text as a genuine example of the sacred creation story of a Polynesian people, true as it is to native poetic style not alone in its composition as a whole but in particular passages, and reflecting old Hawaiian social life and philosophy in its treatment of the birth of life on earth and the myths of the gods.

Photograph by R. J Baker

DAVID MALO KUPIHEA

Enlarged from a snapshot

MRS. MARY KAWENA (WIGGIN) PUKUI

From a snapshot

KILINAHI KALEO OF HANA, MAUI

APPENDIXES

APPENDIX I

The Kalakaua Text

THE PULE HO'OLA'A ALI'I

HE KUMULIPO
- NO
KA-'I-'I-MAMAO
A IA
ALAPAI WAHINE

KA WA AKAHI

1. O ke au i kahuli wela ka honua
2. O ke au i kahuli lole ka lani
3. O ke au i kuka'iaka ka la
4. E ho'omalamalama i ka malama
5. O ke au o Makali'i ka po
6. O ka walewale ho'okumu honua ia
7. O ke kumu o ka lipo, i lipo ai
8. O ke kumu o ka Po, i po ai
9. O ka lipolipo, o ka lipolipo
10. O ka lipo o ka la, o ka lipo o ka po
11.   Po wale ho—'i
12. Hanau ka po
13. Hanau Kumulipo i ka po, he kane
14. Hanau Po'ele i ka po, he wahine
15. Hanau ka 'Uku-ko'ako'a, hanau kana, he 'Ako'ako'a, puka
16. Hanau ke Ko'e-enuhe 'eli ho'opu'u honua
17. Hanau kana, he Ko'e, puka
18. Hanau ka Pe'a, ka Pe'ape'a kana keiki, puka
19. Hanau ka Weli, he Weliweli kana keiki, puka
20. Hanau ka 'Ina, ka 'Ina
21. Hanau kana, he Halula, puka

187

22. Hanau ka Hawa'e, o ka Wana-ku kana keiki, puka
23. Hanau ka Ha'uke'uke, o ka 'Uhalula kana keiki, puka
24. Hanau ka Pi'oe, o ka Pipi kana keiki, puka
25. Hanau ka Papaua, o ka 'Olepe kana keiki, puka
26. Hanau ka Nahawele, o ka Unauna kana keiki, puka
27. Hanau ka Makaiauli, o ka 'Opihi kana keiki, puka
28. Hanau ka Leho, o ka Puleholeho kana keiki, puka
29. Hanau ka Naka, o ke Kupekala kana keiki, puka
30. Hanau ka Makaloa, o ka Pupu'awa kana keiki, puka
31. Hanau ka 'Ole, o ka 'Ole'ole kana keiki, puka
32. Hanau ka Pipipi, o ke Kupe'e kana keiki, puka
33. Hanau ka Wi, o ke Kiki kana keiki, puka

34. Hanau kane ia Wai'ololi, o ka wahine ia Wai'olola
35. Hanau ka Ekaha noho i kai
36. Kia'i ia e ka Ekahakaha noho i uka
37. He po uhe'e i ka wawa
38. He nuku, he wai ka 'ai a ka la'au
39. O ke Akua ke komo, 'a'oe komo kanaka

40. O kane ia Wai'ololi, o ka wahine ia Wai'olola
41. Hanau ka 'Aki'aki noho i kai
42. Kia'i ia e ka Manienie-'aki'aki noho i uka
43. He po uhe'e i ka wawa
44. He nuku, he wai ka 'ai a ka la'au
45. O ke Akua ke komo, 'a'oe komo kanaka

46. O kane ia Wai'ololi, o ka wahine ia Wai'olola
47. Hanau ka 'A'ala'ula noho i kai
48. Kia'i ia e ka 'Ala'ala-wai-nui noho i uka
49. He po uhe'e i ka wawa
50. He nuku, he wai ka 'ai a ka la'au
51. O ke Akua ke komo, 'a'oe komo kanaka

52. O kane ia Wai'ololi, o ka wahine ia Wai'olola
53. Hanau ka Manauea noho i kai
54. Kia'i ia e ke Kalo-manauea noho i uka
55. He po uhe'e i ka wawa
56. He nuku, he wai ka 'ai a ka la'au
57. O ke Akua ke komo, 'a'oe komo kanaka

58. O kane ia Wai'ololi, o ka wahine ia Wai'olola
59. Hanau ke Ko'ele'ele noho i kai
60. Kia'i ia e ke ko Punapuna, ko 'ele'ele, noho i uka

61. He po uhe'e i ka wawa
62. He nuku, he wai ka 'ai a ka la'au
63. O ke Akua ke komo, 'a'oe komo kanaka

64. O kane ia Wai'ololi, o ka wahine ia Wai'olola
65. Hanau ka Puaki noho i kai
66. Kia'i ia e ka Lauaki noho i uka
67. He po uhe'e i ka wawa
68. He nuku, he wai ka 'ai a ka la'au
69. O ke Akua ke komo, 'a'oe komo kanaka

70. O kane ia Wai'ololi, o ka wahine ia Wai'olola
71. Hanau ka Kakalamoa noho i kai
72. Kia'i ia e ka Moamoa noho i uka
73. He po uhe'e i ka wawa
74. He nuku, he wai ka 'ai a ka la'au
75. O ke Akua ke komo, 'a'oe komo kanaka

76. O kane ia Wai'ololi, o ka wahine ia Wai'olola
77. Hanau ka limu Kele noho i kai
78. Kia'i ia e ka Ekele noho i uka
79. He po uhe'e i ka wawa
80. He nuku, he wai ka 'ai a ka la'au
81. O ke Akua ke komo, 'a'oe komo kanaka

82. O kane ia Wai'ololi, o ka wahine ia Wai'olola
83. Hanau ka limu Kala noho i kai
84. Kia'i ia e ka 'Akala noho i uka
85. He po uhe'e i ka wawa
86. He nuku, he wai ka 'ai a ka la'au
87. O ke Akua ke komo, 'a'oe komo kanaka

88. O kane ia Wai'ololi, o ka wahine ia Wai'olola
89. Hanau ka Lipu'upu'u noho i kai
90. Kia'i ia e ka Lipu'u, noho i uka
91. He po uhe'e i ka wawa
92. He nuku, he wai ka 'ai a ka la'au
93. O ke Akua ke komo, 'a'oe komo kanaka

94. O kane ia Wai'ololi, o ka wahine ia Wai'olola
95. Hanau ka Loloa, noho i kai
96. Kia'i ia e ka Kalamaloloa, noho i uka
97. He po uhe'e i ka wawa
98. He nuku, he wai ka 'ai a ka la'au
99. O ke Akua ke komo, 'a'oe komo kanaka

100. O kane ia Wai'ololi, o ka wahine ia Wai'olola
101. Hanau ka Ne, noho i kai
102. Kia'i ia e ka Neneleau noho i uka
103. He po uhe'e i ka wawa
104. He nuku, he wai ka 'ai a ka la'au
105. O ke Akua ke komo, 'a'oe komo kanaka

106. O kane ia Wai'ololi, o ka wahine ia Wai'olola
107. Hanau ka Huluwaena, noho i kai
108. Kia'i ia e ka Huluhulu-'ie'ie noho i uka
109. He po uhe'e i ka wawa
110. He nuku, he wai ka 'ai a ka la'au
111. O ke Akua ke komo, 'a'oe komo kanaka

112. O ke kane huawai, Akua kena
113. O kalina a ka wai i ho'oulu ai
114. O ka huli ho'okawowo honua
115. O paia ['a] i ke auau ka manawa
116. O he'e au loloa ka po
117. O piha, o pihapiha
118. O piha-u, o piha-a
119. O piha-e, o piha-o
120. O ke ko'o honua pa'a ka lani
121. O lewa ke au, ia Kumulipo ka po
122.   Po—no

KA WA ELUA

123. Hanau kama a ka Powehiwehi
124. Ho'oleilei ka lana a ka Pouliuli
125. O Mahiuma, o Ma'apuia
126. O noho i ka 'aina o Pohomiluamea
127. Kukala mai ka Haipu-aalamea
128. O naha wilu ke au o Uliuli
129. O ho'ohewahewa a kumalamala
130. O pohouli a poho'ele'ele
131. O na wai ehiku e lana wale
132. Hanau kama a hilu, a holo
133. O ka hilu ia pewa lala kau
134. O kau[l]ana a Pouliuli
135. O kuemiemi a Powehiwehi
136. O Pouliuli ke kane
137. O Powehiwehi ka wahine

138. Hanau ka i'a, hanau ka Nai'a i ke kai la holo
139. Hanau ka Mano, hanau ka Moano i ke kai la holo
140. Hanau ka Mau, hanau ka Maumau i ke kai la holo
141. Hanau ka Nana, hanau ka Mana i ke kai la holo
142. Hanau ka Nake, hanau ka Make i ke kai la holo
143. Hanau ka Napa, hanau ka Nala i ke kai la holo
144. Hanau ka Pala, hanau ke Kala i ke kai la holo
145. Hanau ka Paka, hanau ka Papa i ke kai la holo
146. Hanau ke Kalakala, hanau ka Huluhulu i ke kai la holo
147. Hanau ka Halahala, hanau ka Palapala i ke kai la holo
148. Hanau ka Pe'a, hanau ka Lupe i ke kai la holo
149. Hanau ke Ao, hanau ke Awa i ke kai la holo
150. Hanau ke Aku, hanau ke 'Ahi i ke kai la holo
151. Hanau ka Opelu, hanau ke Akule i ke kai la holo
152. Hanau ka 'Ama'ama, hanau ka 'Anae i ke kai la holo
153. Hanau ka Ehu, hanau ka Nehu i ke kai la holo
154. Hanau ka 'Iao, hanau ka 'Ao'ao i ke kai la holo
155. Hanau ka 'Ono, hanau ke Omo i ke kai la holo
156. Hanau ka Pahau, hanau ka Lauhau i ke kai la holo
157. Hanau ka Moi, hanau ka Lo'ilo'i i ke kai la holo
158. Hanau ka Mao, hanau ka Maomao i ke kai la holo
159. Hanau ke Kaku, hanau ke A'ua'u i ke kai la holo
160. Hanau ke Kupou, hanau ke Kupoupou i ke kai la holo
161. Hanau ka Weke, hanau ka Lele i ke kai la holo
162. Hanau ka Palani, hanau ka Nukumomi i ke kai la holo
163. Hanau ka Ulua, hanau ka Hahalua i ke kai la holo
164. Hanau ka 'Ao'aonui, hanau ka Paku'iku'i i ke kai la holo
165. Hanau ka Ma'i'i'i, hanau ka Ala'ihi i ke kai la holo
166. Hanau ka 'O'o, hanau ka 'Akilolo i ke kai la holo

167. Hanau ka Nenue, noho i kai
168. Kia'i ia e ka Lauhue noho i uka
169. He po uhe'e i ka wawa
170. He nuku, he kai ka 'ai a ka i'a
171. O ke Akua ke komo, 'a'oe komo kanaka

172. O kane ia Wai'ololi, o ka wahine ia Wai'olola
173. Hanau ka Pahaha noho i kai
174. Kia'i ia e ka Puhala noho i uka
175. He po uhe'e i ka wawa
176. He nuku, he kai ka 'ai a ka i'a
177. O ke Akua ke komo, 'a'oe komo kanaka

178. O kane ia Wai'ololi, o ka wahine ia Wai'olola
179. Hanau ka Pahau noho i kai
180. Kia'i ia e ka Lauhau noho i uka
181. He po uhe'e i ka wawa
182. He nuku, he kai ka 'ai a ka i'a
183. O ke Akua ke komo, 'a'oe komo kanaka

184. O kane ia Wai'ololi, o ka wahine ia Wai'olola
185. Hanau ka He'e noho i kai
186. Kia'i ia e ka Walahe'e noho i uka
187. He po uhe'e i ka wawa
188. He nuku, he kai ka 'ai a ka i'a
189. O ke Akua ke komo, 'a'oe komo kanaka

190. O kane ia Wai'ololi, o ka wahine ia Wai'olola
191. Hanau ka 'O'opukai noho i kai
192. Kia'i ia e ka 'O'opuwai noho i uka
193. He po uhe'e i ka wawa
194. He nuku, he kai ka 'ai a ka i'a
195. O ke Akua ke komo, 'a'oe komo kanaka

196. O kane ia Wai'ololi, o ka wahine ia Wai'olola
197. Hanau ka puhi Kauwila noho i kai
198. Kia'i ia e ka Uwila noho i uka
199. He po uhe'e i ka wawa
200. He nuku, he kai ka 'ai a ka i'a
201. O ke Akua ke komo, 'a'oe komo kanaka

202. O kane ia Wai'ololi, o ka wahine ia Wai'olola
203. Hanau ka Umaumalei noho i kai
204. Kia'i ia e ka 'Ulei noho i uka
205. He po uhe'e i ka wawa
206. He nuku, he kai ka 'ai a ka i'a
207. O ke Akua ke komo, 'a'oe komo kanaka

208. O kane ia Wai'ololi, o ka wahine ia Wai'olola
209. Hanau ka Paku'iku'i noho i kai
210. Kia'i ia e ka la'au Kukui noho i uka
211. He po uhe'e i ka wawa
212. He nuku, he kai ka 'ai a ka i'a
213. O ke Akua ke komo, 'a'oe komo kanaka

214. O kane ia Wai'ololi, o ka wahine ia Wai'olola
215. Hanau ka Laumilo noho i kai

216. Kia'i ia e ka [la'au] Milo noho i uka
217. He po uhe'e i ka wawa
218. He nuku, he kai ka 'ai a ka i'a
219. O ke Akua ke komo, 'a'oe komo kanaka

220. O kane ia Wai'ololi, o ka wahine ia Wai'olola
221. Hanau ke Kupoupou noho i kai
222. Kia'i ia e ke Kou noho i uka
223. He po uhe'e i ka wawa
224. He nuku, he kai ka 'ai a ka i'a
225. O ke Akua ke komo, 'a'oe komo kanaka

226. O kane ia Wai'ololi, o ka wahine ia Wai'olola
227. Hanau ka Hauliuli noho i kai
228. Kia'i ia e ka Uhi noho i uka
229. He po uhe'e i ka wawa
230. He nuku, he kai ka 'ai a ka i'a
231. O ke Akua ke komo, 'a'oe komo kanaka

232. O kane ia Wai'ololi, o ka wahine ia Wai'olola
233. Hanau ka Weke noho i kai
234. Kia'i ia e ka Wauke noho i uka
235. He po uhe'e i ka wawa
236. He nuku, he kai ka 'ai a ka i'a
237. O ke Akua ke komo, 'a'oe komo kanaka

238. O kane ia Wai'ololi, o ka wahine ia Wai'olola
239. Hanau ka 'A'awa noho i kai
240. Kia'i ia e ka 'Awa noho i uka
241. He po uhe'e i ka wawa
242. He nuku, he kai ka 'ai a ka i'a
243. O ke Akua ke komo, 'a'oe komo kanaka

244. O kane ia Wai'ololi, o ka wahine ia Wai'olola
245. Hanau ka Ulae noho i kai
246. Kia'i ia e ka Mokae noho i uka
247. He po uhe'e i ka wawa
248. He nuku, he kai ka 'ai a ka i'a
249. O ke Akua ke komo, 'a'oe komo kanaka

250. O kane ia Wai'ololi, o ka wahine ia Wai'olola
251. Hanau ka Palaoa noho i kai
252. Kia'i ia e ka Aoa noho i uka
253. He po uhe'e i ka wawa

254. He nuku, he kai ka 'ai a ka i'a
255. O ke Akua ke komo, 'a'oe komo kanaka

256. O ke ka'ina a palaoa e ka'i nei
257. E kuwili o ha'aha'a i ka moana
258. O ka opule ka'i loloa
259. Manoa wale ke kai ia lakou
260. O kumimi, o ka lohelohe a pa'a
261. O ka'a monimoni i ke ala
262. O ke ala o Kolomio o miomio i hele ai
263. Loa'a Pimoe i ke polikua
264. O Hikawainui, o Hikawaina
265. O pulehulehu hako'ako'a
266. Ka mene 'a'ahu wa'awa'a
267. O holi ka poki'i i ke au ia uliuli
268. Po'ele wale ka moana powehiwehi
269. He kai ko'ako'a no ka uli o Paliuli
270. O he'e wale ka 'aina ia lakou
271. O kaha uliuli wale i ka po—la
272.   Po—no

KA WA EKOLU

273. O kane ia, o ka wahine kela
274. O kane hanau i ke auau po-'ele'ele
275. O ka wahine hanau i ke auau po-haha
276. Ho'ohaha ke kai, ho'ohaha ka uka
277. Ho'ohaha ka wai, ho'ohaha ka mauna
278. Ho'ohaha ka po-niuauae'ae'a
279. Ulu ka Haha na lau eiwa
280. Ulu nioniolo ka lau pahiwa
281. O ho'oulu i ka lau palaiali'i
282. Hanau o Po-'ele'ele ke kane
283. Noho ia e Pohaha he wahine
284. Hanau ka pua a ka Haha
     Hanau ka Haha

285. Hanau ka Huhu he makua
286. Puka kana keiki he Huhulele, lele
287. Hanau ka Pe'elua ka makua
288. Puka kana keiki he Pulelehua, lele
289. Hanau ka Naonao ka makua
290. Puka kana keiki he Pinao, lele

291. Hanau ka Unia ka makua
292. Puka kana keiki he Uhini, lele
293. Hanau ka Naio ka makua
294. Puka kana keiki he Nalo, lele
295. Hanau ka Hualua ka makua
296. Puka kana keiki he Manu, lele
297. Hanau ka Ulili ka makua
298. Puka kana keiki he Kolea, lele
299. Hanau ke A'o ka makua
300. Puka kana keiki he A'u, lele
301. Hanau ka Akekeke ka makua
302. Puka kana keiki he Elepaio, lele
303. Hanau ka Alae ka makua
304. Puka kana keiki ka Apapane, lele
305. Hanau ka Alala ka makua
306. Puka kana keiki he Alawi, lele
307. Hanau ka 'E'ea ka makua
308. Puka kana keiki he Alaiaha, lele
309. Hanau ka Mamo ka makua
310. Puka kana keiki he 'O'o, lele
311. Hanau ka Moho he makua
312. Puka kana keiki he Moli, lele
313. Hanau ke Kikiki ka makua
314. Puka kana keiki he Ukihi, lele
315. Hanau ke Kioea ka makua
316. Puka kana keiki he Kukuluae'o, lele
317. Hanau ka 'Iwa ka makua
318. Puka kana keiki he Koa'e, lele
319. Hanau ke Kala ka makua
320. Puka kana keiki he Kaula, lele
321. Hanau ka Unana ka makua
322. Puka kana keiki he Auku'u, lele
323. O ka lele anei auna
324. O kahaka'i a lalani
325. O ho'onohonoho a pa'a ka pae
326. Pa'a ka aina o Kanehunamoku
327. Hanau manu ka 'aina
328. Hanau manu ke kai

329. Hanau kane ia Wai'ololi, o ka wahine ia Wai'olola
330. Hanau ka Lupe noho i kai

331. Kia'i ia e ka Lupeakeke noho i uka
332. He po uhe'e i ka wawa
333. He hua, he'i'o ka 'ai a ka manu
334. O ke Akua ke komo, 'a'oe komo kanaka

335. Hanau kane ia Wai'ololi, o ka wahine ia Wai'olola
336. Hanau ka Noio noho i kai
337. Kia'i ia e ka 'Io noho i uka
338. He po uhe'e i ka wawa
339. He hua, he 'i'o ka 'ai a ka manu
340. O ke Akua ke komo, 'a'oe komo kanaka

341. O kane ia Wai'ololi, o ka wahine ia Wai'olola
342. Hanau ke Kolea-a-moku noho i kai
343. Kia'i ia e ke Kolea-lele noho i uka
344. He po uhe'e i ka wawa
345. He hua, he 'i'o ka 'ai a ka manu
346. O ke Akua ke komo, 'a'oe komo kanaka

347. O kane ia Wai'ololi, o ka wahine ia Wai'olola
348. Hanau ka Hehe noho i kai
349. Kia'i ia e ka Nene noho i uka
350. He po uhe'e i ka wawa
351. He hua, he 'i'o ka 'ai a ka manu
352. O ke Akua ke komo, 'a'oe komo kanaka

353. O kane ia Wai'ololi, o ka wahine ia Wai'olola
354. Hanau ka Auku'u noho i kai
355. Kia'i ia e ka 'Ekupu'u noho i uka
356. He po uhe'e i ka wawa
357. He hua, he 'i'o ka 'ai a ka manu
358. O ke Akua ke komo, 'a'oe komo kanaka

359. O kane ia Wai'ololi, o ka wahine ia Wai'olola
360. Hanau ka Noio noho i kai
361. Kia'i ia e ka Pueo noho i uka
362. He po uhe'e i ka wawa
363. He hua, he 'i'o ka 'ai a ka manu
364. O ke Akua ke komo, 'a'oe komo kanaka

365. O ka leina keia a ka manu o Halulu
366. O Kiwa'a, o ka manu kani halau
367. O ka manu lele auna a pa'a ka La
368. Pa'a ka honua i na keiki manu a ka pohaha

369. He au pohaha wale i ka mu-ká
370. O ka hahu 'ape manewanewa
371. O ka holili ha'ape lau manamana
372. O ka manamana o ka hanau po
373. O po wale kela
374. O po wale keia
375. O po wale ke au ia Po'ele'ele
376. O poni wale ke au ia Pohaha, ka po
377. Po—no

KA WA EHA

378. E kukulu i ke 'ahi'a a la'a la
379. O ka 'ape aumoa ka hiwa uli
380. O ho'okaha ke kai i ka 'aina
381. O kolo aku, o kolo mai
382. O ho'ohua ka ohana o kolo
383. O kolo kua, o kolo alo
384. O pane['e] ke alo, o ho'ohonua ke kua
385. O ke alo o ku'u milimili nanea
386. O panoia, o panopano
387. O kane o ka Popanopano i hanau
388. O ka Popanopano ke kane
389. O Polalowehi ka wahine
390. Hanau kanaka ho'olu'a hua
391. Ho'ohua a lau i ka po a'e nei
392. Ia nei la ho'oku'uku'u
393. Ia nei la ho'oka'aka'a
394. Kaka'a kamali'i he'e pu'eone
395. O kama a ka Popanopano i hanau

396. Hanau ka po
397. Hanau ka po ia milinanea
398. Kuka'a ka po ia ki'i nana'a
399. Hanau ka po ia honu kua nanaka
400. Kulia ka po ia 'ea kua neneke
401. Hanau ka po ia ka 'ula maku'e
402. Kula'a ka po ia ka 'ula li'i
403. Hanau ka po ia mo'onanea
404. Kukele ka po ia mo'oni[a]nia
405. Hanau ka po ia pilipili
406. Kukala ka po ia kalakala

407. Hanau ka po ia ka'uka'u
408. Kuemi ka po ia palaka
409. Hanau ka po ia ka ihu kunini
410. Kueli ka po ia kupelepele
411. Hanau ka po ia kele
412. Kali ka po ia mehe[u]he[u]

413. Hanau kane ia Wai'ololi, o ka wahine ia Wai'olola
414. Hanau ka Honua noho i kai
415. Kia'i ia e ke Kuhonua noho i uka
416. He po uhe'e i ka wawa
417. He nuku, he la'i ka 'ai a kolo
418. O ke Akua ke komo, 'a'oe komo kanaka

419. O kane ia Wai'ololi, o ka wahine ia Wai'olola
420. Hanau ka Wili noho i kai
421. Kia'i ia e ka Wiliwili noho i uka
422. He po uhe'e i ka wawa
423. He nuku, he la'i ka 'ai a kolo
424. O ke Akua ke komo, 'a'oe komo kanaka

425. O kane ia Wai'ololi, o ka wahine ia Wai'olola
426. Hanau ka Aio noho i kai
427. Kia'i ia e ka Naio noho i uka
428. He po uhe'e i ka wawa
429. He nuku, he la'i ka 'ai a kolo
430. O ke Akua ke komo, 'a'oe komo kanaka

431. O kane ia Wai'ololi, o ka wahine ia Wai'olola
432. Hanau ka Okea noho i kai
433. Kia'i ia e ka Ahakea noho i uka
434. He po uhe'e i ka wawa
435. He nuku, he la'i ka 'ai a kolo
436. O ke Akua ke komo, 'a'oe komo kanaka

437. O kane ia Wai'ololi, o ka wahine ia Wai'olola
438. Hanau ka Wana noho i kai
439. Kia'i ia e ka Wanawana noho i uka
440. He po uhe'e i ka wawa
441. He nuku, he la'i ka 'ai a kolo
442. O ke Akua ke komo, 'a'oe komo kanaka

443. O kane ia Wai'ololi, o ka wahine ia Wai'olola
444. Hanau ka Nene noho i kai
445. Kia'i ia e ka Manene noho i uka

446. He po uhe'e i ka wawa
447. He nuku, he la'i ka 'ai a kolo
448. O ke Akua ke komo, 'a'oe komo kanaka

449. O kane ia Wai'ololi, o ka wahine ia Wai'olola
450. Hanau ka Liko noho i kai
451. Kia'i ia e ka Piko noho i uka
452. He po uhe'e i ka wawa
453. He nuku, he la'i ka 'ai a kolo
454. O ke Akua ke komo, 'a'oe komo kanaka

455. O kane ia Wai'ololi, o ka wahine ia Wai'olola
456. Hanau ka Opeope noho i kai
457. Kia'i ia e ka Oheohe noho i uka
458. He po uhe'e i ka wawa
459. He nuku, he la'i ka 'ai a kolo
460. O ke Akua ke komo, 'a'oe komo kanaka

461. O kane ia Wai'ololi, o ka wahine ia Wai'olola
462. Hanau ka Nananana noho i kai
463. Kia'i ia e ka Nonanona noho i uka
464. He po uhe'e i ka wawa
465. He nuku, he la'i ka 'ai a kolo
466. O ke Akua ke komo, 'a'oe komo kanaka

467. O hulahula wale ka ne'e [a]na a kolo
468. O ka maewa huelo ka loloa
469. O kukonakona o kukonakona
470. Hele lu wale i ki'o [a]na
471. O ka lepo hune ka 'ai, 'ai—a
472. 'Ai a kau, 'ai a mu-a
473. Ka 'ai [a]na a kauwa hewahewa
474. A pilihua wale ka 'ai [a]na
475. O kele a hana ha-ná
476. O hana mai ulu kunewanewa
477. Ke newa nei ka hele
478. O hele i ka 'aina o Kolo
479. Hanau ka ohana o Kolo i ka po
480. Po—no

KA WA ELIMA

481. O kuhele ke au ia Kapokanokano
482. O ho'omau i ke ahu o Polalouli

483. O ka uli 'iliuli makamaka hou
484. 'Iliuli o ka hiwahiwa Polalouli
485. Moe a wahine ia Kapokanokano
486. O ke kanokano o ka ihu nuku 'eli honua
487. E 'eku i ka moku e kupu a pu'u
488. E ho'opalipali [a]na ke kua
489. Ho'opalipali ke alo
490. O ke kama a pua'a i hanau
491. Ho'ohale uka i ka nahelehele
492. Ho'omaha i ka lo'ilo'i o Lo'iloa
493. O 'umi he au ka moku
494. O 'umi he au ka 'aina
495. Ka 'aina a Kapokanokano i noho ai
496. Oliuliu ke ala i ma'awe nei
497. O ka ma'awe hulu hiwa o ka pua'a
498. Hanau ka pua'a hiwahiwa i ke au
499. Ke au a Kapokanokano i noho ai
500. Moe a po ia Polalouli
501.　　Hanau ka po

502. Hanau ke Po'owa'awa'a, he wa'awa'a kona
503. Hanau ke Po'opahapaha, he pahapaha laha
504. Hanau ke Po'ohiwahiwa, he hiwahiwa luna
505. Hanau ke Po'ohaole, he haole kela
506. Hanau ke Po'omahakea, he keakea ka 'ili
507. Hanau ke Po'oapahu, he huluhulu kala
508. Hanau ke Po'omeumeu, he meumeu kona
509. Hanau ke Po'oauli, he uliuli kona
510. Hanau ka Hewahewa, he hewahewa kona
511. Hanau ka Lawalawa, he lawalawa kela
512. Hanau ka Ho'oipo, he ho'oipoipo kona
513. Hanau ka Hulu, a he 'a'aia kona
514. Hanau ka Hulupi'i, he pi'ipi'i kona
515. Hanau ka Meleoli, he melamela kona
516. Hanau ka Ha'upa, he ha'upa nuinui
517. Hanau ka Hilahila, he hilahila kona
518. Hanau ke Kenakena, he kenakena ia
519. Hanau ka Luheluhe, he luheluhe kona
520. Hanau ka Pi'i'awa'awa, he 'awa'awa kona
521. Hanau ka Li'ili'i, he li'ili'i kona
522. Hanau ka Makuakua, he kuakua kona
523. Hanau ka Halahala, he lei hala kona

524. Hanau ka Eweewe, he eweewe kona
525. Hanau ka Huelo-maewa, he aewe kona
526. Hanau ka Hululiha, he lihelihe kona
527. Hanau ka Pukaua, he kaua hope kona
528. Hanau ka Mehe'ula, he 'ula'ula ia
529. Hanau ka Pu'uwelu, he weluwelu kona

530. O kana ia welu keia
531. Laha ai kama o Lo'iloa
532. O ululoa ka 'aina o Mohala
533. E ku'u mai ana i ka ipu makemake
534. O makemake kini peleleu
535. O mele ke amo a Oma kini
536. A pili ka hanauna a Kapokanokano
537. I ka po nei la—
538.   Po—no

KA WA EONE

539. O kupukupu kahili o Kua-ka-mano
540. O kuku ka mahimahi, o ka pihapiha kapu
541. O ka holo [a]na kuwaluwalu ka linalina
542. Holi [a]na, ho'omaka, ho'omakamaka ka 'ai
543. Ka 'ai ana ka pi'ipi'i wai
544. Ka 'ai ana ka pi'ipi'i kai
545. Ka henehene a lualua
546. Noho po'opo'o ka 'iole makua
547. Noho pupi'i ka 'iole li'ili'i
548. O ka hulu ai malama
549. 'Uku li'i o ka 'aina
550. 'Uku li'i o ka wai
551. O mehe[u] ka 'aki'aki a nei[a] ha'ula
552. O lihilihi kuku
553. O pe'epe'e a uma
554. He 'iole ko uka, he 'iole ko kai
555. He 'iole holo i ka uaua
556. Hanau laua a ka Pohiolo
557. Hanau laua a ka Pone'eaku
558. He nene'e ka holo a ka 'iole 'uku
559. He mahimahi ka lele a ka 'iole 'uku
560. He lalama i ka 'ili'ili
561. Ka 'ili'ili hua 'ohi'a, hua 'ole o ka uka
562. He pepe kama a ka po hiolo i hanau

563. He lele kama a laua o ka po ne'e aku
564. O kama a uli a kama i ka po nei la
565.   Po—no

KA WA EHIKU

566. O kau ke anoano ia'u kualono
567. He ano no ka po hane'e aku
568. He ano no ka po hane'e mai
569. He ano no ka po pihapiha
570. He ano no ka ha'iha'i
571. He weliweli ka nu'u a ho'omoali
572. He weliweli ka 'ai a ke'e koe koena
573. He weliweli a ka po hane'e aku
574. He 'ili'ilihia na ka po he'e mai
575. He 'ili[hia] 'ilio kama a ka po h[an]e'e aku
576. He 'ilio kama a ka po he'e mai
577. He 'ilio 'i'i, he 'ilio 'a'a
578. He 'ilio 'olohe na ka lohelohe
579. He 'ilio alana na ka 'a'alua
580. He manu ke ha'i o Pulepule
581. O mihi i ke anuanu, huluhulu 'ole
582. O mihi i ka welawela i ke 'a'ahu 'ole
583. Hele wale i ke ala o Malama
584. Kanaha'i a ka po i na kama
585. Mai ka uluulu a ka welewele—a
586. Mai ka nahu [a]na a ka nenehe
587. O Hula ka makani kona hoa
588. O ke kaikaina muli o ka Lohelohe no
589. Puka ka pe'ape'a lohelohe
590. Puka ka pe'ape'a huluhulu
591. Puka ka pe'ape'a lau manamana
592. Puka ka pe'ape'a hane'e aku
593. A ka po he'enalu mai i hanau
594.   Po—no

KA WA EWALU

595. O kama auli['i], auli['i] anei
596. O kama i ke au o ka po kinikini
597. O kama i ke au o ka po he'enalu mamao
598. Hanau kanaka o mehelau
599. Hanau kanaka ia Wai'ololi
600. Hanau ka wahine ia Wai'olola

601. Hanau ka po Akua
602. O kanaka i kukuku
603. O kanaka i momoe
604. Momoe laua i ka po mamao
605. Ahinahina wale kanaka e kaka'i nei
606. Ha'ula'ula wale ka lae o ke akua
607. Ha'ele'ele ko ke kanaka
608. Hakeakea wale ka 'auwae
609. Ho'omalino ke au ia ka po kinikini
610. Ho'ola'ila'i mehe ka po he'enalu mamao
611. I kapaia La'ila'i ilaila
612. Hanau La'ila'i he wahine
613. Hanau Ki'i he kane
614. Hanau Kane he akua
615. Hanau o Kanaloa, o ka he'e-haunawela ia
     A—o
616. Hanau ka pahu
617. O Moanaliha
618. Kawaoma'aukele ko laua hope mai
619. Ku-polo-li'ili-ali'i-mua-o-lo'i-po kona muli
620. O ke kanaka ola loa o lau a lau ali'i
621. O kupo, o kupo
622. O kupa, o kupa, kupakupa, ku—pa
623. O kupa kupa, keke'e ka noho a ka wahine
624. O La'ila'i wahine o ka po he'e[nalu] mamao
625. O La'ila'i wahine [o] ka po kinikini
626. Noho i kanaka o ka po kinikini
627. Hanau o Hahapo'ele he wahine
628. Hanau o Hapopo he wahine
629. Hanau o Maila i kapa o Lopalapala
630. O 'Olohe kekahi inoa
631. Noho i ka 'aina o Lua
632. Kapa ai ia wahi o 'Olohelohe Lua
633. 'Olohelohe kane hanau i ke ao
634. 'Olohelohe ka wahine hanau i ke au
635. Noho mai la ia kane
636. Hanau La'i'olo ia kane
637. Hanau Kapopo he wahine
638. Hanau Po'ele-i, hanau Po-'ele-a
639. Ko laua hope mai o Wehiloa
640. Na lakou nei i hanau mai

641. Ka kikiki, ka makakaka
642. Ku nu'u muiona ka muimui ana
643. O kanaka lele wale, o kanaka nei la
      Ua a—o—

KA WA EIWA

644. O La'ila'i, o Ola'i-ku-honua
645. O Wela, o Owe, o owa ka lani
646. Oia wahine pi'ilani a pi'ilani no
647. Pi'iaoa lani i ka nahelehele
648. Onehenehe lele kulani ka honua
649. O kama ho'i a Ki'i i 'o'ili ma ka lolo
650. Puka lele, lele pu i ka lani
651. Kau ka 'omea ke aka 'ula ha'iha'ilona
652. Kau i ka lae, he hua ulu 'i'i
653. Kau i ka 'auwae, he huluhulu 'a
654. Ka hanauna a ia wahine ho'opaha'oha'o
655. Ka wahine no 'Iliponi, no loko o 'I'ipakalani
656. No ka 'aunaki kuku wela ahi kanaka
657. Oia wahine noho i Nu'umealani
658. 'Aina a ka aoa i noho ai
659. I hohole pahiwa ka lau koa
660. He wahine kino paha'oha'o wale keia
661. Me ia ia Ki'i, me ia ia Kane
662. Me ia i Kane a ka po kinikini
663. Moe wale ke au o ia kini
664. He kini ka mamo ka po inaina-u
665. Oia no ke ho'i iluna
666. O ka la'a la'au aoa o Nu'umealani noho mai
667. Ho'okauhua ilaila, ho'owa i ka honua
668. Hanau Hahapo'ele ka wahine
669. Hanau Hapopo ilaila
670. Hanau 'Olohelohe i muli nei
671. O ka 'apana hanauna ia wahine la
672.   Ua—ao—

KA WA UMI

673. O mai la, o La'ila'i ka paia
674. O Kane a Kapokinikini ka pou, o Ki'i ka mahu
675. Hanau La'i'olo'olo i noho ia Kapapa
676. Hanau Kamaha'ina he kane
677. Hanau Kamamule he kane

678. O Kamakalua he wahine
679. O Po'ele-i e-holo, kama
680. O Po'ele-a a-holo, kama
681. O Wehi-wela-wehi-loa
682. Ho'i hou La'ila'i noho ia Kane
683. Hanau o Ha'i he wahine
684. Hanau o Hali'a he wahine
685. Hanau Hakea he kane
686. Hanau ka muki, muka, mukekeke
687. Muka, kukuku, kunenewa
688. Moku, monu, mumule ana
689. Mumule wale ana Kane i ka mule
690. I mule, i ke'eo, i ka maua
691. I ka wahine weweli wale
692. Pe'e e kane ia e ho'ohanau kama
693. E ho'ohanau kama i kana keiki
694. Ho'ole ka lani iaia muli wale
695. Ha'awi i ka 'ape kapu ia Ki'i
696. E Ki'i no ke moe iaia
697. Ha'ili Kane i ka mua, heleu wale
698. Ha'ili o Ki'i o La'ila'i i ka muli lae punia
699. Pehi i ka pohaku hailuku ia Kane
700. O kani ka pahu ke wawa nei ka leo
701. O ka'u ho'ailona ia, ka ka muli
702. Huhu lili Kane moe muli ia mai la
703. O ka ewe o kana muli i muli ai
704. Haku ai kama hanau mua
705. Imua ia La'ila'i, imua ia Ki'i
706. Ka laua kama hanau lani la
707.   Puka—

KA WA UMIKUMAMAKAHI

708. Oia wahine noho lani a pi'o lani no
709. Oia wahine haulani a noho lani no
710. Noho no iluna a iho pi'o ia Ki'i
711. Weli ai ka honua i na keiki
712. Hanau o Kamaha'ina, he kane
713. Hanau o Kamamule, kona muli
714. Hanau o Kamamainau, o kona waena
715. Hanau o Kamakulua kona poki'i, he wahine
716. Noho Kamaha'ina he kane ia Hali'a
717. Hanau o Loa'a ke kane

718.	Loa'a ke kane	Nakelea ka wahine[1]
719.	Le	Kanu
720.	Kalawe	Kamau
	Kulou	Haliau
	Na'u	Ka-le
	'A'a	Hehe
	Pulepule	Ma'i
725.	Nahu	Luke
	Pono	Pono'i
	Kalau	Ma-ina
	Kulewa	Kune
	Po'u	Kala'i
730.	Po'ulua	Kukulukulu
	Pae	Ha'a'a
	Paeheunui	Ki'eki'e
	Hewa	Kulu
	Maku	Niau
735.	Wala	Kunewa
	Piha	Pihapiha
	Mu	Kuku
	Nawai	Hele
	Wawa	Hanehane
740.	Kua'i	'A'anai
	Lu'u	Lu'ule'a
	Mai	Mai'a
	Mai'a	Paua
	Lana	Kilo
745.	Lanalana	Paepae
	Pulu	Lepea
	Puluka	Lelepe
	Pulukene	Lelekau
	Pulumakau	Lelemau
750.	Pulukea	'Umala
	Nekue	Mahili
	Nakai	Napo'o
	Kuleha	Ma-ka
	'Ike	'Ao'ao
755.	Mala	Hu'i
	Malama	Puiki
	Eho	Pulama

1. In text the *o* meaning "of" here is not repeated. The line reads: "Loa'a the husband (or man) of Nakelea the wife," and so on.

Ehoaka	Pulanaia
Ehoku	Malaia
760. Keoma	Haho'oili
Kinohi	Mu'ala
Ponia	Luka
Meu'a	Mamau
Meu'alua	Maukele
765. Ho'olana	Ho'ohuli
Ho'omeha	Memeha
Pula	Kua
Kuamu	Kuawa
Ko'u	Ko'uko'u
770. Meia	Pekau
Kawala	Mahuli
Huli	'Imi
Loa'a	'Oli'oli
Huhu	Le'awale
775. Makuma	Manoa
Manomano	Lauahi
Kini	Mau
Leha	Maua
Pu'a	'Ena
780. Pu'a'ena	'Ena'ena
Wela	Ahi
Maiko	Kulewa
Maikokahi	Kuakahi
Maikolua	Pahila
785. Hilahila	Ho'ohila
Kelau	Lukau
Paio	Haluku
Paia	Kalaku
Keala	Keala'ula
790. Pi'ao	Nai'a
Niau	Kekumu
Launie	Huluhe
Mono	Pa'a
Hekau	Ka'ili
795. Ho'opa'a	Ha
Kalama	Kapala
Helu	Namu
Paila	Opuopu

Halale	Malu
800. Malie	Kalino
Ma'oki	Hulahe
Kaiwi	Iwi'a
Kulea	Kulia
Makou	Koulu
805. Ia'u	Mahea
Iaka	Meia
Makili	Lulu
Heamo	Lou
Heamokau	Makea
810. Pu'ili	Apomai
Pu'ili'ili	Li'ili'i
Pu'iliaku	Heleihea
Mokukapewa	Na'alo
Mokukai'a	Naele
815. Pi'ala	Heleua
Kiamo	Komo
Koikua	Keaho
Koi'ele	Kauhi
Pa'ele	Peleiomo
820. Keomo	Omoomo
Hulimakani	Nanailuna
Nanaikala	Haipule
Kalawela	Kalahuiwale
Kealakau	Hoku
825. Kamau	Meu
'Opala	Wene
Hali	Halima
Haliluna	Halilalo
Halimau	Halelo
830. Halipau	Muakau
Nunua	Nene'e
Nananaka	Lele'io
Oamio	Ololi
Omiomio	Wiwini
835. Aila	Kukala
Ailamua	Heia
Ailakau	Hele
Ailapau	Kaiwi
Manu	Hele'upa

840. Lilio
 Leheluhe
 Kelemau
 Kaumau
 Kaukahi
845. Mauka
 Ohi
 Ikamu
 Kalu
 Kalukalu
850. Lipo
 Lipowao
 Pili
 Pilimau
 Kahale
855. Kahale'ai
 Lawai'a
 Mauaka
 Wana
 Wanawana
860. Wanakaulani
 Wanamelu
 Kaulua
 Wala'au
 Hanehane
865. Hawane
 Heleau
 Hulimea
 Hulimua
 'Ewa
870. Omali
 Huelo
 Niolo
 Pilimai
 Keanu
875. Ka'io
 Haluaka
 Kapuhi
 Ehio
 Kakai
880. Amo

Makini
'Aina
Hinapu
Puoho
Ma'ele
Kai
Laulau
Namu
Moena
Hilipo
Na'o
Naele
'Aiku
Maumaua
Mua
Nu'u
Ka'i'o
Lehu
Kala
Wanakau
Melu
Hulili
Kaohi
Eiaau
Hahane
Kuamu
Ma'aku
'Aiko
Newa
'Ewa'ewa
Malimali
Kakai
Eiaku
Kona
Peleau
Pueo
Kaolo
Mula
Emio
Alakai
Koikoi

	Amoaku	Kuwala
	Helemai	Heleaku
	Onaho	Keanali'i
	Piliko'a	Ukuli'i
885.	Mahinahina	Halepo'i
	Po'opo'o	Nawai
	Omana	Manamana
	Omana'io	Huluheu
	Mana'ina'i	Malana'i
890.	Huluemau	Ka'alo
	Kaluli	Pau
	Nakino	Kinohi
	Nakinolua	Ewalu
	Ukiki	Eau
895.	Uli	Uliuli
	Mele	Melemele
	Lanai	Po'i
	Ha'o	Au
	Pakaikai	Puehu
900.	Moana	Hilo
	Hulu	Makali
	He	Ho'eue
	Makilo	Moi
	Naua	'Upa
905.	Ua	Hama
	Pele'u	Hamahuna
	Mahina	Hina
	Mahinale	Ulukua
	Mahinale'a	Palemo[2]
910.	Pipika	Kuhinu
	Mahele	Pu'unaue
	Kaohi	Kaohiohi
	Kona	Konakona
	Iho	Pelu
915.	Kula'a	Mailu
	Kuamau'u	Holehole
	Pahili	Halulu
	Keia	Luluka
	Maki'oi	Meihiolo
920.	Helehele	Pineha

2. "The sea that made the chiefs fall down," *Ke kai o Kahinali'i.*

	'Aukai	Milo
	Moekau	Helemau
	Huluau	Pulama
	Melemele	Milokua
925.	Kumuniu	Pilia
	Amoi	Akua
	Kunewa	Hulema
	Pahilo	Pili'aiku
	Napo'i	Ka'ale
930.	Kulana	Nawa
	Kakau	Po'ipo'i
	Holeha	Hulupehu
	Pa'ani	Malana'opi
	Lewa	Kukelemio
935.	Pihaulu	Hoiha
	Kelewa'a	Kinohili
	Kaki'o	Hiliha
	Hulipena	Miko
	Mokiweo	Pakala
940.	Kapalama	Kepo'oha
	Kapalamalama	Kepo'olimaha
	Wikani	Kamakolu
	Kapehi	Kaluku'u
	Hiwa	Kahiwahiwa
945.	Pano	Kekaliholiho
	Opelau	Maha
	Mahilu	Kaene
	Ho'olewa	Waiau
	Kumau	Kahaka
950.	Papalele	Kukala
	Haole	Kuwahine
	Makua	Kaluakekane
	Leho	Holomau
	Opikana	Nahenahe
955.	Helemaka	Liko
	Kukuhale	Hinaulu
	Pohakukau	Hinamai
	Helua	Kalani
	Komokomo	Malie
960.	Po'ele'ele	Ho'olua
	Nuku'ele'ele	Papakele

	Mama	Papakapa
	Hamama	Malele
	Kuemi	Kulua
965.	Opiliwale	Kapoulena
	Ahulimai	Mahinu'ele
	Ma'ikomo	Pelemau
	Hununu	Kamanu
	Ho'olohe	Nawaikaua
970.	Kumaua	Kulukaua
	Koikoi	Hau
	Mau'awa	Kolokolo
	Kelelua	'A'a
	Mukana	Mahi'opu
975.	Mahili	Wili
	Kukona	Naka
	Kanawai	Hapele
	Lohilohi	Hapeleau
	Apikili	Nohilo
980.	Ho'omaku	Nohalau
	Olepe	Makau
	Kala	Heleana
	Hulipau	Hulimakeau
	Makohi	Hulimakele
985.	'O'opuola	Nahalau
	Niuhuli	Nakuli'i
	Ohao	Nakumau
	Nu'u	Helemai
	Lena	Palemo
990.	Ahiahi	Opihi
	Ahiahihia	Ounauna
	Ahiakane	Wanaku
	Ahiakapoloa	Kikala
	Ahiakapokau	Hapu'u
995.	Ahiakulumau	Makani
	Ahiakamake	Kilau
	Ahiaka'olu	Honika
	Pohinakau	Hilahea
	Moulikaina	Ho'omaka
1000.	Ho'oku	Nanana
	Manaweulani	Laukunu
	Ho'omailu	Puluea

Mailu
Polehua
1005. Pu'ulele
Hamohulu
I'amama
Kuinewa
Holopulau
1010. Makanewanewa
Melia
Humuhumu
Ukianu
Ukinala
1015. Ukikamau
Ukilelewa
Ukinahina
Ho'opulu
Nahiole
1020. Mukiki
Kiola
Mulemulea
Kukawa
Kamio
1025. Ho'omu
Hailau
Ho'omauke'a
Pulune
Kuaua
1030. Moeiho
Manu'ala
Kolealea
Hilohilo
Maluipo
1035. 'Awaia
Ho'ohinu
Eapu
Ialo
Heiau
1040. Hei'aumana
Pulemo
Kaukeoa
Helemua

Lehuane
Keahu
Noelo
Noe'ula
Noenoe
Pilimau'u
Hinakona
Helepuau
Melemele
Palamau
Nenue
Ilimaka
Keohoko
Laumeki
Nilea
'Olo'olohu
Kealapi'i
Makino
I'ai'a
Helelu
Maika'iwa
Molemole
Unauna
Pamakani
Muli
Kahe
Wailuhi
'Imihia
Kawele
Kauwewe
Hokelona
Hoki'i
Milo
Ohouma
Uluoha
Makalewa
Pi'ioha
Ho'ohiwa
Maluolua
Hi'ileia
Puainea

	Kalele	Wamakona
1045.	Paepae	Lima'auki
	Keoa	Puameli
	Kapouhina	Kuamaulu
	Kapouhinaha	Hoku'a'ala
	Ho'opi'opi'o	Pi'onu'u
1050.	Ho'opi'oaka	Pi'oanuenue
	Ho'olahalaha	Pulau
	Ho'omahilu	Makua
	Nanewa	Peleuwao
	Nanawa'a	Oma
1055.	Ho'okilo	Pilikamau
	Kumeheu	Leleawa
	Leleiluna	Mainahu
	Halekumu	Kimonaue
	Halepaio	Holio
1060.	Halemoeanu	Ke'oke'o
	Haleluakini	Mali'i
	Halekuamu	Noio
	Ha'iola	Laulaha
	Kalelemauliaka	Miloha
1065.	Ko'iniho	Naku
	Po'oku	Paleamakau
	Hale'imiloea	Hilohilo
	Pani'oni'o	Liho
	Kealakike'e	Maiau
1070.	Oiaku	Kaniho
	Huini	Naihu
	Pa	'Ai'ano
	Pana	Koliau
.	Panakahi	Alia'oe
1075.	Pa'ikekalua	Piliwale
	Pu'ukolukolu	Hele'iamai
	Napu'ueha	Ho'okonokono
	Palimakahana	Helemaia
	Waiakea	Hepahuno
1080.	Kaeamauli	'Eleiku
	Kokoi'ele	Maumau
	Kaholooka'iwa	Heoioi
	Kalelenohinalea	Aluaku
	Pana'akahiahinalea	Helule

1085.	Panaikaluakahinalea	Painaina
	Pu'ukoluakukahinalea	Noakawalu
	Napu'uikahakahinalea	Piliamoa
	Palimawaleahinalea	Manu
	Akahiakaea'akilolo	Lekeamo
1090.	Paluaakaea'akilolo	Kelekeau
	Pu'ukoluakaea'akilolo	'Umikaua
	Pu'uhakahaa'akilolo	Mailo
	Pu'ulimakaeaaka'akilolo	Nihohoe
	Akahikeewe	Paliiuka
1095.	Paluakeewe	Paliikai
	Paukolu	Makaimoimo
	Pu'uhakeewe	Lauohokena
	Pulimakaewe	Piu
	Waiakaeakaewe	Nahinahi
1100.	Kamauliakaewe	Kamehai
	Koieleakaewe	Ulupo
	Kuaiwaakaewe	Newaiku
	Henahuno	Puhemo
	Panakahikenahu	Lahilahi
1105.	Panaluakenahu	Kaukeahu
	Panakolukenahu	'Ulalena
	Panahakenahu	Eiawale
	Lewelimakenahu	Konukonu
	Paakaeakenahu	Uli
1110.	Omaulikenahu	Na'ina'i
	Ko'ielehakenahu	Pilomoku
	Kuaiwakelekenahu	Nahae
	Hekaunano	Welawela
	Papio	Lo'ilo'i[3]
1115.	Manu'akele	Kealo
	Kaunuka	Kukamaka
	Maki'i	Auhe'e
	Kupololi'ili[4]	Ha'ihae
	Kupoka	Milio
1120.	Kupokanaha	Hamunu
	Kupone'e	Naia
	Kupohaha	Pakau

3. "The second sea that made the chiefs fall down," *Ka lua o ke kai o Kahinali'i*.

4. See l. 619.

	Kupoko	Hemolua
	Kupo-e	Naio
1125.	Kupou ·	Kelekele
	Kupolele	Hapulu
	Kupololo	Napulu
	Kupolili	Kuamo'o
	Kuponakanaka	Mu'umu'u
1130.	Kupohilili	Mo'onawe
	Kupohalalu	Helua
	Kupohelemai	Poiwa
	Kupokalalau	Nana
	Kupolahauma	Nakulu
1135.	Kupoli'ili'i	Eiamae
	Kupolona'ana'a	Lelehewa
	Kupolomaikau	Kimopu
	Kupolohelele	Holi
	Kupolopa'iuma	Kupolupa'iuma
1140.	Kupoloha'iha'i	Luli
	Kupolokeleau	Makeamo
	Kupolonaunau	'Imo
	Kupoloahilo	Lua
	Kupolomakanui	Hulili
1145.	Kupolomaiana	Manu
	Kupolokahuli	Hulu
	Kupololili	Namaka
	Kupololililili	Pulupuli
	Kupololalala	Naku
1150.	Kupolohalala	Ahi
	Kupololuana	Hoaka
	Kupolola'ila'i	Lelea
	Kupolola'iolo	Hanau
	Kupolola'imai	Ilimai
1155.	Kupolola'iaku	Ho'oilo
	Kupolohilihili	Makanalau
	Kupolomalimali	Hulipumai
	Kupolo'ale	Leleiluna
	Kupolo'imo	Holo'oko'a
1160.	Kupolokalili	Uliuli
	Kupolomene	Hiwauli
	Kupolohulu	Kinopu
	Kupolohulilau	Makiao

	Kupolohulimai	Makiaoea
1165.	Kupolokamana'o	'Ewa
	Kupolokeweka	Lukona
	Kupolokulu	Eapa'ipa'i
	Kupolonehea	Hulihele
	Kupolohaliu	Maliu
1170.	Kupolonakunaku	Uliau
	Kupolo'ololo	Kio'io
	Kupolo'ololi	Holeaku
	O Polo	Nolu
	Polohili	Kau
1175.	Polokau	Uli
	Polouli	Polo
	Polopolo	Hamu
	Polohamu	Nini
	Polonini	Ha'iha'i
1180.	Poloha'iha'i	Hei
	Poloheihei	Hanu'ai
	Polohanu'ai	'Ewa
	Polomahimahi	Kolo
	Poloaku	Malu'ape
1185.	Polomai	Pelepele
	Eliakapolo	Pua'a
	Ekukukapolo	Pua'akame
	Halimaikapolo	Uluea
	Ho'opoloiho	Hiamanu
1190.	Poloku	Paka
	Polokane	Leleamia
	Polohiwa	Halu
	Polomua	Menea
	Popolomea	Miomio
1195.	Popolohuamea	Omo
	Popolokai'a	Lanaki
	Polonananana	Manahulu
	Polomakiawa	La'ohe
	Poloanewa	Peleaku
1200.	Polohauhau	Nanale
	Polohehewa	Huamua
	Polomehewa	Hewa
	Poloula'a	Makolu
	Poloahiwa	Hiwa

1205.	Polo'ula	'Ula
	Polowena	We-na
	Poloimu	Mohalu
	Polokakahia	Kanakau
	Polo'i	'I'i
1210.	Polo'i'i	Hipa
	Polohi-pa	Pe-pa
	Polohi-pakeke	Meao
	Polohi-pakaka	Lahiki
	Polohi-helehele-lahiki	Kahiki
1215.	Polohi-paukahiki	Ka'ahiki
	Polohilele	Haumea
	Poloahaumea	Ahıluna
	Poloahiluna	Kaumai
	Polokaumai	Kaulani
1220.	Polokaulani	Kamakani
	Poloikamakani	Ikai
	Poloikai	Kamehani
	Poloikamehani	Maumau
	Poloimaumau	Mauna
1225.	Poloimauna	La'au
	Poloila'au	Kanahele
	Poloikanahele	Kukulu
	Poloikukulu	Ho'omoe
	Poloiho'omoe	Hanahana
1230.	Poloihanahana	Ka-haiau
	Polokahiau	Luahiko
	Poloikalua	Hiko
	Poloahiko	Kahá
	Poloikaha	Lima
1235.	Poloihilima	Waiku
	Poloioaiku	Mauli
	Polomauli	Koiele
	Polokokoiele	'I'iwa
	Polokuaiwa	Hemo
1240.	Polohemo	Nahunahu
	Polokina'u	Oli'iloa
	Poloki'i	Mano
	Pololi'i	Halula
	Polowaikaua	Pomea
1245.	Li'ili	Auau

	Li'iliauau	Kamau
	Li'ilikamau	Holiholi
	Li'ilili'ili	Nanaahu
	Li'ilihalula	Hole
1250.	Li'ilimama	Holehole
	Li'ilimanua	Pilimau
	Li'ilihakahaka	Ho'ohene
	Li'iliha	Iwiaku
	Li'ilihemoaku	Lanikama
1255.	Li'ilikaumai	'Iliuli
	Li'iliaolo	'Olo'olo
	Li'ilipihapiha	Nu'unu'u
	Li'ilinu'unu'u	Helelima
	Li'ilihelelima	Auli
1260.	Li'iliau	Nolunolu
	Li'ilimiha	Haleakeaka
	Li'ilinania	. Puluka
	Li'ilipelu'a	Maluli
	Li'ilimahimahi	Makauma
1265.	Li'ilikaliaka	Nahili
	Li'ilimeleau	Poloa
	Li'ilileoleo	Popoko
	Li'ililimanu	Po'imo'imo
	Li'ilikapili	Poiauwale
1270.	Li'iliholowa'a	Poilumai
	Li'iliholomau	Poinanaia
	Li'ilikalele	Nanana
	Li'ilikaili	Nanaue
	Li'ilipoipo	Nahuila
1275.	Li'iliwalewale	Meia
	Li'ilihanahana	Kulaimoku
	Li'ilihuliana	Pihi
	Li'iliwahipali	Pililau
	Li'ilinohopali	Ma'ele'ele
1280.	Li'ilinohoana	Kauhale
	Li'ilikauhale	Palia
	Li'ilipulepule	Pule
	Li'ili-la	Halawai
	Li'ili-hou	Leleipaoa
1285.	Li'ili-kaki'i	Miliamau
	Li'ili-kahuli	Kulana

Li'ili-homole	'Iwa'iwa
Li'ili-pukaua	Luna
Li'ilililolilo	Kaua
1290. Li'ililanalana	Lilo
Li'ililanakila	Kila
Li'ililana-au	Kilaua
Li'ilimalana	Mana
Li'iliahula	Lana
1295. Li'ilipukiu	Piko
Li'ilipaluku	Hulikau
Li'ilima'ema'e	Pakapaka
Li'i'oki'oki	Li'ili'i
Li'iali'ili'i	Lilioma
1300. Li'iakauli'ili'i	Manukele
Li'iakamama	Mama
Li'iamama	Paepae
Li'ipaepae	Umu
Li'iumu	Ki'i
1305. Li'iluaki'i	Kini
Li'iluakini	Lohi
Li'imolohi	Nahele
Li'ikau'unahele	'Upa
Li'ia'upa	Li'awa
1310. Li'imuli'awa	Newaku
Li'inewaku	Mali
Li'ihomali	Pulama
Li'ipulama	Palama
Li'ipalama	'Ohinu
1315. Li'i'ohinu	'Omaka
Li'i'omaka	'Olua
Li'ipau	Kaneiwa[5]
O 'A	O Li'i
Ali'i	La'a
1320. Ali'ila'a	Aka
Ali'iaka	Mau
Ali'imau	Ali'i
Ali'iali'i	Pohea
Ali'ipo'i	Mi'i
1325. Ali'ikono	Pahu

5. "The third sea that made the chiefs fall," *Ke kolu o ke kai o Kahinali'i.*

	Ali'ipahu	'Ume
	Ali'i'ume	Hala
	Ali'ihala	Poniponi
	Ali'iponi	Kelenanahu
1330.	Ali'ilanahu	Ka'eka'ea
	Ali'ikaea	Hohonupu'u
	Ali'ihonupu'u ⎫ Opu'upu'u ⎭	Kaeahonu
	Ali'ilehelehe	Lehelehe
1335.	Ali'imakolu	Hinakolu
	Ali'inohouka	Mauka
	Ali'ihimuhani	Haui
	Ali'ileleiona	Lopiana
	Ali'iwala'au	Kukeleau
1340.	Ali'ikuwala	Mana'a'ala
	Ali'ikomokomo	Lupuhi
	Ali'iaku	Ikuwa
	Ali'inewa	Mania
	Ali'ikuhikuhi	Lahulahu
1345.	Ali'ikilo	Loa
	Ali'ikiloloa	Pokopoko
	Ali'ikilopoko	Anana
	Ali'iemi	'Ami'ami
	Ali'ikolo	Lepau
1350.	Ali'ihelu	Lepeake
	Ali'iheluone	Malamu
	Ali'ipu'uone	Nahakea
	Ali'ikamanomano	Ho'ouli
	Ali'ihukeakea	Pololani
1355.	Ali'ipauku	Kalakala
	Ali'inana	Huli
	Ali'ikilokilo	Kelea
	Ali'ikuloluna	Halululu
	Ali'ikilolono	Kalahai
1360.	Ali'ikiloau	Kanamu
	Ali'ikilohonua	Heanaipu
	Ali'ikilouli	Ho'owili
	Ali'ikilokai	'Ume
	Ali'ikilonalu	'Ohi
1365.	Ali'ikilohulu	Pelapela
	Ali'ikiloahu	Oheohe

	Ali'ikilomakani	Malumalu
	Ali'ikilola	Lipoa
	Ali'ikilohoku	Kanulau
1370.	Ali'ikilomalama	Nahele
	Ali'ikilomakali'i	Ho'opulu
	Ali'ikilokau	Kakeli'i
	Ali'ikiloho'oilo	Hulu
	Ali'ika'ana'au	Lono
1375.	Ali'ika'anamalama	Kea
	Ali'ika'anaua	Papahuli
	Ali'ikilomo'o	Mo'olio
	Ali'ikilokua	Kilohi
	Ali'ikiloalo	Anapu
1380.	Ali'ikilohope	A-aa
	Ali'ikilomua	Pehe
	Mua	Wanaku
	Muapo	Haina
	Muahaka	Kulamau
1385.	Mualele	Hilipo
	Muakaukeha	Keanukapu
	Muahale	La'apilo
	Muahalekapu	Ho'ohali
	Muaanoano	Nauia
1390.	Muakekele	Ipu
	Muahaipu	Kahiko
	Muakahiko	Wa'awa'a
	Muawa'a	Po'i
	Muapo'ipo'i	Helenaku
1395.	Muakamalulu	Kaukahi
	Muahele'i	Lulu
	Muakohukohu	Mo'olelo
	Muakahukahu	Kapili
	Muaoma	Kahu
1400.	Muanalu	Anoano
	Muanaluhaki	Nalu
	Muanalupopo'i	Poki'i
	Muanalukalohe	Nanaku
	Muanaluha'ikakala	Moku
1405.	Mualala	Ho'onahu
	Muahaipu	'Api'api
	Muapule	Mahoa

	Muahanu'ala	Ahia
	Muaikekele	Mulemule
1410.	Muaipoipo	'Akia
	Muakalaiki'i	Lena
	Muakawa'a	'Auhuhu
	Muaiopele	La'aumele
	Muaiopola	La'ala'au
1415.	Muapali	Wahine
	Muaho'opo	Kikana
	Muaunu	Ui-a
	Muaha'i	Kahuli
	Mualupe	'Eli'eli
1420.	Muakala	Mo'omo'o
	Muawekea	Kapu
	Muahilo	Lau
	Muakahu	Eiwa
	Muakahukahu	Hiliahu
1425.	Mua'ama'ama	Kaomi
	Muaahilo	Auwe
	Muaanoa	Olopule
	Muaale'ale'a	Ka'imai
	Muainakalo	Kinika
1430.	Muaohupu	Niniha
	Muaikauka	Niniahu
	Muaikumuka	Moemole
	Muaikaunukukanaka	Mokukaha
	Muaokalele	Opilopilo
1435.	Muaokahaiku	Meheia
	Muaokahanu'u	Kamanuha'aha'a
	Muaokalani	Lele'amio
	Muamamao	Aumalani
	Muanu'unu'u	Kahakaua
1440.	Muaokamoi	Holi
	Muaokaha'i	Haehae
	Muaokeoma	Mano
	Muaokekahai	Opelele
	Muaoka'oliko	Ehu
1445.	Muaokapahu	Kapilipili
	Muaokahana	Hapoe
	Muaokahanai	Hunu
	Muaokaipu	Ohekele

	Mua'ume'umeke	Pukapu
1450.	Muapo'i	Ponouli
	Muaahuliau	Lehiwa
	Muaipapio	Keleauma
	Muailoiloi	Pohopoho
	Lo'imua	Nanio
1455.	Lo'ikahi	Pae
	Lo'ilua	Pililauhea
	Lo'ilo'i	Manukoha
	Lo'ikalakala	Kanaia
	Lo'iloloi	Naio
1460.	Lo'ilolohi	Puhimaka
	Lo'inuilo'i	Kalino
	Lo'ilo'ikaka	Kalaniahu
	Lo'iakama	Poepoe
	Lo'iiopoe	Hiloauama
1465.	Lo'ilo'inui	Uhuau
	Lo'ipouli	Moku
	Lo'imia	Leleiona
	Lo'iapele	Haikala
	Lo'iahemahema	Nakulu
1470.	Lo'iakio	Kukala
	Lo'ialuluka	Hi'ipoi
	Lo'iahamahamau	Olo
	Lo'i'olo'olo	Papa'a
	Lo'ikolohonua	Hano
1475.	Lo'iipulau	Mahoe
	Lo'ianomeha	Kaloa
	Lo'ikinikini	Pokipoki
	Lo'imanomano	Kinikahi
	Lo'ilo'imai	Holiolio
1480.	Lo'ilo'ikapu	Alohi
	Lo'ilo'ikala	Aheaka
	Lo'ilo'inahu	Niao
	Lo'ilo'ipili	Wali
	Lo'iahuahu	Waleho'oke
1485.	Lo'ikulukulu	Nohopali
	Lo'ipilipa	Nohinohi
	Lo'ipilipili	Mahealani
	Lo'ihalalu	Palimu
	Lo'ihalululu	Kahiona

1490.	Lo'ilo'ilele	Lukama
	Lo'ilo'ipa	Kahikahi
	Lo'ipakeke	Waikeha
	Lo'iloipo	Manini
	Lo'ilo'ipololo	Hinalo
1495.	Lo'iipololo	Oamaamaku
	Lo'ikamakele	Lahi
	Lo'ihi'aloa	Keleakaku
	Lo'imanuwa	Lahipoko
	Lo'ikalokalo	Pauha
1500.	Lo'i'ihi'ihi	Kaheka
	Lo'ihilimau	Pi'opi'o
	Lo'imoemoe	Ho'okaukau
	Lo'ipilopilo	Ho'oiloli
	Lo'iko'iko'i	Puapua
1505.	Lo'iko'i'i'i	Mahiapo
	Lo'iloloilo	Kulukau
	Lo'iloloilo[?]	Kupe'e
	Lo'iloloikapu	Kealanu'u
	Lo'ilalolo	Kinana
1510.	Lo'ilo'inaka	Pulelehu
	Lo'ilo'ila	Milimili
	Lo'ilo'ikopea	Apoapoahi
	Lo'iimauamaua	Pola
	Lo'iikuki'i	Houpo
1515.	Lo'iimanini	Kakiwi
	Lo'iipukapuka	Polinahe
	Lo'iomilu	Ipulau
	Lo'iomiliapo	Nahawiliea
	Lo'iomakana	Ho'olaumiki
1520.	Lo'iokanaloa	Palahalaha
	Lo'ioki'iki'i	Hulikahikeoma
	Lo'iihi'ikua	Kahiliapoapo
	Lo'iihi'ialo	Kaheihei
	Lo'iokanaha	Hilipalahalaha
1525.	Lo'iikeluea	Apuwaiolika
	Lo'iopilihala	Ohiohikahanu
	Lo'iomalelewa'a	Palakeaka
	Lo'iii'ele'ele	Mimika
	Lo'ipo	Kilika, hanau o
1530.	Pola'a—	

1531. Hanau ka 'ino, hanau ke au
1532. Hanau ka pahupahu, kapohaha
1533. Hanau ka haluku, ka haloke, ka nakulu, ka honua naueue
1534. Ho'iloli ke kai, pi'i ka mauna
1535. Ho'omu ka wai, pi'i kua a hale
1536. Pi'i konikonihi'a, pi'i na pou o Kanikawá
1537. Lele na ihe a Kauikahó
1538. Apu'epu'e ia Kanaloa, Kanikahoe
1539. Hanau o Poelua i ke alo o Wakea
1540. Hanau ka po'ino
1541. Hanau ka pomaika'i
1542. Hanau ka moa i ke kua o Wakea
1543. Make Kupolo-li'ili-ali'i-mua-o-lo'ipo
1544. Make ke au kaha o piko-ka-honua; oia pukaua
1545. Hua na lau la nalo, nalo i ka po liolio

KA WA UMIKUMAMALUA

	Opu'upu'u ke kane	La'aniha ka wahine
	Opu'upe	Pepe
	Opu'umauna	Kapu'u
	Opu'uhaha	Leleiao
1550.	Opu'ukalaua	Mauka-o
	Opu'uhanahana	Kilokau
	Opu'uhamahamau	Halalai
	Opu'ukalauli	Makele
	Opu'ukalakea	Opu'u'ele
1555.	Opu'ukalahiwa	Opu'umakaua
	Opu'ukalalele	Lelepau
	Maunanui	Makelewa'a
	Maunane'e	Hulipu
	Maunapapapa	Kanaua
1560.	Maunaha'aha'a	Ha'alepo
	Maunahiolo	Hane'ene'e
	Pu'ukahonua	Lalohana
	Ha'akuku	Wa'awa'a
	Ha'apipili	Ha'amomoe
1565.	Kanioi	Ha'akauwila
	Puanue	Lalomai
	Kepo'o	Kau-a-wana
	A-'a'a	Ho'oanu
	Piowai	'A'amoa

1570. Nauanu'u   Makohilani
      Ha'ulanuiiakea   Huku
      Mahikoha   Hinaho'oka'ea
      'O'opukoha   Kumananaiea
      Hawai'i   Ulunui
1575. Kekihe-i   Kekila'au
      Makuaikawaokapu   Ikawaoelilo
      Makaukau   Hahalua
      Kalolomauna   Kaloloamoana
      Kalolopiko   Kalolo'a'a
1580. 'A'a   Waka'au
      Kauwila   Uhiuhi
      Palipali   Palimoe
      Punalauka   Punalakai
      Pihe'eluna   Pihe'elalo
1585. Malana'opi'opi   Hika'ulunui
      Malanaopiha-e   Pihaehae
            Hanau Kıhala'aupoe he Wauke
            Hanau o 'Ulu he 'Ulu
            Hanau ko laua muli o
      Kepo'o   Halulu
      Oliua   Kauikau
      Kikona   Ka'imai
1590. Ho'opulupulu   Auna
      Ho'olehu   Lapa'i
      Ka'ulunokalani   Kahele
      Ho'ouka   'Aluka
      Kanalu   Hakihua
1595. Po'i   Lenawale
      Paepaemalama   Kaumai
      Kaulana   Kaulalo
      Pala'au   Paweo
      Nuku'ono   Hopulani
1600. Pouhana   Hanaku
      Kaiwiloko   Kamaka
      Leua   Ka'oiwi
      Ho'okahua   Ho'omalae
      Kuiau   Ku'iaeonaka
1605. Kapawaolani   Kaini'o
      Manamanaokalea   Kaukaha
      'Auku'u   Koha

	Kakahiaka	Ku'ua
	Kapoli	Ho'opumehana
1610.	Kimana	Kalimalimalimalau
	Polohilani	Kalanimakuaka'apu
	Kahilinaokalani	Hemua
	Kapaia	Ho'olawakua
	Kakai	Manawahua
1615.	'O'ili	Mohala
	Kapaeniho	'Oke'a
	Kaupeku	Kapua
	Ka'ope'ope	Kuka'ailani
	Nakia	Ho'omaua
1620.	Ko'ele	Lohelau
	Huakalani	Kaunu'u'ula
	Nu'uko'i'ula	Meheaka
	Kaioia	Meheau
	Kalalomaiao	Ho'oliu
1625.	Hakalaoa	Kulukau
	Kekoha	Mahikona
	Pipili	Ulukau'u
	Ka'ulamaokoke	Kapiko
	Ka'ulakelemoana	Ho'omau
1630.	Hi'ikalaulau	Hamaku
	Hainu'awa	'Ulahuanu
	Laukohakohai	Ho'olilihia
	Opa'iakalani	Kumukanikeka'a
	Opa'ikumulani	Kauikaiakea
1635.	Liahu	Kapohele-i
	Kanikumuhele	Ho'omauolani
	Ho'opililani	Nawihio'ililani
	Ohemokukalani	Kauhoaka
	Pilihona	Mahinakea
1640.	Ho'omahinukala	Paliho'omoe
	La'iohopawa	Kuaiwalono
	Kuliaimua	Ho'opi'alu
	La'aumenea	Mahiliaka
	Ho'opiliha'i	Holiliakea
1645.	Kiamanu	Pu'unaueakea
	Ho'opa'ilimua	Ho'opi'imoana
	Nakukalani	Kaukealani
	Naholokauihiku	'Apo'apoakea

Pepepekaua
1650. Ho'omaopulani
Kukulani
Kukauhalela'a
Kukaimukanaka
Kukamokia
1655. Kukahauli
Kukamoi
Kukaluakini
Ho'opilimoena
Ho'opailani
1660. Lohalohai
Kelekauikaui
Kanikania'ula
Keleikanu'ulani
Keleikanu'upia
1665. Keleikapouli
Kelemalamahiku
Ho'ohiolokalani
Ho'opihapiha
Ho'opalipali
1670. Mihikulani
Maunaku
Ho'oholihae
Pi'ipi'iwa'a
Kakelekaipu
1675. Nakiau'a'awa
Nanue
Napolohi
Ho'ohewahewa
Milimilipo
1680. Ku'emakaokalani
Po'opo'olani
Ka'iliokalani
Ho'oipomalama
Kunikunihia
1685. Paniokaukea
Polomailani
Polohiua
Kukukalani
Ho'olepau

Puhiliakea
Ahuahuakea
Awekeau
Waka'aumai
Hiliapale
Hauli
Lele'imo'imo
Ho'oahu
Pu'epu'e
Kahiolo
Mahikona
Lauhohola
Mokumokalani
Meimeikalani
Palimaka
Pihana
Opi'opuaka
Ku'uku'u
Ho'opalaha
Ho'onu'anu'a
Kuka'alani
Poupehiwa
Kalelewa'a
Hinapahilani
Naukelemauna
Laulaulani
Po'iao
Kuhimakani
Lonoaakaikai
Ho'opalepale
Miliho'opo
'Ohuku
Heanalani
Kiloahipe'a
Kaikainakea
Mali'iluna
Pokaukahi
Nakao
Heiheiao
Pani'oni'o
Holoalani

1690. Nu'ualani   Pahiolo
      Lanipahiolo   Mukumulani
      Ho'omukulani   Newa'a
      Ho'onewa   Kua'a'ala
      Lanuku'a'a'ala   Pilimeha-e
1695. Ho'opilimeha-e   Niniaulani
      Maninikalani   Kalaniku
      Ho'onakuku   Nahunahupuakea
      Lanipuke   Kalolo
      Ahukele   'O'ilialolo
1700. Pi'oalani   Pi'oalewa
      Miahulu   Pahulu
      Minialani   Ki'ihalani
      .Kumakumalani   Ho'ouna
      Ho'opilipilikane   Pilikana
1705. Nu'akeapaka   Holiakea
      Palela'a   Palikomokomo
      Palimoe   Palialiku
      Paliho'olapa   Palimau'ua
      Palipalihia   Paliomahilo
1710. Hanau Paliku
      Hanau Ololo   Ololonu'u
      Hanau Ololohonua   Olalohana
      Hanau Kumuhonua   Haloiho
      { O Kane [k]
      { O Kanaloa he mau mahoe
1715. { O Ahukai [ka muli loa]   Holehana
      Kapili   Kealona'ina'i
      Kawakupua   Helea'eiluna
      Kawakahiko   Kaha'ulaia
      Kahikolupa   Lukaua
1720. Kahikoleikau   Kupomaka'ika'eleue
      Kahikoleiulu   Kanemakaika'eleue
      Kahikoleihonua   Ha'ako'ako'aikeaukahonua
      Ha'ako'ako'alauleia   Kaneiako'akahonua
      Kupo   Lanikupo
1725. Nahaeikekaua   Hane'eiluna
      Keakenui   Laheamanu
      Kahianaki'iakea   Luaanahinaki'ipapa
      Koluanahinaki'iakea   Ha'anahinaki'ipapa
      Limaanahinaki'iakea   Onoanahinaki'ipapa

1730. Hikuanahinaki'iakea   Waluanahinaki'ipapa
       Iwaanahinaki'iakea   Lohanahanahinaki'ipapa
       Welaahilaninui   Owe
       Kahikoluamea   Kupulanakehau
1734. Wakea i noho ia Haumea, ia Papa, ia Haohokakalani, hanau o
       Haloa
       O Haloa—no

KA WA UMIKUMAMAKOLU
(HE LALA NO KA WA UMIKUMAMALUA)

1735. Paliku ke kane   Paliha'i ka wahine
1736. Palika'a   Palihiolo
1737. Lakaunihau   Keaona
1738. Nalaunu'u   Pu'ukahalelo
1739. Kapapanuinuiauakea   Ka'ina'inakea
1740. Kapapaku   Kapapamoe
1741. Kapapaluna   Kapapailalo
1742. 'Olekailuna   Kapapapa'a
1743. Kapapanuialeka   Kapapahanauua
1744. Kapapanuikahulipali   Kapapai'anapa
1745. Kapapanuiakalaula   Kapapaholahola
1746. Kapapaki'ilaula   Kapapaiakea
1747. Kapapai'aoa   Kapapapoukahi
1748. Kapapauli   Kapapapoha
1749. [Hanau] o Kapapa-pahu ka mua, Ka-po-he'enalu mai kona
       hope noho
1750. Ka-po-he'enalu ke kane   Kamaulika'ina'ina ka wahine
1751. Kaho'okokohipapa   Mehakuakoko
1752. Papa'iao   Mauluikonanui
1753. Papahe'enalu   Hanauna
1754. Hanau a iloko o Pu'ukahonualani o Li'aikuhonua, o kona
       muli mai, o Ohomaila
1755. Ohomaili ke kane   Honuakau ka wahine
1756. Kehaukea   Kualeikahu
1757. Mohala   Lu'ukaualani
1758. Kahakuiaweaukelekele   Hinawainonolo
1759. Kahokukelemoana   Hinawai'oki
1760. Mulinaha   'Ipo'i
1761. Hanau o Laumiha he wahine, i noho ia Kekahakualani
1762. Hanau o Kaha'ula he wahine, i noho ia Kuhulihonua

1763. Hanau o Kahakauakoko he wahine, i noho ia Kulani'ehu
1764. Hanau o Haumea he wahine, i noho ia Kanaloa-akua
1765. Hanau o Kukauakahi he kane, i noho ia Kuaimehani he wahine
1766. Hanau o Kauahulihonua
1767. Hanau o Hinamanoulua'e he wahine
1768. Hanau o Huhune he wahine
1769. Hanau o Haunu'u he wahine
1770. Hanau o Haulani he wahine
1771. Hanau o Hikapuanaiea he wahine, ike [i]a Haumea, o Haumea no ia
1772. O Haumea kino paha'oha'o, o Haumea kino papawalu
1773. O Haumea kino papalehu, o Haumea kino papamano
1774. I manomano i ka lehulehu o na kino
1775. Ia Hikapuanaiea pa umauma ka lani
1776. Pa ilio ia wahine o Nu'umea
1777. O Nu'umea ka 'aina, o Nu'upapakini ka honua
1778. Laha Haumea i na mo'opuna
1779. I'o Ki'o pale ka ma'i, ka'a ka lolo
1780. Oia wahine hanau manawa i na keiki
1781. Hanau keiki puka ma ka lolo
1782. Oia wahine no o T'ilipo o Nu'umea
1783. I noho io Mulinaha
1784. Hanau Laumiha hanau ma ka lolo
1785. O Kaha'ula wahine hanau ma ka lolo
1786. O Kahakauakoko hanau ma ka lolo
1787. O Haumea o ua wahine la no ia
1788. Noho ia Kanaloa-akua
1789. O Kauakahi-akua no a ka lolo
1790. Ho'ololo ka hanauna a ia wahine
1791. Ha'ae wale ka hanauna lolo
1792. O Papa-huli-honua
1793. O Papa-huli-lani
1794. O Papa-nui-hanau-moku
1795. O Papa i noho ia Wakea
1796. Hanau Ha'alolo ka wahine
1797. Hanau inaina ke ke'u
1798. Ho'opunini ia Papa e Wakea
1799. Kauoha i ka la i ka malama
1800. O ka po io Kane no muli nei
1801. O ka po io Hilo no mua ia

1802. Kapu kipaepae ka hanu'u
1803. Ka hale io Wakea i noho ai
1804. Kapu ka 'ai lani makua
1805. Kapu ka 'ape ka mane'one'o
1806. Kapu ka 'akia ka 'awa'awa
1807. Kapu ka 'auhuhu ka mulemulea
1808. Kapu ka 'uhaloa no ke ola loa
1809. Kapu ka la'alo ka manewanewa
1810. Kapu ka haloa ku ma ka pe'a
1811. Kanu ia Haloa ulu hahaloa
1812. O ka lau o Haloa i ke ao la
1813.   Pu—ka—

KA WA UMIKUMAMAHA

1814. Li'aikuhonua ke kane	Ke'akahulihonua ka wahine
1815. Laka	Kapapaialaka
1816. Kamo'oalewa	Lepu'ukahonua
1817. Maluapo	Laweakeao
1818. Kinilauemano	Upalu
1819. Halo	Kinilauewalu
1820. Kamanookalani	Kalanianoho
1821. Kamakaokalani	Kahuaokalani
1822. Keohookalani	Kamaookalani
1823. Kaleiokalani	Kapu'ohiki
1824. Kalali'i	Keaomele
1825. Malakupua	Ke'ao'aoalani
1826. Ha'ule	Loa'a
1827. Namea	Walea
1828. Nananu'u	Lalohana
1829. Lalokona	Laloho'oaniani
1830. Honuapoiluna	Honuailalo
1831. Pokinikini	Polelehu
1832. Pomanomano	Pohako'iko'i
1833. Kupukupuanu'u	Kupukupualani
1834. Kamoleokahonua	Ke'a'aokahonua
1835. Paiaalani	Kanikekoa
1836. Hemoku	Pana'ina'i
1837. Makulu	Hi'ona
1838. Milipomea	Hanahanaiau
1839. Ho'okumukapo	Ho'ao
1840. Lukahakona	Niaulani

1841. Hanau o Kupulanakehau he wahine
1842. Hanau o Kulani'ehu he kane
1843. Hanau o Koi'aakalani
1844. O Kupulanakehau wahine
1845. I noho ia Kahiko, o Kahiko-luamea
1846. Hanau o Paupaniakea
1847. O Wakea no ia, o Lehu'ula, o Makulukulukalani
1848. O ko laua hope, o kanaka 'ope'ope nui
1849. Huihui a kau io Makali'i, pa—'a
1850. Pa'a na hoku kau i ka lewa
1851. Lewa Ka'awela, lewa Kupoilaniua
1852. Lewa Ha'i aku, lewa Ha'i mai
1853. Lewa Kaha'i, lewa Kaha'iha'i
1854. Lewa Kaua, ka pu'uhoku Wahilaninui
1855. Lewa ka pua o ka lani, Kaulua-i-ha'imohai
1856. Lewa Puanene, ka hoku ha'i haku
1857. Lewa Nu'u, lewa Kaha'ilono
1858. Lewa Wainaku, lewa Ikapa'a
1859. Lewa Kikiula, lewa Keho'oea
1860. Lewa Pouhanu'u, lewa Ka'ili'ula
1861. Lewa Kapakapaka, lewa Mananalo
1862. Lewa Kona, lewa Wailea
1863. Lewa ke Auhaku, lewa Ka-maka-Unulau
1864. Lewa Hinalani, lewa Keoea
1865. Lewa Ka'aka'a, lewa Polo'ula
1866. Lewa Kanikania'ula, lewa Kauamea
1867. Lewa Kalalani, lewa Kekepue
1868. Lewa Ka'alolo, lewa Kaulana-a-ka-la
1869. Lewa Hua, lewa 'Au'a
1870. Lewa Lena, lewa Lanikuhana
1871. Lewa Ho'oleia, lewa Makeaupe'a
1872. Lewa Kaniha'alilo, lewa 'U'u
1873. Lewa 'A'a, lewa 'Ololu
1874. Lewa Kamaio, lewa Kaulu[a]lena
1875. Lewa o Ihu-ku, lewa o Ihu-moa
1876. Lewa o Pipa, lewa Ho'eu
1877. Lewa Malana, lewa Kaka'e
1878. Lewa Mali'u, lewa Kaulua
1879. Lewa Lanakamalama, lewa Naua
1880. Lewa Welo, lewa Ikiiki
1881. Lewa Ka'aona, lewa Hinaia'ele'ele

1882. Lewa Puanakau, lewa Le'ale'a
1883. Lewa Hikikauelia, lewa Ka'elo
1884. Lewa Kapawa, lewa Hikikaulonomeha
1885. Lewa Hoku'ula, lewa Poloahilani
1886. Lewa Ka'awela, lewa Hanakalanai
1887. Lewa Uliuli, lewa Melemele
1888. Lewa Makali'i, lewa Na-huihui
1889. Lewa Kokoiki, lewa Humu
1890. Lewa Moha'i, lewa Kauluokaoka
1891. Lewa Kukui, lewa Konamaukuku
1892. Lewa Kamalie, lewa Kamalie-mua
1893. Lewa Kamalie-hope
1894. Lewa Hina-o-na-lailena
1895. Lewa na Hiku, lewa Hiku-kahi
1896. Lewa Hiku-alua, lewa Hiku-kolu
1897. Lewa Hiku-aha, lewa Hiku-lima
1898. Lewa Hiku-ono, lewa Hiku-pau
1899. Lewa Mahapili, lewa ka Huihui
1900. Lewa Na Kao
1901. Lu ka 'ano'ano Makali'i, 'ano'ano ka lani
1902. Lu ka 'ano'ano akua, he akua ka la
1903. Lu ka 'ano'ano a Hina, he walewale o Lonomuku
1904. Ka 'ai a Hina-ia-ka-malama o Waka
1905. I ki'i [i]a e Wakea a Kaiuli
1906. A kai ko'ako'a, kai ehuehu
1907. Lana Hina-ia-ka-malama he ka
1908. Kaulia a'e i na wa'a, kapa ia Hina-ke-ka ilaila
1909. Lawe [i]a uka, puholuholu ia
1910. Hanau ko'ako'a, hanau ka puhi
1911. Hanau ka inaina, hanau ka wana
1912. Hanau ka 'eleku, hanau ke 'a
1913. Kapa ia Hina-halako'a ilaila
1914. 'Ono Hina i ka 'ai, ki'i o Wakea
1915. Kukulu i ki'i a paepae
1916. Kukulu kala'ihi a lalani
1917. Ki'i Wakea moe ia Hina-kaweo'a
1918. Hanau ka moa, kau i ke kua o Wakea
1919. 'Alina ka moa i ke kua o Wakea
1920. Lili Wakea, kahilihili
1921. Lili Wakea inaina uluhua
1922. Papale i ka moa lele i kaupaku

1923. O ka moa i kaupaku
1924. O ka moa i ka haku
1925. O ka 'ano'ano ia a Ka'eo'eo
1926. E halakau nei i ka lewa
1927. Ua lewa ka lani
1928. Ua lewa ka honua
1929. I ka Nu'u no

KA WA UMIKUMAMALIMA

1930. O Haumea wahine o Nu'umea i Kukuiha'a
1931. O Mehani, nu'u manoanoa o Kuaihealani i Paliuli
1932. Liholiho, 'ele'ele, panopano lani 'ele
1933. Kamehanolani, o Kameha'ikaua
1934. Kameha'ikaua, akua o Kauakahi
1935. I ke oki nu'u i ke oki lani o Haiuli
1936. Ha'alele i ka houpo huhu lili punalua
1937. Kau i ka moku o Lua, o Ahu a Lua, noho i Wawau
1938. Wahine akua wahine o Makea
1939. O Haumea wahine o Kalihi o Ko'olau
1940. Noho no i Kalihi i kapa i ka lihilihi o Laumiha
1941. Komo i ka 'ulu, he 'ulu ia
1942. O kino 'ulu, o pahu 'ulu, o lau 'ulu ia nei
1943. He lau kino o ia wahine o Haumea
1944. O Haumea nui aiwaiwa
1945. I aiwaiwa no Haumea i ka noho
1946. Nonoho i na mo'opuna
1947. I ka moemoe i na keiki
1948. Moe keiki ia Kau[a]kahi, o Kuaimehani ka wahine
1949. Moe mo'opuna ia Kauahulihonua
1950. O Hulihonua ka wahine
1951. Moe mo'opuna ia Haloa
1952. O Hina-mano'ulua'e ka wahine
1953. Moe mo'opuna ia Waia, o Huhune ka wahine
1954. Moe mo'opuna ia Hinanalo, o Haunu'u ka wahine
1955. Moe mo'opuna ia Nanakahili, o Haulani ka wahine
1956. Moe mo'opuna ia Wailoa, o Hikopuaneiea ka wahine
1957. Hanau o Ki'o, ike [i]a Haumea
1958. Ike [i]a o Haumea he pi'alu'alu
1959. He konahau, he konakona
1960. He 'awa'awa iná ka wahine
1961. 'Awa'awahia a mulemulea

1962. I hainá, eu, ai'a, he wahine pi'i-keakea-e
1963. Ua pi'alu ke kua, pi'alu ke alo
1964. Ke'ehina ka umauma, pa hiolo Nu'umea
1965. Nauau papa pa umauma 'ilio ka wahine
1966. Ia Ki'o laha na li'i
1967. Mòe ia Kamole i ka wahine o ka nahelehele
1968. Hanau o Ole ke kane o Ha'i ka wahine
1969. Pupue ke kane   Kamahele ka wahine
1970. Manaku   Hikoho'ale
1971. Kahiko   Kaea
1972. Lukahakona   Ko'ulamaikalani
1973. Luanu'u   Kawaoma'aukele
1974. Ki'i   Hinako'ula
1975.   Hanau o 'Ulu, hanau O Nana'ulu
1976. 'Ulu ke kane   Kapunu'u ka wahine
1977. Nana   Kapulani
1978. Nanaie   Kahaumokuleia
1979. Nanaielani   Hinakina'u
1980. Waikalani   Kekauilani
1981. Kuheleimoana   Mapu'uaia'a'ala
1982. Konohiki   Hakaululena
1983. Waolena   Mahui'e
1984. Akalana   Hina-a-ke-ahi
1985. Hanau Maui mua, hanau Maui waena
1986. Hanau Maui-kiki'i, hanau Maui-a-ka-malo
1987. O ka malo o Akalana i humea
1988. Ho'okauhua Hina-a-ke-ahi, hanau he moa
1989. He huamoa ke keiki a Hina i ho'okauhua
1990. 'A'ohe ho'i he moa o ka moe ana
1991. He moa ka ka hanau ana
1992. Alala ke keiki, ninau Hina
1993. 'A'ohe ho'i he kanaka o ka moe ana he keiki ka
1994. He keiki aiwaiwa na Hina-a-ke-ahi
1995. Ukiuki Kia['i]-loa ma laua o Kia['i]-a-ka-poko
1996. O na kaikunane ia o Hina
1997. O na kia['i] elua iloko o ke ana ha
1998. Paio haká Maui, hina ua kia['i]
1999. Kahe ka wai 'ula i ka lae o Maui
2000. O ka ua mua ia a Maui
2001. Ki'i i ka pu 'awa hiwa a Kane ma laua o Kanaloa

2002. O ka ua alua ia a Maui
2003. O ka ua akolu ke ku'eku'e o ka 'ahu'awa
2004. O ka ua aha o ka 'ohe a Kane ma laua o Kanaloa
2005. O ka ua alima o ka paehumu[?]
2006. O ka ua aono o ka anu'u
2007. Nu[n]u Maui, ninau i ka makuakane
2008. Ho'ole Hina, " 'A'ole au makua
2009. O ka malo o Kalana o ka makua ia"
2010. 'Ono i ka i'a na Hina-a-ke-ahi
2011. A'o i ka lawai'a, kena Hina-a-ke-ahi
2012. "E ki'i oe i ko makuakane
2013. Aia ilaila ke aho, ka makau
2014. O Manai-a-ka-lani o ka makau ia
2015. O ka lou [a]na o na moku e hui ka moana kahiko"
2016. Ki'i [a]na ka ala'e nui a Hina
2017. Ke kaikuahine manu
2018. O ka ua ahiku [o] na ua a Maui
2019. O ke kupua e'u nana i ho'olou
2020. Ke 'a, ka waha, ka opina o Pimoe
2021. O ka i'a 'Aimoku e halulu ai ka moana
2022. Lilo Pimoe moe i kaina a Maui
2023. Ulu aloha o Mahanaulu'ehu
2024. O kama a Pimoe
2025. Lawena uka ai Maui i na i'a koe ka pewa
2026. I ho'ohalulu a'e Kane ma laua o Kanaloa
2027. O ka ua a hikilele 'iwa a Maui
2028. Ola Pimoe ma ka pewa
2029. Ola Mahanaulu'ehu ma ka hi'u
2030. Lilo Hina-ke-ka ia Pe'ape'a
2031. O ke akua pe'ape'a o Pe'ape'a
2032. O ka ua ho'olawa ia a Maui
2033. I waluhia ka maka o Pe'ape'a-makawalu
2034. Kikeke ka ua ia Moemoe
2035. Kilika ke kaua a Maui i ka La
2036. I kipuka 'ahele a Maui
2037. Lilo makali'i i ka La
2038. Lilo ke kau ia Maui
2039. Inu i ka wailena ma ke kuna
2040. O Kane ma laua o Kanaloa
2041. O kaua i ka ho'upa'upa
2042. Puni Hawaii, puni Maui

2043. Puni Kauai, puni Oahu
2044. I Kahulu'u ka ewe i Waikane ka piko
2045. Ha'ule i Hakipu'u i Kualoa
2046. O Maui-a-ka-malo
2047. O ka ho'okala kupua o ka moku
2048.   He moku—no

KA WA UMIKUMAMAONO

2049. Maui ke kane	Hinakealohaila ka wahine
2050. Nanamaoa	Hinakapa'ikua
2051. Kula'i	Hinaho'opa'ia
2052. Nanakua'e	Keaukuhonua
2053. Kapawa	Kukuluhiokalani
2054. Heleipawa	Ko'oko'okumaikalani
2055. Hulumalailena	Hinamaikalani
2056. 'Aikanaka	Hina'aiakamalama
2057. Hanau o Punaimua, o Hema, o Puna i muli	
2058. 'Aha'i Hema i ke apuela o Luamahaheau	
2059. Hanau Kaha'i-nui-a-Hema	Hinaulu'ohi'a
2060. Wahieloa ke kane	Ho'olaukahili ka wahine
2061. Laka	Hikawaolena
2062. Luanu'u	Kapokulei'ula
2063. Kamea	Popomaile
2064. Pohukaina	Huahuakapolei
2065. Hua	Hikiiluna
2066. Paunuikaikeanaina	Manokalililani
2067. Huanuiekalala'ila'ikai	Kapoea
2068. Paunuikuakaolokea	Kapuho'okia
2069. Haho	Kauwilai'anapu
2070. Palena	Hikawainui
2071. Hanau Hanala'anui, hanau Hanala'aiki	
2072. Hanala'aiki ke kane	Kapukapu ka wahine
2073. Mauiloa	Kauhua
2074. Alau	Moeikeana
2075. Kanunokokuheli'i	Keikauhale
2076. Lonomai	Kolu
2077. Wakalana	Kawai
2078. 'Alo	Puia
2079. Kaheka	Ma'ilou
2080. Mapuleo	Kama'eokalani
2081. Paukei	Pa'inale'a

2082. Luakoa ke kane   Hina'apo'apo ka wahine
2083. Kuhimau   Kaumana
2084. Kamaluohua   Kapu
2085. Lo'e   Waoha'akuna
2086. Kahokuohua   Hikakauwila
2087. Kaka'e   Kapohanaupuni
2088. Kaulahea   Kapohauola
2089. Kahekili   Hauanuihoni'ala
2090. Hanau o Kawauka'ohele, o Kelea-nui-noho-ana-'api'api, he
   wahine
2091. Noho [Kelea] ia Kalamakua
2092. Hanau La'ielohelohe, noho ia Pi'ilani, [hanau Pi'ikea]
2093. O Pi'ikea noho ia 'Umi, [hanau] o Kumalae-nui-a-Umi
2094. Nona ka Pali haili kauwa
2095. Kumalaenui-a-'Umi ke kane, o Kumunuipuawale ka wahine
2096. Makua ke kane, ka wohi kukahi o ka moku
2097. Kapohelemai ka wahine, he wohi ali'i kapu, ka ho'ano
2098. O 'I, ia 'I ka moku, ka haina kanaka
2099. Ke kaulana 'aina i Pakini
2100. Ka 'ohi'a ko, ke ku'ina o ka moku o Hawaii
2101. Ia Ahu, ia Ahu-a-'I, ia Lono
2102. Ia Lono-i-ka-makahiki ho'i

APPENDIX II

Textual Notes

Since Hawaiians were not precise in the use of such technical elements as punctuation and capitalization, I have referred their use to each particular case without strictly following the printed text. The small initial *k* in the manuscript, moreover, is often indistinguishable from the capital. Lists of names, even those of plants and animals, I have regularly capitalized for emphasis. The difficult question of the compounds with *po* I have met by referring each to its probable meaning as a personified generative agent or as a time element and have capitalized or not accordingly. Punctuation within the line, occasionally noted in the text, has depended upon the meaning of the passage. Since in Hawaiian chants each line is, in general, complete in itself, I follow the usage of the text in omitting altogether end stops.

The insertion of the apostrophe or *hamsa* to indicate the catch in the voice, by no means lost in Hawaiian speech, where an original voiced glottal or nasal has become soundless, remained unmarked by the missionaries who reduced the language to written form and was indicated, and that unevenly and only when occurring within the word, by Parker's 1922 revision of Andrew's dictionary of 1865. Yet it is of first importance in distinguishing two unrelated words otherwise spelled alike but derived from different roots and carrying different meanings. No Hawaiian today can be an infallible guide for the exact voicing of a chant no longer to be heard in oral recitation. I have, however, depended upon native authority, especially upon Mrs. Mary Pukui, for correction of this omission, with occasional help from Dr. Buck and Dr. Emory, and with generous assistance in verification by Dr. Elbert, philologist in charge, with Mrs. Pukui and Dr. Emory, of a new revision of the Hawaiian dictionary.

Corrections from the Kalakaua text have, on the whole, been inconsiderable, and variations in this text from the manuscript seldom occur. Certain passages, such as the star names and the Maui

241

name song, are, however, exceptions. They seem to have come from a different source and to have been set down by an illiterate. Changes from the text have been made only after careful comparison with variant texts or on the advice or with the approval of native interpreters. Important variations in meaning have been based upon the interpretation of the whole passage. All changes from the Kalakaua text are here noted. Reference is made to Kukahi's printed version, cited as "Ku"; to the manuscript source, cited as "MS"; and, for the genealogies, to the Kamokuiki book, cited as "Kms." In a few cases comparisons are quoted from the reprint of Kukahi in *Aloha*, from Bastian, and from Poepoe's rough manuscript, all cited by name. Star names are checked from Mrs. Makemson's list.

TITLE

Text writes -*amamao*, prose note has -*i-mamao*.

CHANT ONE

Line

3.	Ku writes *kukai-aka*.
6.	Capitalization of the Prologue follows manuscript. Text capitalizes *walewale*, the first *lipolipo* in line 9, *la* and *po* in line 10.
7, 8.	Text is without commas; Ku is here followed.
8.	*Aloha* writes *welawela*.
12.	The line is connected with 11 in text; I follow *Aloha* in text and translation.
15.	Ku omits the final *puka* throughout.
15–17.	Ku writes *Hanau ka Ukukoakoa, he Akoakoa kana Hanau ke koe enuhe eli hoopuu honua, he koe kana.* *Aloha* translates: "The Ukukoakoa [coral insect] gave birth to the Akoakoa [coral] The earth-raising insect gave birth to the angleworm."
24.	Misprinted *Pioo* in text.
27.	Written *Makaiaulu* in MS and text.
30.	Omitted in Ku.
32.	Poepoe writes *Pipi*.
33, 34.	Lines inverted in text; text capitalizes *kane*.
35.	*Akaha* in text and MS.
37.	MS reads *He pou hee i ka wawa.*
38.	Comma after *nuku* irregularly in both text and MS.

Line
39.	Text writes *a oe* as two words.
42, 48.	No hyphen in text.
60.	Text writes *ko Punapuna koeleele*.
65, 66.	Text reads *Puaiki* and *Lau aki*.
71.	Text has *Kikalamoa*.
72.	Ku writes *momoa*.
83.	Text reads *Limukala*.
107, 108.	Text reads *Hulu-waena* and *Huluhulu Ieie*.
112.	Kukahi prefers *hue-wai*.
114.	Text has *kahuli*, capitalizes *Honua*.
115.	All texts read *O paia*.
116.	Text capitalizes *Hee*, writes *ka po*.
118, 119.	Ku follows English alphabetical order, *a, e, o, u*.
120.	Text has *koohonua*.

CHANT TWO (CHANT THREE IN MS)

Ku omits lines 141–43, 145–47, 153–55, 157, 158, 161, 164, 166, 173, 174, 191, 192, 197, 198, 209, 210, 215, 216, 221, 222, 251, 252, 262–67, and all refrains after the first.

124.	*Poleliuli* in MS; text writes *kalana*.
127.	Text and MS write *haipu aalamea*.
129, 130.	All four words capitalized in MS.
131.	Ku capitalizes *Ehiku*.
132.	Text and MS write without, Ku with, commas. Ku proposes *a hilo, a holo*.
134, 135.	Text and MS write *kau ana* (see l. 124); Ku writes *kaulana* and *Kuemiemi*.
138.	Ku precedes *holo* with a comma throughout: "it swims."
139.	Text has *moana*.
146.	Text omits the first *ke*.
149.	Ku writes *Ka ao*.
159.	Text omits the first *ke*.
162.	Text misprints *Nuku Moni*.
164.	Text has *Pakukui*.
173.	Text writes *Haha*.
179.	Text has *ke Pahau*.
197.	Written *Puhi kauwila* in text.
209.	Text writes *Pakukui*.
210.	Written *Laukukui* as one word.
221.	Written *Kapoou* in text.

Line
265.   Text writes *Pulehulehu*.
266.   Text and MS write *a ahu*.
268.   Ku has comma after *moana*.

CHANT THREE (CHANT TWO IN MS)

Ku omits lines 280, 299, 300, 311–14, 330, 331, 342, 343, 360, 361, and
all refrains but the first.

278.   Text writes *a poniu au aeaea;* Ku as here.
279.   Text writes *haha;* Ku capitalizes.
280.   Omitted in text; MS as here.
284.   Text has *Hanuu kupua;* Ku as here. No capital for *haha.*
285, 286.   Text writes *haha* and *hahalele.*
303.   Text has *alai.*
304.   Text has *apapani.*
311.   Text has *moha.*
317.   Text reads *ke kaiwa.*
321.   Text has *unauna.*
323.   Text reads *a nei.*
324.   Text has *kakakai.*
331.   Text writes *lupe aloke;* MS has *lupe alake.*
336.   Text has *naio.*
340.   Text has *ao.*
342.   Text and MS write *amoku.*
360.   Text has *noeo.*
368.   Text has *pokaha;* Ku capitalizes.
370.   Ku writes *hehu.*

CHANT FOUR

Kukahi omits lines 403–12, 426, 427, 438, 439, 462, 463, 469–72, 476,
and repeats the refrain but once.

378.   Text reads *ke ahia a laa la;* Ku has *ke ahi a Laa la,* and
              the queen so translates: "the fire of Laa there."
379.   Text reads *kahiwauli;* Ku has *hiwauli* and *apeaumoa.*
381.   Text has *a kolo mai;* Ku capitalizes *Kolo.*
383.   Ku writes *kolokua* and *koloale,* hyphenated in *Aloha.*
384.   Text reads *O pane ke alo.*
387.   Text and MS have *Kaneaka Papanopano;* Ku writes *kane
              a ka po panopano.*
388.   MS has *po panopano.*
390.   Text reads *hooluahua;* Ku has *hoolua.*
391.   Text and MS have *aa nei;* Ku has *po laa nei.*

Line
392, 393. Ku writes in one line.
394. Text has *pue one*.
395. Text reads *po panopano;* Ku has *Popanopano*.
397, 398. Ku has *Milinanea* and *Kiinaanaa*.
399, 400. Text reads *puananaka;* Ku writes in one line.
401, 402. Text reads *kaula makue* and *kaulalii*.
409. Text has *kaihukunini*.
412. Text has *mehemehe*.
414. Text has *honua* for *honu*.
436. Text and MS read *Wawa*.
456. *Okeope* in text; *O keope* in MS.
467. The termination *na* is a contraction for the progressive form of the verb, as also in *ki'ona* (l. 470); *'aina* (ll. 473, 474). Kukahi writes *nee ana*, but *aina*.
468. Ku has *lo-loloa*.
473, 474. Text has *kauwa-hewahewa;* MS capitalizes; Ku writes *ka ua hewahewa*.
475, 476. Ku renders this: *O kele a hano, hano mai ulu kune-wanewa*.

CHANT FIVE

Ku omits lines 490–94, 497, 498, 505, 510–15, 516–27, 531–33, 535.
486. Ku writes *kano*.
487. Ku writes *a kupu*.
490. Text capitalizes *Kama*.
491. Text has *uku*.
492. Text reads *Loi loa*.
493, 494. Text capitalizes *Umi*.
496. Text writes *O Liuliu*.
515. Text has *Meleuli . . . melemele*, perhaps referring to the brown-haired *'ehu* people.
516. Text has *haupo . . . haupo;* Bastian writes *haupe*.
520. Text has *pii Awaawa*.
521. Text has *Aliilii*.
525. Text has *Huelo Maewa*.
526. Text has *Hulu Liha*.
535. Text has *Mele*.

CHANT SIX

539. Text writes *Kupukapu* and *Kuakamano*.
541. Text has *holonaa* and *linolino;* Ku has *holo ana*.

Line

542.	Text has *Hoolino;* Ku has *Holino.*
543, 544.	Ku writes in one line.
545.	Ku writes *a-lualua.*
546.	Text has *popoo;* Ku has *poopoo.*
548.	Text has *huluai;* Ku has *hulu ai.*
549, 550.	Ku writes in one line.
551.	Text capitalizes *Mehe* and writes *a nei haula;* Ku has *kaula.*
552, 553.	Text capitalizes *Lihilihi* and *Peepee;* Ku writes in one line.
556, 557.	Text without, Ku with, capitals.
558, 559.	Ku writes *iole uka, iole kai.*
562, 563.	Text writes *pohiolo,* but *po nee aku;* Ku with capitals.
564.	Text writes *auli;* Ku has *a Uli.*

CHANT SEVEN

567–69.	Ku runs together and capitalizes *Kapohaneeaku* and *Kapohaneemai.*
572.	Ku writes *ka ai aole koe koena.*
574.	Ku writes *ilihia.*
575, 576.	Ku omits; text writes *iliililio, po nee aku.*
577.	Text without comma; Ku writes *loa* for *aa.*
579.	Ku writes *no ka kalua.*
580.	Text has *kehai;* Ku writes *He manu ke kai opulepule.*
581.	Text without comma.
582.	Text reads *i kea ahu ole;* Ku has *i ke aahu ole.*
586.	Text writes *nahuno;* Ku has *nahu'na*
587.	Text writes *hula ka makani;* Ku capitalizes *Hula.*
588.	Text writes *lohelohe.*
590.	Omitted in Ku.
593.	Text misprints *hohee.*

CHANT EIGHT

595.	Text reads *auli, auli a Ke;* MS has *a-uli, auli a Ne;* Ku has *a Uli a Ne.*
596.	Text and MS read *ka Pokini;* Ku has *Pokinikini.*
597.	Text writes *hee nalu.* In Kms, page 1, *Kapohaneeaku* is the child (*keiki*) of *Kapohiolo* and *Kapohanee,* and parent by the woman *Kapohanee mai* of *Lailai,* the twins *Kane* and *Kii, Kaheehaunawele, he ia* (a fish), *he mau Pahu,* and the long-lived man named at lines 617–19.

Line
598.   Bastian writes *e mehe lau;* Ku has *Mehelau.*
602, 603. Ku writes in one line.
610.   Text writes *me he Kapoheenalu mamao.*
614.   Text writes *Akua.*
615.   Written *Kaheehaunawela* in text and MS; *Kaheehauna-*
          wele in Ku and Kms; Malo, page 333, has *Haunawelu.*
          Kms calls him "a fish" (*he ia*).
619.   No hyphens in text.
622.   Text capitalizes *Kupakupa.*
624–26.   Text capitalizes *Kapoheemamao* and *Kapokinikini* and
          sets off with commas in the first two lines.
627–30.   These names are absent from the Kms genealogies.
635, 636. Text capitalizes *Kane.*
638.   Text writes *Poelei* and *Poelea.*
641.   Text capitalizes *Kikiki.*

The text here is obscure. Some would make Maila wife to Ki'i the
man (*kane*) and mother to the children listed; others, La'ila'i
under the name of La'i'olo, born after her return to the god Kane.

CHANT NINE

644.   No hyphens in text.
645.   Text reads *O owela, o owe.*
647.   Text has *Piiaoalani.*
648.   *O Onehenehe* in text and MS. Text has *ku ka honua;*
          MS reads *ku lani ka honua;* Bastian has *ka lani.*
649.   Text writes *kii.*
650.   MS reads *Puka ku lele.*
651.   Text has *haihai lona.*
656.   Text has *kuku ahi;* MS as here.
657.   MS reads *nuu mealani.*
662.   MS reads *Kanaokapokinikini;* text has *Kane a Kapo-*
          kinikini.
663.   MS has *oia kini.*
664.   Text reads *he mamo ka pa ina ina-u.*
666.   Text has *laalaau.*
667.   Text reads *hoo-wa.*
668.   Text and MS have *haha poele.*
670.   Text writes *O Lohelohe.*

CHANT TEN

673.   ⌐ Text reads *O Maila;* Bastian writes *O maila.*
675.   Text writes the name without a capital.

Line
679, 680.   *Kama* capitalized in text; names written in one word, *Poeleieholo*, etc.
681.   Text has *Wehiwelawehi loa*.
689.   Text has *kane*.
693.   Text writes *i kama keiki*.
697.   Text has *kane*.
701.   Text writes *kaka muli*; MS as here.
702.   Text has *kane*. Some would write *Maila*.
703.   Text reads *o ka o kana muli*.

CHANT ELEVEN

708.   Text writes *Piolani*.
712–16.   Kms, page 2, gives to Kii and Lailai the children Kama-
            haina, Kamamule . . . Kamakalua; to Kane and Lailai
            those named above. Cf. lines 676–85 and Ku, page 59.
716.   Text has *Hali*.
768.   Text has *Kuamuu*.
982.   *Heleaua* in text.
994.   Text uses hyphens: *Ahia-ka-po-kau*.
1021.   Text writes *Ia-a*.
1082–1101. Names of wives do not follow MS.
1094–1102. Text writes as two words, capitalized: *Akahi Keawe*
            (Keawe the first), etc.
1144.   Text write *Kupa*. . . .
1182.   Text inserts an initial *Ku*.
1223.   Text writes *Kamehana*.
1231.   Text writes the name with the *O* emphatic.
1258.   Text writes *Helelinaa*.
1272.   Text writes *Onanana*.
1314.   Text has *Lupalama*.
1348.   Text uses the *O* emphatic.
1455.   Text writes *Pa-e*.
1531–35.   Text capitalizes *mauna, ino, au, pahupahu, pohaha, halu-
            ku, naueue,* and *kuaahale*.
1553.   Text writes *Kanakulu*.
1534.   Text writes *Hoi loli*.
1536, 1537. Text writes *Piikonikonihia* in one word, *Kani ka wa* in
            three words.
1540, 1541. Text writes *po ino* and *pomaikai*.
1542.   Text capitalizes *moa* and *kua*.
1543.   Text is without hyphens.

Line

1544. Text capitalizes *Aukaha Opikokahonua,* writes *Oia pu kaua;* Ms is without capitals but writes *Oiapu.*

CHANT TWELVE

Genealogies in this and the last section are substantially the same in Kms, with minor variations not here noted. From line 1624 the genealogy to Wakea differs in Kms, indicating that a different line of descent has been followed.

1554, 1555. Text has *Opuele* and *Opumakaua.*

1587. Kms, page 23, carries a note on Halulu, reading thus in translation: "This Halulu was a woman and from her came the bird Halulu whose bones now rest in the government house [*sic*]. In the mele of Kahikinui-auaimoku she was said to be the first wife of Kahiki-waieke who sailed from Upolo of Kohala."

1656. Text has *Kuku Moi.*

1665. Text misprints *Kellikapuli.*

1713. *Kamiele* is wife in Ku.

1716–26. See Kms, page 35; Ku, page 60; Fornander, *Polynesian Race,* I, 181.

1732. Text misprints *-lauinui.*

1734. Commonly written *Ho'ohokukalani.*

CHANT THIRTEEN

1735. This section is called in the text *He lala no ka wa umikumamalua* (a branch of the twelfth section). From this point the emphatic *O* precedes the male names on genealogies listed in the next four sections, indicating a different source from that of earlier branches (see Kms, p. 33; Ku, pp. 59–60, for the *Paliku* genealogy).

1749. Text has *mai kona hope noho.*

1753. Text misprints *Hanauua.*

1754, 1755. *Ohomaila* and *Ohomaili* follow text.

1765. *Kuaimehana* in text, but see line 1948.

1760–66. Kms, page 33, names the same four women as daughters of Maulinaha and Hipoi, with Kukauakahi and Kahuhu as sons of Haumea by Kanaloa and Kauaimehani wife of the first, Kauahulihonua of the second. Ku, page 60, agrees with the Kalakaua text.

1779. Text writes *kio.*

Line
1783.   Kms writes *Maulinaha.*

1784.   Text misprints *Launihau.*

1792–94.   Text is without hyphens.

1799, 1800.   Text capitalizes *Malama* and *Muli.*

CHANT FOURTEEN

1815.   Genealogy from Laka in Kms, page 34; Fornander, Kumuuli genealogy, *Polynesian Race,* I, 184–85.

1844.   Text misprints *Kupulaua.* . . .

1847.   Kms writes *Wakea he alii, Makulu he kauwa, Lihauula he kahuna* (". . . a chief . . . a servant . . . a priest").

1850–1900.   Text is exceedingly corrupt. Star names are not consistently capitalized, commas are omitted between pairs, parts of a compound name often separated without hyphens. Corrections are from Makemson's alphabetical star list.

1858.   Text writes *i ka paa.*

1861.   Text writes *Kapakapa, ka lewa.* . . .

1862.   Written *Waileia* in text.

1866.   Text misprints *Lawa.*

1869.   Written *Huo* in text.

1870.   Text writes *Lewalewa lewa.* . . .

1874.   Written *Kaululena* in text.

1875.   Perhaps *Ihu-moe.*

1881.   Text writes *Hinaieeleele.*

1892–93.   Perhaps Makemson's *Maile-mua* and *Maile hope.*

1894.   Text has *Hinaona lailena.*

1897.   Text has *Hikuhana.*

1898.   Text has *Hiku-oni.*

1901.   Text reads *Lu ka anoano makaliianoano ka lani.*

1906.   Text has *ahuahu.*

1907.   Text reads *Hinaiaakamalama.*

1908.   Text reads *Kauliaae ina Waa kapa ai hina-ke-ka ilaila.*

1909.   Text writes *uku* and *puhaluholu.*

1910.   Text capitalizes the second *hanau.*

1913.   Text has *Kapa ai* and *hinahalakoa.*

1914.   Text writes *hina.*

1920.   Text writes *Kahilihili.*

1929.   Hyphenated throughout in text.

CHANT FIFTEEN

Line

1930. Text reads *ku kuihaa*.

1931. Text capitalizes *Nuu*.

1932. No commas in text.

1941. Text has *uluhe*.

1951, 1952. Text writes *Ae ka wahine* on the second line; hence the queen translates, "Yes, the wife."

1955. Text misprints *Nauakahili*.

1960. Text has awaawaina.

1962. Text writes *e Uaia* and *pii-keakeae;* no commas.

1966–69. Names are without capitals from *kio* to *pupue*.

1968. Text has *ka kane*.

1973, 1974. Text writes *luanuu* and *kii*.

1976. Text has *ka Punuu*.

1984. Text is without hyphens.

1985, 1986. Text has *Maui a kamalo*.

1987. Text capitalizes *Malo*.

1988. Text writes *Hina a keahi*.

1989. Text misprints *hookahua*, puts a comma after *keiki*.

1995. Text reads *kialoa* and *kia akapoko*.

1997. Text has *kane* and misprints *Kaualoa*.

2001. Text has *na kia*.

2004. Text writes *kane*.

2005. Text reads *pae he uma*.

2007. Text has *Nuu*.

2009. Text has *kalana*.

2010, 2011. No hyphens for names.

2014. No hyphens, perhaps *Mana-ia-ka-lani*.

2016. Text has *Kii* and *ahina*.

2018. Text corrupted to *ahi kuna ia a Mui*.

2020. Text reads *Kaopina*, without commas.

2022. Text reads *i ka ina a Maui*.

2023. In the Kms genealogy, Mahanauluehu is wife of Maui-a-Kalana and mother of Nanamaoa. In Fornander and in the genealogy of the sixteenth section, line 2049, she is called *Hina-kealohaila*.

2025. Text reads *ina ia Koekapewa*.

2026. Text separates *a e*.

2029. Text has *makahiu*.

Line
2030, 2033. Names are not hyphenated.
2034.   Text reads *Kike ke kaua*.
2044.   Text has *kewe*.
2046, 2047. Text capitalizes *Malo* and *Hookala*.

CHANT SIXTEEN

2049.   For the Kumulipo genealogy begun at lines 1951–84 and
             continued in this section, see Kms, pages 36–37, 39–40,
             called *Ke Kuamoo o Haloa* ("The Lineage of Haloa");
             Malo, page 312, as far as *Palena;* Ku, page 61; For-
             nander, *Polynesian Race,* I, 190-91, 193. Fornander
             omits *Kapawa*.
2059.   Text has *Kahainuia Hema*.
2075.   Text writes *Kei Kauhale* for the wife and omits *ka
             wahine*.
2090, 2091. *He wahine*, omitted in the first line, opens the second.
2098, 2099. Text capitalizes *Ia* and Kaulana.
2102.   Text is without hyphens.

APPENDIX III

References

a) KUMULIPO BIBLIOGRAPHY

PRINTED SOURCES

1. BASTIAN, ADOLF. *Die heilige Sage der Polynesier: Cosmogonie und Theogonie.* Leipzig, 1881.
2. *He pule ho'ola'a ali'i. He Kumulipo no Ka-I-amamao a ia Alapai-wahine* ("A Prayer for the Consecration of a Chief, a Kumulipo for Ka-I-amamao and [Passed on] to the Woman Alapai").
3. *An Account of the Creation of the World According to Hawaiian Tradition. Translated from original manuscripts preserved exclusively in her majesty's family, by Liliuokalani of Hawaii. Prayer of Dedication. The Creation for Ka I i mamao, from him to his daughter Alapai wahine, Liliuokalani's greatgrandmother. Composed by Keaulumoku in 1700 and translated by Liliuokalani during her imprisonment in 1895 at Iolani Palace and afterward at Washington Place, Honolulu; was completed in Washington, D.C., May 20, 1897.* Boston, 1897.
4. KUKAHI, JOSEPH L. *He kumulipo, he moolelo Hawaii,* pp. 1–98. Honolulu, 1902. (In two parts, pamphlet.)
5. "The Kumulipo: Legendary Story of Creation" [originally written in the Hawaiian language by JOSEPH KUKAHI] [*Ke Kumulipo: Moolelo o ka hanaia ana o Hawaii Nei*], *Aloha: An English and Hawaiian Magazine,* Vol. I (June 15–September 1). Honolulu, 1928.

MANUSCRIPT SOURCES PRESERVED IN HAWAIIAN MANUSCRIPT COLLECTION OF BISHOP MUSEUM, HONOLULU

6. He Pule Heiau. He Kumu Lipo no Alapai Wahine ("A Temple Prayer. A Beginning in Deep Darkness for the Woman Alapai"). Haw. MS Col. LI².

7. No Kumulipo no ("Concerning the Kumulipo"). Haw. MS Col. LI.
8. POEPOE, J. M. He mele kuauhau Kumulipo ("A Genealogical Chant of Kumulipo"). (To line 442 with comments upon "Kamokuiki's Genealogy of Kumulipo.") Haw. MS Col. LI³.
9. ROCK, DR. JOSEPH. English translation of Bastian's translation and notes. Haw. MS Col.
10. Helps in Studying the Kumulipo Chant. Haw. MS Col. LI⁴.

DISCUSSION

11. ACHELIS, TH. *Uber Mythologie und Cultus von Hawaii: Sonder-Ausdruck aus dem "Ausland."* Braunschweig, 1895. (Pamphlet of 82 pp.)
12. TREGEAR, EDWARD. "The 'Creation Song' of Hawaii," *Journal of the Polynesian Society*, IX (Wellington, N.Z., 1900), 38–46.
13. CURTIS, MATTOON M. "Ancient Hawaiian Theories as to the Nature and Origin of Things," *Hawaiian Almanac and Annual for 1919* (Honolulu, 1918), pp. 79–93.
14. STOKES, JOHN F. G. "An Evaluation of Early Genealogies Used for Polynesian History," *Journal of the Polynesian Society*, XXXIX (Wellington, 1930), 7–13.
15. BUCK, PETER (TE RANGI HIROA). Vikings of the Pacific, pp. 242–48. New York, 1938.

b) LIST OF REFERENCES

ALEXANDER, MARY C. *William Patterson Alexander*. New Haven, 1881.

ANDREWS, LORRIN. *A Dictionary of the Hawaiian Language*. Honolulu, 1865.

BECKWITH, MARTHA W. *Hawaiian Mythology*. New Haven, 1940.
——. "Hawaiian Shark Aumakua," *American Anthropologist*, XIX (Lancaster, Pa., 1917), 503–17.
——. "Polynesian Story Composition," *Journal of the Polynesian Society*, LIII (Wellington, 1944), 177–203.
——. *The Hawaiian Romance of Laieikawai*, by S. N. Haleole. Original publication, Honolulu, 1863. Translation, Bureau of American Ethnology Report 35. Washington, 1919.
——. See KEPELINO.

BUCK, SIR PETER (TE RANGI HIROA) *Ethnology of Mangareva* (Bernice Pauahi Bishop Museum Bull. 157). Honolulu, 1938.

——. *Mangaian Society* (Bernice Pauahi Bishop Museum Bull. 122.) Honolulu, 1934.

——. *Vikings of the Sunrise.* New York, 1934.

ELLIS, WILLIAM. *Polynesian Researches during a Residence of Nearly Eight Years in the Society and Sandwich Islands.* 2d ed. 4 vols. London, 1831–39.

EMERSON, JOSEPH S. *The Lesser Hawaiian Gods.* ("Papers of the Hawaiian Historical Society," No. 2.) Honolulu, 1892.

EMERSON, DR. N. B. *Unwritten Literature of Hawaii: Sacred Songs of the Hula* (Bureau of American Ethnology Bull. 38.) Washington, 1909.

——. *See* MALO.

EMORY, KENNETH F. "The Tahitian Account of Creation, by Mare," *Journal of the Polynesian Society,* XLVII (Wellington, 1938), 45–60.

——. "The Tuamotuan Creation Chant," *ibid.,* XLVIII (Wellington, 1939), 1–29.

——. "Tuamotuan Concepts of Creation," *ibid.,* XLIX (Wellington, 1940), 69–136.

——. "Additional Illustrations of Tuamotuan Creation," *ibid.,* LII (Wellington, 1943), 19–21.

FIRTH, RAYMOND. "Marriage and the Classificatory System of Relationships," *Journal of the Royal Anthropological Institute of Great Britain,* LX (London, 1930), 235–68.

——. *We the Tikopia: A Sociological Study of Kinship in Primitive Polynesia.* London, 1936.

——. *The Work of the Gods in Tikopia.* ("Monographs on Social Anthropology published for the London School of Economics and Political Science.") London, 1940.

FORNANDER, ABRAHAM. *An Account of the Polynesian Race.* 3 vols. London, 1878–85.

——. *Collection of Hawaiian Antiquities and Folklore.* Translated by JOHN WISE; edited by THOMAS G. THRUM. (Bernice Pauahi Bishop Museum, "Memoirs," Nos. 4, 5, 6.) Honolulu, 1916–19.

GILL, REV. WILLIAM WYATT. *Myths and Songs from the South Pacific.* London, 1876.

GREEN, LAURA. *Folk-Tales from Hawaii.* Honolulu, 1928.

GREEN, LAURA, and PUKUI. *Legend of Kawelo and Other Hawaiian Folk Tales.* Honolulu, 1930.

GREY, SIR GEORGE. *Polynesian Mythology and Ancient Traditional History of the New Zealand Race, as Furnished by Their Chiefs and . . . (Priests).* 2d ed. Auckland, 1885.

HANDY, EDWARD S. C. *Marquesan Native Culture*. (Bernice Pauahi Bishop Museum Bull. 9.) Honolulu, 1923.

HANDY, EDWARD S. C., and PUKUI. *The Hawaiian Planter*, Vol. I. (Bernice Pauahi Bishop Museum Bull. 161.) Honolulu, 1940.

HENRY, TEUIRA. *Ancient Tahiti, Based on Material Recorded by J. M. Orsmond*. (Bernice Pauahi Bishop Museum Bull. 48.) Honolulu, 1928.

HOBBS, JEAN. *Hawaii: A Pageant of the Soil*. Palo Alto, Calif., 1935.

Ka Moolelo Hawaii ("Hawaiian Traditions"). Written by Hawaiian students and corrected by one of the instructors, adding dates and occasionally sentences and paragraphs. Lahainaluna, 1838.

KAMAKAU, SAMUEL M. "Moolelo Hawaii" ("Hawaiian Traditions"), *Ke Au Okoa* (newspaper). Honolulu, 1869-71. Translation in manuscript, Bishop Museum collection.

KEPELINO. *Traditions of Hawaii*. Edited by MARTHA WARREN BECKWITH. (Bernice Pauahi Bishop Museum Bull. 95). Honolulu, 1932.

KING, CAPTAIN JAMES. *A Voyage to the Pacific Ocean under the Direction of Captains Cook, Clerk, and Gore, in his Majesty's Ships the Resolution and Discovery . . . in the Years 1776, 1777, 1778, 1779*, Vol. III. 3 vols. London, 1784.

KRÄMER, DR. AUGUSTIN. *Die Samoan-Inseln*, Vol. I. 2 vols. Stuttgart, 1902.

LUOMALA, KATHERINE. *Maui-of-a-Thousand-Tricks: His Oceanic and European Biographers*. (Bernice Pauahi Bishop Museum Bull. 198.) Honolulu, 1949.

LYONS, CURTIS. "The Song of Kualii, of Hawaii, Sandwich Islands," *Journal of the Polynesian Society*, II (Wellington, 1893), 163-78.

MAKEMSON, MAUD. *The Morning Star Rises*. New Haven, 1941.

MALO, DAVID. *Hawaiian Antiquities (Moolelo Hawaii)*. Translated from the Hawaiian by DR. N. B. EMERSON; edited by W. D. ALEXANDER. Honolulu, 1903.

MÜHLMANN, WILHELM E. "Die Geheime Gesellschaft der Arioi...," *Internationales Archiv fur Ethnographie*, Vol. XXXII, Suppl. Leyden, 1932.

PARKER, REV. HENRY. *A Dictionary of the Hawaiian Language by Lorrin Andrews*. Revised. Honolulu, 1922.

PUKUI, MARY KAWENA. "Games of My Hawaiian Childhood," *California Folklore Quarterly*, II (Berkeley, 1943), 205-20.

——. *Ke Awa Lau o Pu'uloa* ("The Many-harbored Sea of

Pu'uloa"), pp. 56–62. (Hawaiian Historical Society Reports, No. 52.) Honolulu, 1943.

———. "Songs of Old Kau," *Journal of American Folklore*, LXII (1949), 247–58.

———. See GREEN AND HANDY.

RIVERS, W. H. R. *The History of Melanesian Society*. 2 vols. Cambridge, England, 1914.

SMITH, S. PERCY. *The Lore of the Whare-wananga: Teaching of the Maori College on Religion, Cosmogony, and History*, Part I: *Te Kauwae-runga or "Things Celestial."* ("Memoirs of the Polynesian Society," Vol. III.) New Plymouth, N.Z., 1913.

———. "Some Paumotu Chants," *Journal of the Polynesian Society*, XII (Wellington, 1913), 221–42.

STOKES, JOHN F. G. "An Evaluation of Early Genealogies Used for Hawaiian History," *Journal of the Polynesian Society*, XXXIX (Wellington, 1930), 1–42.

———. *Index to "The Polynesian Race" by Abraham Fornander*. Honolulu, 1909.

THRUM, THOMAS G. *More Hawaiian Folk Tales: A Collection of Native Legends and Traditions*. Chicago, 1923.

———. *See* FORNANDER.

TITCOMB, MARGARET. "Kava in Hawaii," *Journal of the Polynesian Society*, LVII (Wellington, 1948), 105–71.

TREGEAR, EDWARD. *A Maori-Polynesian Comparative Dictionary*. Wellington, 1887.

WHITE, JOHN. *The Ancient History of the Maori: His Mythology and Traditions*. 6 vols. Wellington, 1887.

[PRINTED IN U S A]